The Harvest Reaped

From TVs to IVs at Age 50+

Sam Gendler, Md.

THE HARVEST REAPED
FROM TVS TO IVS AT AGE 50+

iUniverse books may be ordered through booksellers or by contacting:

iUniverse
1663 Liberty Drive
Bloomington, IN 47403
www.iuniverse.com
1-800-Authors (1-800-288-4677)

ISBN: 978-1-4917-6258-5 (sc)
ISBN: 978-1-4917-6259-2 (hc)
ISBN: 978-1-4917-6257-8 (e)

Library of Congress Control Number: 2015904850

Print information available on the last page.

iUniverse rev. date: 05/19/2015

To my beloved parents
Rebecca and Clement Gendler
who devoted their lives through the Great Depression and beyond
to instilling in their three sons an avid desire
for wisdom, honesty and fairness,
and the mandate to pass these attributes on
to their children and grandchildren

Contents

Part II

Foreword

The driving forces and hardships that we all have to endure in life often make us who we are. But, it is what we extract from these experiences that separate us from the average person. It is so sad to encounter people trapped in a life of boredom and feeling helpless to change their lot. We are all limited by our life span, which we can lengthen or shorten to some extent. These days there is a tremendous amount of information around on leading healthier lives. It's such a pitiful waste to shorten our lives with smoking, drugs or lack of exercise. After all, being a human being is one of the most incredible miracles of our universe. We may be the only such miracles in the entire universe.

We owe it to ourselves, our families and this wonderful planet that we live on to spend our lives in a way that improves ourselves and everyone around us. If we can enjoy our short time on earth so much the better. The purpose of the Harvest Reaped is to show you how to try to avoid being trapped in a boring, non-productive life and to capture the best possible outcomes for you and your loved ones.

Such was my life, with all its twists and turns of fate, and all its demands and rewards that should be appreciated by a broad cross section of people. In addition to the many obstacles I encountered along my journey, my life was strongly shaped by my family, friends and mentors, so, I have included them in this effort, although their names may have been changed.

In the various schools that I had attended, I was often helped and guided by mentors who paid an inordinate amount of attention to me. In retrospect, they recognized that I had an unusual potential for a very bright future - when all I could see was the endless dimness of my meager surroundings. For the most part, these mentors were mostly my teachers, but I took that for granted not realizing that I was getting more than my share of attention. Astonishingly, they ignored that I was often shabbily dressed as a child or teen-ager due to the grinding poverty in which my family lived.

Although I always loved to read, I was shy and unsure of myself. But my teachers saw more of a future for me than I could ever fathom. As a teen-ager, my friends often called me "professor" as I was more interested in reading books than most of them. Still, the fact that I was poorer than most of them made me feel inferior and I couldn't foresee that I would ever amount to much or one day be considered well off, financially. Indeed, it wasn't until I was half way through high school that I started to realize that I had any potential at all and what some of the possibilities were.

As my life shaped up favorably, with its ups and downs, I developed a keen appreciation of the sciences, medicine, mathematics, and engineering. Oddly enough, it was from my math background, especially after studying the laws of probability, I came to the conclusion that there were too many unique events in my life to be so easily dismissed as pure chance. That led me to the possibility of a guiding force watching over me. As my parents had a very hard life, they naturally felt the lack of such a guiding power and even claimed to be atheists or agnostics at times. Yes, my life was hard much of the time but dire circumstances didn't stop me from attaining special goals I kept setting for myself.

From TVs to IVs, I am now into my 90s and living in California with Teresa, my wonderful wife. I hope that the story of my life will provide a lot of inspiration that will help encourage others- and add a little humor as well – in the anecdotes that follow. My intent is for the reader to come away with the knowledge that it is never too late to pursue one's dream and change the course of one's life.

I started writing Harvest Reaped many times but never got past the first 50 pages. A few years ago, when I cut back on my practice hours, I was able to find the time to dedicate myself to writing the complete book. It was exciting to me to review the high points in my life and even the set-backs.

My "Ham" radio days put me in contact with the world, beginning in my mid-teens. I moved amateur radio to the back burner gradually as email and texting became the way to go in communication. I still treasure my amateur station license, W2KEE, which I have held for the past 53 years. I still love the sciences and have devoted my recent reading to the structure of the Cosmos.

I have a special request for the readers of Harvest Reaped. When I reached certain points in the book where there were electronic or medical matters involved, I dedicated some paragraphs to the technical aspects. To the non-technical reader, please feel free to skip over those parts in the book. They are for the technical readers who prefer to learn how things work.

Sam Gendler, M.D.

Part I

Clement and Rebecca

My Romanian mother was born in Paris, known as the City of Lights and Capital of the Arts, at the turn of the twentieth century. As was common in those days, she was born to nomadic immigrants traveling throughout Europe looking for work. Her father was seeking employment as an itinerant tailor. It was an exhaustive effort and one that kept the family trekking through various parts of Egypt, Turkey and France before reaching their final destination, America.

After her father passed away from tuberculosis, the rest of the family decided that they would move to the United States. They had heard the proverbial tale that the streets were paved with gold. Several female family members had already preceded them and one had married a successful gentleman with an upholstery business located in the Bronx, just north of Manhattan.

It was uncertain that my mother would ever see the sidewalks of New York as she was immediately turned down for emigration at the port of debarkation, in Italy. This was due to a chronic eye infection, probably trachoma caused by chlamydia trachomatis, endemic in that era.

Only in her teens, she was treated by a kindly physician who burned away the eye membrane that had developed using a "blue stone" that I believe to have been copper sulfate. The membrane that formed in these infections could lead to total blindness if left untreated. (Chlamydia is an organism somewhere between a virus and a bacterium which presently causes infection of the genitals, but rarely of the eyes.)

After frequent treatments, which she often described as sheer torture, she was able to emigrate and join the rest of her family. Like others before her, she landed in lower Manhattan with many other Jewish immigrants – along with Irish, Italian, Polish and other ethnic groups.

By comparison, my father was born in Eastern Europe, somewhere in the triangular Russian/Prussian/Austrian area that existed then. It had carried the name of Poland for many centuries until 1795. Until then, the Poles made many unsuccessful attempts to restore their own country. The area was finally reassembled as Poland after the three powers that had occupied the area were defeated in the first World War. Poland was then established as a democracy under President Josef Pielsucki. Poland remained free until September 1, 1939, when it was invaded and occupied by the German invaders. My ancestors there were hard-working, long-lived farmers. My father told me that his grandfather, in Poland, had died at age 105 from the exertion of cutting down a tree and trying to carry it away.

Although it would still be some years before they met, they were only teenagers when they arrived in New York City via Ellis Island, located in Upper New York Bay.

Perhaps it was because Ellis Island was the country's busiest port of immigration that mistakes were often made, resulting in strange reinventions of the family name. Perhaps there should have been a sign that read Newcomers Beware. Even the initial interviewing process was usually performed without any interpreters present. Indeed, it is believed that my father, who entered the new land as Clement Gendler, was born as Korda Paniecki. Since several of my uncles had already immigrated prior to his arrival and now bore the name, Gendler, which became my father's newly assigned name forevermore.

Another oddity is that the original family name, Paniecki, was usually reserved for nobility, which is puzzling since our family history is that of hard working peasants. Even the acquired name, Gendler, a variant of the English word "handler," implies that the so-named person keeps a sharp eye out for great bargains that he can quickly buy and sell, and turn over for profit. Clement Gendler was not of that ilk.

As a student in New York City's Rand School, an educational facility based on the principles of socialism in 1906, he not only learned about socialism but also met the very pretty Rebecca Goldenberg, the woman whom he would later marry and who would one day become my mother.

Portal to the New Land

Before the story unfolds about my parents and the life they made in the new land, one that produced three sons who would grow up to have very successful lives and families of their own, it is important to stop here and realize the rarified atmosphere of Ellis Island, especially for newcomers.

Anyone who is second, third or even fourth generation of the immigrants that came through there should visit to Ellis Island. Although the view would have been sighted from the steerage area of each ship as it approached land, the nearby Statue of Liberty on Liberty State Park, in all of her majesty, must have been a thrilling sight for the immigrants. Anyone would be moved by its history of the different cultures, ethnic groups and races that had entered through that portal to a new land and new life. So many hopes and dreams.

It's no small wonder the first and greatest lines of Emma Lazarus's sonnet, still give me goose bumps whenever I read or recite it. It appears on a bronze plaque that was placed in the pedestal at the base of the statue in 1903:

> *"Keep ancient lands, your storied pomp!" cries she*
> *With silent lips. "Give me your tired, your poor,*
> *Your huddled masses yearning to breathe free,*
> *The wretched refuse of your teeming shore.*
> *Send these, the homeless, tempest-tost to me,*
> *I lift my lamp beside the golden door!"*

The New Colossus, Emma Lazarus, 1903

So, the question is, where did the tempest-tost all go? Most of the impoverished immigrants arriving in Ellis Island joined their families living in Manhattan. A small percentage of them found their families living in other destinations, such as German immigrants to Wisconsin, and Polish immigrants to upstate New York or Illinois. However, a vast number of immigrants who originally settled in Manhattan eventually moved to newer areas of Brooklyn and the Bronx.

In Manhattan, at the time, there was tremendous population density with families packed into old tenement buildings which stood side-by-side with no space between them. The individual apartments ran from the front to the back of the building in two rows with windows for light and ventilation at the front and back of the apartment, as well as an air-shaft between. They were called railroad flats. This high density, coupled with poor nutrition and long, working hours with little pay, led to a high rate of the dreaded disease tuberculosis or TB.

As is typical with TB, the patient suffers from a cold for a week or two and the illness continues with a chronic cough. After a few months of coughing, the phlegm appears bloody. There is also a general wasting away of the patient and overall exhaustion from the disease which was called "consumption" in those days. Since there were no antibiotics then, tuberculosis was usually fatal.

It was quite common to see, perhaps, a gaunt, elderly man seated in the bay window of his house who was constantly coughing and blotting his lips with a cloth after each and every coughing spell. After a few months of that, he no longer appeared at the window. Everyone around would know what that meant. As TB is highly contagious even to this day, I test regularly for TB and always with positive results. Yet I always receive negative results on my chest x-rays which indicates that I don't actually have TB, but that I had been exposed in earlier days.

There is a fascinating true story from that time that concerns a popular French author, Louis Saranac, who lived in Manhattan at the time. In the height of his career, Saranac went through the physical sequence that I have described above. When the bloody sputum presented itself, he went to his family physician who, upon examining

4

him, told him that he should hurry to finish any stories that he had started as he had only a few months left to live.

Given this edict, Saranac rented a small cabin at the shore of a lovely lake in the Adirondack Mountains in upstate New York, where he had always enjoyed a quiet respite while writing his books. It was the most beautiful location he had ever known. He kept busy writing his books and the cough faded. He enjoyed the fresh air and pure water of the setting, and lived a long life, returning to New York City only to attend the funerals of the very physicians that had, earlier, pronounced his death sentence.

Saranac's example was widely studied and soon the Saranac Sanatorium was erected next to the same lake, which was renamed Lake Saranac, in his honor. The philosophy of good diet, ample sunlight and fresh clean air was widely copied and has gone on to either save or improve the lives of many.

Get Back In There

I was born Samuel Enoch Gendler in 1921 to immigrant parents living in Brooklyn, New York.

As her first-born, my mother often told me the circumstances of my birth. When she experienced her first labor pains, my father took her to a small private hospital where she was placed in a bed and the doctor summoned. As I was a first child, the nurses assumed that there would be a lengthy labor. When I began to "crown", the nurses panicked and actually tried to push my head back up the birth canal. The doctor finally arrived and successfully completed the birthing process but, according to my mother, I was one ugly baby with a swollen bruised head.

My brother, Paul Herbert, arrived three years later and was followed by our next brother, Lawrence Herman, another three years later. The intrusion by my brothers into our family altered the close bonds that I felt with my mother. As my brother Paul grew up, I came to believe that he was her favorite. She would frequently comment on his beauty when he was a baby and how handsome he was as he grew older. I always felt that I was the "ugly duckling." This was a sentiment that was upsetting to me and greatly contributed to my feelings of insecurity.

As my mother was not working, she spent lots of time reading to me and, as a result, I learned how to read at the young age of three. As a young family, we lived a Bohemian-style existence and I was somehow instilled at a young age with the idea that my parents were communists (whatever that was). My dad read the communist newspaper, *The Daily Worker,* which almost always showed cartoons of big-bellied capitalists surrounded by bulging sacks of dollar bills. He also read *The New York Times* but, shucks; it had no comics and therefore was of little interest to me. (In my teens, I used to joke around with my pals a lot and one of my favorites was to paraphrase the communist captions by asking, "Why should only the capitalists have big bellies? Why shouldn't we give the working girls big bellies too?" Well, you had to be there.)

More than that, my dad was largely self-taught, quite well read and highly intelligent. At home, we had two books. They were *Das Kapital,* by Karl Marx and *The Origin of Species,* by Charles Darwin. I opened them a few times but didn't take much interest in them. I found myself far more interested in ten-cent pulp magazines like *Doc Savage* and *The Shadow,* which were sold in monthly editions. Doc Savage was the Superman of my generation. He could defend the poor and oppressed against hordes of bad guys with a little help from a motley crew of supporters and his dazzling fists. It was not until my teen years that I began to read widely and discovered the joys of science.

The Laying of the Bancas

I marveled at my father's resourcefulness. He not only believed in socialism but the therapeutic powers of massage. In my childhood my legs developed a bow-legged curvature probably due to a vitamin D deficiency and a resulting malady called Rickets. By definition, this deficiency decreases absorption of calcium from the intestine and causes the mineralization of bones, making them soft and bendable under weight-bearing activities. Today, Rickets is rare. Vitamin tablets and supplements are cheap and plentiful, and our modern day generation worships the sun, whilst sunlight fosters Vitamin D production in the skin.

According to my parents, it was my father's massage therapy that helped straighten my legs - not to mention sun exposure later on in life, as well.

Dad didn't believe in doctors and had great faith in other home remedies. One of them was the Compresses. Whenever we had sore throats, my father would wrap a piece of flannel cloth or toweling around our necks. If our glands swelled up, he massaged our throats quite vigorously. Yup, massaging and compressing were the mainstay of our medical care and in the comfort of our home.

It wasn't just doctors Dad didn't believe in, he also didn't believe in germs. Once, when I was running on the sidewalk, I dropped an empty glass milk bottle that I was carrying. A piece of the glass cut my knee. My dad tore a piece of cloth from an old but clean sheet, and wrapped it around the knee to stop the flow of blood. Since dad didn't believe that germs existed, he claimed that the bacteria beneath the microscope lens were nothing more than tiny specks of dirt.

Sometimes, stronger tactics were required. When my brother Paul was about four months old, he became very ill. My parents blamed the illness on the lack of heat in the apartment which was furnished, only in the kitchen, by a wood burning stove. When he didn't respond to my father's standard therapy, my parents called in an old world practitioner to "lay on bancas." This was a miraculous procedure performed with small, thick glass cups or bancas, and alcohol. It involved the practitioner pouring a little alcohol into the banca, swishing it around, pouring the excess alcohol back in the bottle and then lighting the resulting vapor in the cup. This was then pressed against my little brother's back and as it cooled the vapor condensed and the decreased pressure sucked in the flesh. The cup remained fixed in place on the back, still quite warm. Soon, his upper back was festooned with a number of bancas. The theory was that the bancas sucked out all of the poisons from the body. My folks said that they were sure he was dying but after the procedure he soon recovered. He did not pass away until seventy five years later, after having lived a full life.

A Soup Bowl Full of Fries

We were extremely poor and food was scarce at times but we were often helped by meager handouts from various social service organizations. Clothing was passed down from me, the oldest, to Paul who was next, and then to Larry, the third in line. Larry swears to this day that he sometimes had to wear our mother's hand-me-downs as well.

Accordingly, we were frequent visitors to the second hand clothing shops whenever there were a few extra dollars to be had. When things got better, food was more plentiful. Yet most of the proteins we ingested came from cheap cuts of meat like flank steak. This was cut thinly and covered our platter with the tips of the steak hanging over. Whatever was served was devoured quickly, probably due to the competition among us, with a separate soup bowl filled with French fried potatoes.

In those early years, Dad had been in the business of manufacturing woman's dresses. He failed at that. His older brother, Israel Gendler, had loaned him five-hundred dollars to help him get started, but dad was never able to repay it - a sore point in our family.

Later on, he was employed as an insurance agent for the Metropolitan Insurance Company. As the economy faltered, my father's insurance business ran into trouble. The policy holders were poor people whom my dad had to visit each week and collect sums of twenty-five to fifty cents a week or so. As the economy got intensively worse, the customers sometimes couldn't pay the tiny premiums which meant their policies would lapse. My father would attempt to keep that from happening by paying the money from his own pocket.

He ran into trouble when he could no longer sustain the premiums from his own income and, soon enough, he was out of the insurance business. From then on, he went through a series of low paying jobs, finally working for many years as a truck driver for a bakery. I remember him leaving early in the morning before sunrise and coming home at night dog-tired. My mother helped, working as a seamstress but, in those days, her wages were very low.

Ramona, I hear the Mishameltzabar!

I don't remember how old I was when I engaged in my first business venture. On week-ends, I would buy pretzels from a small pretzel manufacturing plant located in a nearby store-front. I would pay one cent each for the pretzels and the owner loaned me the basket from which to sell them. I'd take my basket of pretzels to small parks in the neighborhood and sell the pretzels for two cents each which would occupy me for a whole day. I would eat any leftovers or share them with my brothers. I never realized that I was violating my parents' staunch socialistic principles by selling pretzels at an outrageous 100 percent markup.

I found the whole enterprise entertaining and was fascinated by the manufacturing process used to make the pretzels. The flour and water were mixed in a big vat and then forced through an opening to make a long thick ribbon of dough. As the ribbon was squeezed out, it was cut into lengths. These lengths would then be twisted into a double-bow by an artful flip of the wrist, and laid onto a moving conveyer belt which carried it into the baking oven.

It was hard work for an "ugly duckling" but I was strong. Perhaps that's because my mother was a great fan of a physical culture guru of the time, Bernar McFadden (he was very firm about dropping the "d"). I do know that he made liberal use of medicine balls since we had many in our home.

My mother also got the idea, somehow, that heavy cream was healthy and beneficial for growing boys. So, when we could afford it, she would buy some heavy cream for us and pour it over chocolate pudding, a great favorite of ours. Well, we did grow up big and strong as she had hoped, but both Paul and I needed coronary artery bypass grafts later on in life. No wonder!

There were other treats too as we also grew up on the delightful taste of coffee with lots of sugar and cream – as well as the less delightful taste of Postum which consisted of toasted cereal grains. We preferred to "Tink Ahn", two Jewish words that we learned in our multi-lingual neighborhood. The two words mean "dip in", and describe our favorite goody. It consists of a fresh roll, which used to cost a few cents, and we would tear off chunks for dipping into a bowl of coffee or chocolate milk.

Like all children we loved chocolate but the most interesting way to buy it back then was to purchase "a two-cent pick." The "pick" consisted of going to the candy store where you picked a chocolate candy with a cream center from an open box. You bit into it and, if the cream was pink instead of white, you got a prize. If it wasn't, well, you ate the "pick" and the chocolate tasted great just the same.

Our upbringing was further developed by my mother's cultural interests. She had an excellent singing voice in the Contralto range and had learned to play the piano. Once, she purchased a used one for about fifty dollars, on the installment plan, which was a way of charging things. She loved to practice at the piano and sing operatic and classical pieces. I remember one of her favorites was named "Ah, Sweet Mystery of Life," a rather happy song she liked to share with us. Sometimes she would teach us very sad songs which would always bring tears to our eyes.

Her endless anecdotes were chosen, no doubt, to impress us about dangers we might experience in life. This one, I believe, was meant to teach us not to steal.

Oh, I served seven years in state prison
And seven more years I have to serve
For throwing a man down in an alley,
And stealing his gold watch and chain.
Oh, if I had the wings of an angel

Over these prison walls would I fly
Back to the arms of my mother
And there, I would lie down and die.

Sad, sad and lonely sitting in this prison
All alone, all alone
Thinking of my little baby brother
And the days when I was home.

There were more parts to the song but I can't remember them. I once googled the song but an entirely different version came up. I presume that my mom didn't modify or embellish the lyrics just to teach her boys that crime doesn't pay.

My mother's talents and musical abilities were wasted on me because, despite our being raised in this musical environment, I was more of a listener than a performer, meaning I was tone deaf. I can't vouch for the singing ability of my brothers but one, Larry, told me that he had sung songs at various parties and been complimented each time.

When I was about seven years old, I used to sing a popular song named "Ramona." The first few lines went, *"Ramona, I hear the mission bells afar, Ramona, ringing out our song of love,"* and so on. What I heard was: *"Ramona, I hear the mishameltzabar,"* etc. It was not until years later that I realized the error of my ways and was able to sort out the correct wording.

While we may have been poor, life was very entertaining and most of that can be attributed to my mother. When my brothers and I were very young, we were fascinated by her stories about Kiezeleh Meizeleh, a mischievous, little mouse that was always getting into tough scrapes and miraculous escapes. These stories later fascinated our children and grandchildren. Too bad it never occurred to me to record these when tape recorders appeared on the scene.

There were also long stories she told us about families like the Rosenblatts, with lots of intrigue, and twists and turns in the plots. In those tales, many of the characters were elderly, ignored and neglected, or husbands who were under the influence of their spendthrift wives. The wives dressed expensively, ate out in fancy restaurants, and paid lots of attention to *their* side of the family. Fortunately, I did manage to record a few of these before she passed away about twenty five years ago.

Mother was so interactive with the three of us, sometimes taking us to movies like *Sorrell and Son*, a silent film released in 1927 which was based on a novel by Warwick Deeping, and which later was made into a TV miniseries in 1984. As I recall part of the plot, the son married a young, pretty woman and they lived on an island. In the middle of a raging storm, the young wife ordered her husband to row to the mainland to buy a pair of stockings for her. Sadly, he was drowned at sea.

My mother also seemed to live in a life of her own as we would often find slips of paper around the house with special words, proverbs or phrases that had caught her fancy. For example, "A bird in the hand" or "Paris in the Spring", the place where she was born.

Beware of Clay Pots

When children leave their mother's side and struggle to find their way in the world, they can be misguided and misled. These events are known as the dark moments of life, as simple and innocent as they may seem now. Here are some of mine that I remember all too well:

A few weeks after I was chosen to be the flag bearer at my elementary school, someone must have forgotten to tell me that the flag carrier was chosen for a specific period only and mine had ended. I was terribly embarrassed by the whole affair. With shoulders slumped downward, I inched back to my class with my tail between my legs and I probably cried myself to sleep that night.

In high school, we had a music appreciation class where we learned short musical phrases to many of the classical music pieces. This class introduced me to many of the famous symphonies and opera pieces which are so dear to me now. For example, we sang to Shubert's *Unfinished*

Symphony, Mascagni's *Caballero Rusticana*, and Tchaikovsky's *March Slav*. Despite my inability to carry a tune, I loved the music. In one of our classes, my teacher called upon me to sing a few lines of a piece of music we were studying. In my fright, I sang the verses in a high pitched, quavering voice, landing off-key on several notes. Having failed at that exercise, my teacher then called on one her favorites, a classmate of mine that never missed a note - although he did have a rather raspy voice.

When he was finished, our teacher turned to me and said, "It's too bad that such a beautiful voice is wasted on someone who can't read music." I blushed - another of life's dark moments!

That's not to say there weren't any bright moments in my young life. One of these revolved around the family radio. Somehow, my parents were able to buy a Majestic radio console, again on the installment plan. It was a fine piece of furniture and, when the radio was connected to a long wire antenna on the roof, we could listen to our programs. Mine were "Chandu, the Magician" and "The Shadow Knows," which I would hurry home from school to hear. My two brothers and I would also listen to the great Sunday evening programs until Eddie Cantor closed with "I Love to Spend Each Sunday with You," a bittersweet memory because it signaled our having to get ready for school the next day and then bedtime.

I remember one day when I should have stayed home rather than go to school. I was in junior high at the time and we were doing some experiments with strips of magnesium which, under the right conditions, can burn in the air like a firework's sparkler. I had volunteered to bring in a small clay flower pot for the experiment. We had a small one on the fire-escape outside of my parents' bedroom that was filled with earth, but the flower had long since died so I grabbed it. I took it to school but, when we performed the experiment, the magnesium flared up in the pot uncontrollably with clouds of smoke filling the area with the unmistakable smell of urine. How could that happen? Well, one or both of my parents were probably using it as a chamber pot and, under the right conditions, that's what happens to magnesium.

The Scottsboro Nine

At around the same time, the Young Communist League was having a social gathering for young boys and girls of the neighborhood. Admission was free but we had to sign a petition to "Free the Scottsboro Boys" first. I vaguely understood that they were nine young Afro-Americans accused, and then convicted, of raping two white girls. The evidence appeared to be shaky and the penalties drastic, especially since it happened down south. The case raised an international furor and dragged on for many years. As it turned out, charges were dropped for four of the boys and the remaining five received sentences ranging from seventy five years in prison to death.

The appeals reached the US Supreme Court twice. During and after World War II, I worried about whether any of the petition lists that I had signed might make problems for my career, but there was never a problem with my clearance. (There is a very recent effort, which has recently gained momentum to grant a full pardon to the Scottsboro boys, post mortem or alive.)

Patrusky Will Get You For This!

Nothing was more of a mystery to me than the great Patrusky, a man who would haunt me for most of my growing years. One time when we were very young children, my father had been working somewhere away for many weeks. It was a cold night when we heard a knock at the door. We were visited by a sinister figure that my mother later identified only as Patrusky. He was accompanied by a silent, menacing character whose name was not known. Patrusky grilled my mother about my father's whereabouts, which she denied knowing. As far as I could figure, Patrusky was some loan-shark who had loaned my father some money. We were terrified as he threatened dire consequences if my father didn't pay up. While I don't know how the matter was resolved, Patrusky is the name my mother would use like a weapon to scare us whenever we misbehaved. She would say, "If you boys don't stop, I'll get Patrusky after you!"

Accordingly, the Patrusky name was used a lot in our household as we could have easily qualified as three cases of ADHD had that diagnosis existed back then. Dad was a strict disciplinarian enforcing us with a very large razor-strap. During the day, my mom threatened us with punishment for our scandalous, outlandish behavior. She would report our behavior to my father when he got home that night. But night would seem far away, although as it, and Dad, approached, we started to slow down in fear of our fate.

As my father opened the door, mom would blurt out, "Let me tell you what they did today."

The three of us immediately scattered to the far corners of our small apartment. I rushed to my haven, which meant sliding under the bed. Dad handled that one with a broomstick as he lifted the mattress off the bed. The wire loop springs permitted the passage of the handle from above to the floor, gradually forcing me to the periphery and, of course, the razor-strap. Had it been another decade, I could have rushed to the telephone to call the authorities and report the abuse. But the telephone was in the corner candy store, the call would have cost an enormous sum of one nickel, and there were no laws in place to do anything about it.

Fortunately, Mom would switch from accuser to defender and place herself between Dad and whichever one of us was under attack. She would say, "That's enough, he's learned his lesson." I don't ever recall needing any suturing or bandaging, which is surprising.

The Alligator Pit

As the oldest of three brothers, I was responsible for taking mine to the movies on Saturday mornings. The films that interested us were "serials." The good guys were usually in white cowboy outfits and the bad in black cowboy outfits. They were about one-half hour in duration and always ended with the good guy and his beautiful girl-friend in great peril. It was hard to wait a whole week until the next episode to see how they got out of these situations. Then they would suffer another disaster and you had to wait until the following week. And so it went. Our parents had to come up with fifteen cents for the three of us each Saturday, which was no mean task in those days. It got worse when inflation set in and the price doubled to thirty cents.

It is hard sometimes to remember just how wild we were, especially when Paul and I routinely ganged up on our little brother, Larry. We scared him into thinking that there was an alligator pit under the bedroom floor, and that all we had to do was press a button for the floor to slide open so we could drop him into the open jaws of the hungry alligators. Such tall tales were probably reinforced by those Saturday morning trips to the movies. I'm sure that we were sent there so that our parents could get a little R 'n' R. Larry is well past Medicare age but I am sure he is still afraid of alligators. Sorry to say, Larry still sports a scar on his forehead from our horseplay.

Our reputation as the terrible Gendler threesome spread far and wide. We were seldom invited to visit family members. Our parents would be told that they only could come again without us. One scenario that I recall involved a visit to an uncle's family. They lived on the first floor above a store. Upon arrival, we were fascinated by a wooden case containing twelve seltzer bottles on the upper landing and, by the time we left, all had been reduced to shattered glass on the street floor by the Gendler Three. As we left, our host shook his fist at us and shouted at Clement and Becky never to bring us again.

My brother, Paul, could make things even more complicated. One Saturday, when we were walking home from the movies, I was holding a hand of each brother in my own. As we crossed the street, Paul suddenly yanked his hand loose and bolted in front of a passing car. He was knocked down and broke his clavicle or collar bone. Surprisingly, my dad was very understanding and Paul recovered after sporting a shoulder support for a few weeks. Still, things could have been much more serious.

Sometimes, it seems, they were. Once we lived on the third floor of an apartment building. I had my own room while my two younger brothers shared a room. While doing some work on my *rig*, a term we used for radio amateur equipment, I glanced out of my bedroom window which faced the back of a similar building with a shared yard between us. I could see kids running through the rooms of the opposite apartment at the same level across the way. There were no adults around and I was certain that two of those hooligans were my brothers. I kept looking out. In the midst of a game of Hide and Seek that they were playing, two of the hiders had taken to hanging out of the back windows. I yelled at them to get back inside, which they did. I always suspected that the two boys hanging from the windows were none other than my brothers.

One afternoon, while my parents were at work, I was at my rig again and my brother, Paul, had a visiting friend. They were playing Hide and Seek again and Paul's buddy hid in a closet. A problem arose when he lit a rolled-up piece of newspaper with a match in order to provide some light inside the closet. Dad's only suit caught fire and they yelled for me. I ran to the closet and told them to close the closet door tightly to starve the fire of oxygen. It sort of worked as the house didn't burn down but the pants ended up as a pair of knickers instead. That night my parents had to scour the neighborhood to find us.

Although the oldest child, I was no innocent either, especially when there was a chemistry set around. Once, Paul was going to be punished for something by Dad so he locked himself in the bathroom. Paul always claimed that he heard me tell Dad that I had an idea to get him out of the bathroom. I don't remember that portion of the incident but, if so, I was probably currying favor to count against whatever my next transgression would be. Paul stated that he noticed a piece of cardboard with a burning piece of sulfur on top sliding into the bathroom under the door. He claimed that, at first, he opened the bathroom window and hung his upper body outside to get some oxygen. Then, he staggered to the bathroom door to open it while almost asphyxiated. I don't remember the event quite that way but, when you consider my potassium chlorate experiment, Paul may have been right.

That's because the experiment in question had its genesis in an article I read in *Popular Mechanics* magazine. The article explained how potassium chlorate forms an explosive mixture when mixed with sugar and set on fire. That very chemical was available at the corner drug store and cheap. I had some spending money and, being quite inquisitive, I bought some potassium chlorate, put it in a shoebox, and mixed it with sugar. As white powder, it looked innocent enough so I took it with me to school by subway and showed it to my science teacher. He reacted by sending me home immediately with instructions to flush it down the toilet bowl. Fortunately there were no accidents that day as I quickly followed his orders. Little did the subway riders suspect that the kid beside them with the bushy hair had, within his possession, in a shoe box, a science experiment with such threatening consequences.

Getting our Window "Broke"

We moved apartments often. It would be years before my mother explained to me that we had to move or we would have been evicted for not paying the rent. In those days, landlords were sometimes desperate to rent their apartments so they offered several free rent months called concessions. My parents would move into an apartment during the concession period and then move out when it expired, before paying any rent. One year was the longest we ever lived in one place. When I came back home from Stuyvesant High School by subway, the first day after one of our moves, I couldn't even remember our new address. I don't know how I got to the new apartment but I suspect that my mother walked the neighborhood until we crossed paths.

Another reason we moved a lot was because of roaches. Whenever my mother found a cockroach in our home, it meant an immediate search for another place to live. Any bug found strolling along on one of our dishes, or in our pots and pans, meant they had to be thrown away. My mother was one of those constant hand washers which we now label as having obsessive-compulsive behavior but we didn't have a name or remedy for it then.

We lived mostly in Brooklyn, New York. We also spent some years in the Bronx amidst the same poor neighborhoods as Colin Powell, our former Secretary of State. While my brothers and I were born in the Williamsburg section of Brooklyn, we eventually moved to the Brownsville section which was the stomping grounds of Murder, Inc., later known as the Jewish mafia. It has been said that they used the sparsely inhabited Canarsie section of Brooklyn as the burial grounds for their murder victims.

I was in my mid-teens around then and, unknown to any one of us, we probably rubbed shoulders with some of the mafia members that preyed on the shopkeepers in the area. Thinking back, when two technically inclined friends of mine and I were making an extra few dollars by repairing radios, we rented a dilapidated store in Brownsville to use as a repair site. The store was at the basement level of an apartment building called a tenement. The rent was twelve dollars a month and we opened it each evening after we got home from school.

One evening, a big guy came into the store and offered to sell us protection. We looked at him and asked, "Protection from what?" He replied, "From getting your windows broke."

We told him that we couldn't afford the few dollars a month that he was demanding. We closed the operation shortly thereafter with the windows remaining intact. He probably left us alone since we were young kids and, obviously, slim pickings.

The Russians Are Coming!

As with most teenagers, I became obsessed with cars and developed a burning desire to learn how to drive. As my family couldn't afford a car, I had to beg for a chance to learn on someone else's. At the time, my father was employed by a large bakery owned by the Goshman Brothers and I occasionally earned a few dollars after school by helping out in the bakery. One of their more popular products was Russian Health bread; thirteen square slices of black bread in a cellophane wrapper. There was a small conveyor belt feeding the long loaves of Russian Health bread, which were sliced automatically with the slices still stacked as though intact. My job was to pick up a stack of thirteen slices and slap them onto the cellophane and then shift the package to the heat sealer. I grew quite adept at grabbing thirteen slices, no more, no less, without even counting. This work earned me a few dollars a week.

One additional benefit to this job involved the younger Goshman, Albert. He was a rough-and-tough type and the younger brother of Morris Goshman. Albert was enormously strong - probably from kneading huge mounds of dough. I once saw him arguing with the local tailor. The exchange got heated and Albert swung his powerful right arm and smashed it into the face of his weaker adversary. The tailor took off with blood dripping from his face. That's the kind of guy Albert was.

It was this same Albert that let me chauffer him around town, seated on the rear seat, on a particular mission. With only a learner's permit, I would drive him to different restaurants where I would park the car. He would then give me some small change to go into the restaurant and order a sandwich on his Russian Health Bread. If the sandwich which was served was counterfeit, I was told to refuse to pay for it stating that it was not Goshman's authentic Russian Health Bread.

Of course, Albert Goshman had singled out those particular restaurants, which he knew were not his customers. It was uncomfortable for me to carry this out, but my desire to practice for my driving test overcame such discomfort.

An additional problem that faced me was that, under New York City law, unlicensed drivers with learner's permits were only allowed to practice in designated areas. Yet no one challenged my driving around with the younger Goshman, until Albert decided to work over some restaurants in lower Manhattan – "maybe break their windows?" The crowded narrow streets made driving difficult and parking was impossible. Driving along a particularly narrow and congested street, a traffic officer motioned for me to stop the car and pull over. I didn't understand what the problem was but I braked to a stop and cranked the window open. As he was about to say something to me, Albert protested, "Officer, leave him alone. He's only a learner." I cringed but the overworked officer wiped his brow, looked at me, and at Albert, and exclaimed "Jesus! Be careful and get out of this traffic."

A Motley Crew

Looking back, it seems that I was always ashamed of something. I recall my embarrassment when my parents went with me one evening to my school for Parents' Day. We were all poorly dressed and when my mother spoke to my teacher, she used a falsetto voice. I never knew why she did this. I just assumed that it came from her operatic aspirations. There I was, this little, freckled- face, bushy-haired kid with a smile that sported a twisted tooth, which I concealed with my tongue. Charming. Over the years, the tooth straightened itself out all right, but we were an odd sight on a day meant for good impression.

Eventually, I did make a good impression. As I got into the early teens, I became interested in the sciences, particularly radio and electronics. I built some radio receivers from scrap parts that I found lying around. My science teacher in elementary school, Mr. Fiedler, quickly saw my talent and potential, and it was he who first urged me to become an engineer. At the time, I understood that to be someone that drives locomotives, but he set me straight and was my first mentor.

In high school I met Dr. Alexander Joseph, who later taught at the Bronx High School of Science. Both of them, Mr. Fiedler and Mr. Joseph, profoundly influenced my life. I visited Dr. Joseph much later in life, but when I tried to find any record of him nothing showed up. There had been an early principal at the school whose title and given name was Dr. Alexander. I guess it is possible that he had preferred earlier in his career not to use his family name but I never knew of it.

I never got to see him again. So, thank you Dr. Alexander Joseph, for being one of my mentors.

The Boss Comes First

I might have impressed my academic mentors, but I didn't exactly make grade with any of the bosses I encountered while still in my teens. Since the Great Depression caused unbelievable hardships on a global level, with its giant unemployment rates and low wages, my family went through particularly hard times. To help the family, my father who earned twenty dollars a week as a truck driver, tried to get me some afterschool employment, even though it only paid two to three dollars a week. Every little bit helped.

One job he arranged for me was behind the counter of a delicatessen in Rockaway, Queens. I was about thirteen years old and my duty included drawing beer from the large dispensers into mugs. Due to my inexperience, I only filled the mug two-thirds full with the remainder by foam. The customers complained bitterly about the foam collar but I soon learned how to draw the beer to the top of the mug with little or no foam. Of course, that pleased the customers but not the owner, and I was soon fired.

Sometime later, my parents got me a job delivering beauty supplies. I was a front-seat passenger for an elegantly dressed man who sold beauty supplies to beauty shop operators and hair dressing shops. The supplies were kept in the trunk of my employer's car and I had to deliver the order to the shops, which were usually several stories. After several deliveries on that first afternoon, he shocked me by putting his hand on my crotch and asking me to show him what I had there. I flipped out and opened the door on my side and ran away. My parents were angry about the inappropriate gesture, of course, and that was the end of my afternoon job.

Another job I took was with a tailor near my home in Brooklyn. He was willing to pay me three dollars a week to deliver dry-cleaned garments after school in the neighborhood. I arrived at one home with a garment that a young woman was eagerly waiting for. When I handed it to her, I was surprised to see that she was wearing nothing but a pink slip. I blushed deep red. I had been raised with no sisters and didn't take such a presentation lightly. She obviously noticed that I had been staring at her and immediately covered up. Her parents must have gotten involved as I soon lost that job as well.

Enter the Rosenbergs

While disease and illness are two topics that someday I would know volumes about, at fourteen I was mostly concerned with studying for my radio amateur license and passing the FCC exam. I passed and was assigned a Radio Amateur Station License, call sign W2KEE. While I still maintain the license, I have not had the time in recent years to practice the hobby that once brought me so much pleasure. These days the internet, email, and smart phones, do all the communicating.

In pursuit of the license, I had studied the exam with a neighbor who was four years older than me, whom I will call Joel B. He too passed the exam and got his license on the first try but we lost contact. Due to the four year difference in our ages, it was not unusual to find that older teens were being secretly recruited to fight for the Spanish Government against the rebels led by General Francisco Franco. Many died in Spain or were imprisoned.

Years later, I noticed that Joel's call listing in the Radio Amateur Call Book had disappeared. I wouldn't learn why until the Los Angeles Times ran a feature article about an infamous American electronics engineer who had dishonored his country and immigrated to the USSR after WWII. This has contributed greatly to the USSR's development of anti-aircraft radar systems. Joel's work was credited with helping to shoot down American planes during the Korean and Vietnam wars. The newspaper reported that he was greatly honored by the USSR with a large apartment in Leningrad and a huge salary of seven hundred rubles a month, unusual for his rather modest title.

The paper also pointed out that when Joel had become a senior he had applied for, and received, social security benefits from the United States Social Security Administration. The furor generated by the article was due to the indignation that this turncoat was trying to immigrate back to the USA.

Consequently, our congress was considering passing a law specifically excluding him from continuing to receive any benefits or ever returning to the US. I learned more about him. He had been under investigation over the years by the US government as he had been reported to have been a classmate of Julius Rosenberg and Martin Sobell while attending City College in New York. If you know your history, you know that Julius Rosenberg and his wife, Ethel Rosenberg, were executed in 1953 for passing military secrets to the USSR. Martin Sobell was imprisoned for espionage in 1951 and released in 1969.

Coincidentally, during World War II, I worked for a while at a small electronics factory as a production line supervisor which was producing a combination transmitter-receiver for the US Signal Corps. In one incident, I argued with the resident Signal Corps inspector, at the plant, about trying to pass one of the units with a trivial problem, at least in my opinion. His area supervisor, the very same Julius Rosenberg, was visiting the plant that day when he stormed over to me and, quite angrily, told me that I was sabotaging the war effort.

One can easily understand that some years later when reading about the case, I was shocked to read about Julius Rosenberg being arrested and accused of espionage. I looked up his name in the telephone directory and called his home. His wife, Ethel Rosenberg, answered and I told her of my surprise at the news. I related that, in my brief encounter with him, I found him intensely protective of our country. She reassured me that it was all some kind of gross mistake.

Shortly thereafter, I was shocked when I read in the local papers that she, too, was arrested. Given the situation, it is my honest suspicion that my conversation with her was listened to by the authorities.

As we were caught up in the Cold War mentality at the time, the case received enormous publicity around the world and the subsequent executions were criticized internationally as being excessive. It was only recently that I learned that they had been involved with Joel B. before he had moved to the Soviet Union.

Young Sam, the Student

Early in my school career, I was skipped through the second half of my fifth semester in elementary school. Later, I was also moved into the Rapid Advance Program of my junior high school. This latter move compressed four years of junior high into two years. My mentors had drilled into me the idea of applying to leading high schools. I took the exams and was admitted into Stuyvesant High School in Manhattan.

While Stuyvesant High School's reputation was excellent at the time, it has since developed to become one of the greatest high schools in the United States, one with many illustrious graduates.

Every morning I had to wake up early to catch the train from Brooklyn to Manhattan. The subway train ran on an elevated structure in my area, and was always tightly packed. As a fifteen year old boy, when pressed against the right person and of the right gender, I occasionally found the packing in of passengers to be a stimulating experience.

On one of those subway trips, I was hanging on to one of the overhead hangers and reading one of my school books when I noticed that I was facing an attractive, well-dressed young woman who was sitting opposite me and reading her folded newspaper. I felt the upper edge of the newspaper poking my sensitive areas repeatedly and quite accurately. I didn't budge from the position, even as the car emptied out leaving me the only one standing. She chose not to look up. When she finally got off, at the station before my 14th Street destination, it appeared that several of the men in the car ran after her. I don't know what they hoped to achieve by pursuing her this way, or if they even dared to approach her, but events like that happened only once in a while. More often than not, my forty five minute ride to the 14th Street station was hot, boring, and uneventful, without any room to even open a book.

When I graduated from Stuyvesant at the tender age of sixteen, I enrolled at the College of the City of New York, CCNY. The depression was still in full force so the school was hard pressed to accommodate its burgeoning but poor student body. Almost all of my required courses for the first semester were closed at registration. Years later, I learned that the college would have made an exception for me, if I had presented a note from an employer regarding my job responsibilities. Unfortunately, I didn't know that at the time. Besides, I had no job. On a daily basis I had an early subway ride from Brooklyn to the northern tip of Manhattan which took almost two hours, then a class or two, lots of time off, maybe another class later on in the day, and another two-hour trip home to Brooklyn.

Whenever I had an extra twenty-five cents I would head downtown to the Paramount Theatre, an opulent venue that is now owned by Long Island University and used for classroom space. I would watch live bands playing while we danced in the aisles. Singers like Frank Sinatra and band leaders like Artie Shaw, Benny Goodman, Tommy and Jimmy Dorsey gave my daily grind a big lift.

Pedal to the Metal

I had to drop out after my first year of CCNY for lack of funding. My brothers were moving up and also getting ready for college too. At seventeen, I found a job as a wireman at the Precision Apparatus Company which made vacuum tube testers. Little did I know at the time that those little tubes would be the start of my scientific career, one that would lead me to the Gemini I space mission. The company was located in the Williamsburg section of Brooklyn, at the waterfront near the Brooklyn Navy Yard, a few miles from where I was born. From the windows of the plant, I could see a drab warehouse nearby that had a sign announcing what was a strange name to me at the time, Pfizer. Precision offered me a job that paid 25 cents per hour for eight hours a day, seven days a week. Since Saturday was paid for at one and a half times, and Sunday was paid at double, I figured I could earn about $19 a week.

At the time, a new car cost about $900, rents in our lower class apartments were about $20 per month, a man's suit cost about $20, a hot dog on a roll cost was about 15 cents, a pack of cigarettes cost about 25 cents and a Hershey bar cost 5 cents.

When I reached the age of eighteen, I took my first driving test and passed. Since I had started working at seventeen, I saved about a dollar a week. When I had saved $25, I bought a used car with about forty thousand miles on its speedometer. That was about the lifetime limit of the average used car in those days. With very little horsepower available, I would try to zoom along with the optimism of youth. It was a puny effort with lots of exhaust smoke trailing behind, caused by burning oil escaping the worn piston rings.

Regarding this little dynamo of a car, one incident made a big impression on me for life. It happened on Atlantic Avenue in Brooklyn, the area where there was an overhead structure for the Long Island Railroad trains heading into Manhattan. Several cars, including mine, had stopped for a red light. I was gunning the motor intermittently, ready to zoom off when the light turned to green. When the light changed, I stomped down on the gas pedal but halted when the car to my left didn't budge at all. Fortunately, my car had only moved forward about a foot when I noticed that an enormous Mack Truck was zooming across Atlantic Avenue from the left. I would have been killed if I had not halted my charge forward. More than seventy years later I still relive this scenario.

These older cars, and trucks, had mechanical brakes, not hydraulic ones. This meant that tramping down on the brake pedal pulled on a bundle of four, flexible steel cables, each connected to the brake shoe of the respective wheel. Imagine trying to get equal stopping force on each of the four wheels simultaneously. In those days, we were really were driving by the seat of our pants.

Bernie and Bummy

Sometimes we were living by the seat of our pants too. Still in my teens, I would get together with a group of friends after work that I had gotten to know in the Brownsville section of Brooklyn, one of Murder, Inc.'s stamping grounds.

We all came from poor families. Eventually we worked our way out of poverty. My closest friend, Bernie Gold, was a stocky red-head. He never got past the 10th grade but he had a quick mind and an amazing sense of humor. His first job was working at a glove factory, punching out a design consisting of tiny perforations in the back of each glove. In those days of cheap labor, at two dollars a day, it was more economical to employ a strong man to use a heavy steel block, shaped somewhat like a hammer, to pound on another heavy steel block with sharp pins projecting from the opposite face. This had to be done in one stroke and resulted in Bernie developing powerful shoulder and upper extremity muscles.

This development came in handy. We were often challenged by other groups in our neighborhood. I was never much of a fighter but Bernie was, so I got used to holding his sweater or jacket while he pounded away at someone who didn't like the way we looked at him. He was good at being the pounder but one day Bernie bit off more than he could chew.

We were strolling along one evening when we noticed that some young boys, on bicycles, were taunting the small girls walking ahead of us. Naturally, Bernie and I yelled at them to stop. An older guy on a bicycle came peddling furiously from behind.

He shouted at us, "Who said that?"

Bernie responded with, "I did!"

They quickly shed their sweaters.

I held Bernie's sweater as usual, while the other guy assumed a professional stance and pounded Bernie with lightning fast fists. Bernie tried to defend himself but he was no match for this professional fighter. I tried to help by grabbing this guy's arms to pull him away and was shocked that they felt so solid.

I did manage to intercede though, and they both quieted down. The opponent identified himself as Al Bummy Davis, a contender for the lightweight world championship. Bernie asked how well he did. Bummy answered lousy. Poor Bernie. With all those lumps Bernie had a lot of explaining to do when he got home.

Bummy had been born into our Brownsville neighborhood as Albert Davidoff. Just a few years after that episode he was shot to death at a holdup in a bar by an armed robber. When the robber ran out of the bar with the money he had stolen from the bar, it was Bummy Davis who ran after him yelling at the robber to drop his loot. The robber turned and fired the shot that killed the contender for the lightweight world championship, as well as a veteran of WW II.

Bernie also served. He joined the US Air Force during WW II and was stationed in England. His job as an airplane mechanic was to patch up and quickly refuel the bombers and fighter planes that returned from missions over Europe so that they could take off again.

After the war, he dropped all of those skills. His wife, Roz, took over the home repairs as it seemed that Bernie had even forgotten which end of a screwdriver was the handle. Upon his discharge from the military, he bought a used pickup truck. He would call on candy and grocery stores and sell them candy and cookies in a role he called a Wagon Jobber. The going was very rough for Bernie as he sold mostly to people of the poor Puerto Rican areas of Manhattan. He persevered despite having to endure long waits for the owner of each tienda to finish attending to the customers before paying attention to Bernie's sales pitch.

One day, while he was waiting in a busy store, a Hispanic truck driver came in with some cookies called galletas, pronounced gal-YET-as. These are a great treat in Puerto Rico and in the Puerto Rican neighborhoods of New York City. The store owner left his customers and rushed over to the driver and accused him of passing up his store for the past few weeks. The owner of the tienda expressed disappointment at how small the amount of galletas was in the present delivery. Bernie, always quick on the draw, listened in astonishment and noted the company name and address painted on the truck. He looked up the company, Tropical Crackers, and visited the factory. He introduced himself to the owner, whom we will call Señor Garcia.

The timing proved perfect in that Sr. Garcia was having lots of problems trying to control his fleet of delivery trucks and was drowning in complaints from customers caused by undependable deliveries. Bernie convinced him that he could take over the sales and delivery end of the business. These promises proved true as Bernie controlled the delivery men who no longer could decide whether or not they wanted to work a particular day. If they goofed off more than once or twice, they found that they no longer had a job. He continued to run his own truck but delivering only the tropical crackers known as galletas.

Sr. Garcia treated Bernie as his one and only son since he was single and childless. Bernie prospered and, years later, when Sr. Garcia was in trouble with the IRS for not being able to come up with the withholding tax, Bernie bought him out. Sr. Garcia had made the gross mistake of falling in love with a Mexican movie star and trying to satisfy her desire for jewelry and furs. Many decades and several acquisitions later, Bernie had moved his operations to a giant building in the Bronx and became one of the largest candy and food distributors in the Northeastern United States.

Bernie passed away in 2004 at the ripe age of eighty four when he suffered a heart attack after a bout with pneumonia. He had an indwelling defibrillator for several years which had kicked in, episodically. As a very young child, his mother had been told by the doctor that he had a heart murmur and that she shouldn't spend a lot of money on him as he wouldn't last very long. Bernie proved that doctor wrong.

Another childhood friend of mine was Bob, short for Sidney Barbanel. Bob had more of an allowance than I had. His mother would give him a few dollars to spend compared to my twenty five cents a week. Although his father had passed away when he was a child, his mother was inventive, selling aprons, dresses, stockings and other sundries to local women from her ground floor apartment. Like me, he studied at a top high school, Brooklyn Technical High School, commonly referred to as Brooklyn Tech.

Bob had a successful career and was able to help me in my own. His contributions will appear later in this work.

In Memory of Paul

The passing of my younger brother Paul was sadder still. He started out in life as a successful student at Townsend Harris High School located in New York City, which was and is still one of the city's top schools. After graduation, he entered the US Army during wartime and saw active duty in France and Germany. He was wounded in the Battle of the Bulge and discharged from the army as being disabled.

Despite his disabled status, Paul was an outstanding athlete and achiever. He excelled in tennis, Ping-Pong, hand-ball, billiards and even chess. He enrolled in Clemson University and graduated with honors. Paul chose teaching as a career and took a position in the New York City school system as an English teacher. Over the years, he progressed to the position of chairman of the department.

Paul married Rochelle Rothman, who was also a school teacher, and they had two children, Ellen and Seth, who are now successful physicians in the New York area. They are each widely quoted and respected in their professions - Ellen Gendler, in dermatology, and Seth, in gastroenterology. When they were children, Paul and his family moved into a new home in Bellmore, Long Island, at around the same time that I moved my family to West Hempstead, Long Island.

Paul continued his upward climb by advancing to assistant principal, and then principal, of his school. He would become assistant superintendent of his home school in Bellmore, LI, and then superintendent of schools for his home school system, as well as chairman of the school board of his home community. Later, he became superintendent of schools in Rye, New York, located in Westchester County, just north of the city. As a highly reputed reformer of troubled school systems, he put in place various control methods including the necessity of a doctor's note whenever a teacher called in sick, which drastically reduced the high teacher absentee rate.

A lot of teachers resented the new controls and soon took a proactive stance stirring up the small community. The small city of Rye, including the school board, was split into pro and con Paul Gendler factions. Seeing the turmoil in the community, Paul negotiated an end to his contract. He left the area and went on to better things. Soon after, he took a position on the campus of the University of Bridgeport in Connecticut with an organization that placed small schools on various college campuses around the US. These schools taught English to foreign students before they entered their freshman year of college in the United States.

Another reason Paul decided to work outside of New York State was that he had reached the age where he could draw upon his pension if he no longer worked within the state. While he found the concept of the foreign language training program was good, he was not content with the way it was achieved. He was invited several times to the home office of the organization in California but, in Paul's opinion, they did not respond adequately to his advice. He gambled with his pension and savings by leaving the organization and forming his own, the Language Institute for English (LIFE). He set up a curriculum and hired teachers for a school on the campus of Fairleigh Dickinson University in New Jersey. He researched the foreign student situation and visited the various countries in Europe and Asia, interviewing sales representatives in selected countries. The Language Institute for English picked up steam and thrived expanding onto more campuses.

After several years, Berlitz expressed an interest in acquiring it and made Paul an offer. A purchase agreement was proposed in the order of $3,000,000 but, at the top level of the Berlitz organization, the contract was rejected. The next year, the LIFE organization earned an amazing pre-tax amount of about $1,000,000 and negotiations reopened. The Berlitz people finally acquired it for about $4,000,000. Paul remained as a consultant for the organization for a few years and then retired to Boca Raton, Florida.

Paul and I stayed in very close touch over the years by telephone, after we moved out of Long Island, New York. I bragged about him to any one that would listen and he told me that he did the same about my career. When I had to put my electronics company through reorganization via bankruptcy, he advised me to take a job as a shop teacher in electronics. He counseled me that it was obvious that I was not a very good businessman, and that I would enjoy summer vacations and a regular paycheck. His so-called advice only hardened my resolve to keep on going and to show him. Now I wonder if his egging me on like that was his true intention all along. I never asked him.

We communicated frequently, exchanging the latest jokes and riddles, as well as brainstorming each other's problems and successes.

Our parents who did much of our babysitting when our children were young were supremely proud of their own off-spring. From our humble beginnings, they received enormous gratification at our successes while we never shared our failures with them.

When I succeeded in my medical career, Paul would not take medical advice from me. He told me that his doctors were board-certified and graduates of New York University where Paul had studied and taught. In his opinion, that made them paramount in the medical field. Meanwhile, I had done very well at my medical schooling, which I absorbed with great zeal. I was also less enthusiastic about the medical care Paul himself was receiving.

We lost Paul in 2005 at the age of seventy nine after a devastating attack of influenza despite the fact that he had received a flu vaccine shot. The disease shut down vital organs and he battled the illness for several months of intensive care with a tracheostomy in place. But, as the vital organs were finally returning to normal functioning, he suffered a stroke and died shortly thereafter.

An enormous crowd attended his funeral services in his home city of Boca Raton, Florida. The eulogies were heartbreaking and all of them, including mine, were unanimous in that he was outstanding in so many ways. While Rebecca and Clement had handed us some wonderful genes, in retrospect, I lacked the *good at sports* gene and we both missed the *carrying a tune* genes.

My Kid-Brother Larry

Our youngest brother, Larry, despite the induced alligator phobia, led a relatively normal childhood through the hungry times. When Larry finished high school, he enlisted in the US Navy just as World War II was winding down. During one of his leaves, he became ill with an upper respiratory infection and I recommended that he stay in bed an extra day to recuperate. Confident of my advice, I wrote a long note to his superior officer on his behalf on a blank sheet of paper. I had no better document since this happened many decades before I became a medical doctor. When he returned to his base a day late the Navy allowed him to continue his recuperation with a week in the brig.

After the war, Larry became a prizefighter and had modest successes in the ring. His greatest success was in not suffering any broken bones or scarring. After his fighting career, he worked as a photographer, sometimes in his own business and other times working for others. He married a pretty blonde named Lila Marks and they had three children; Robert, Susan, and Mindy.

After a stint as a high school wrestler, Robert also opted for medicine as a career. He went to medical school in France but was able to transfer to the Mount Sinai School of Medicine located in New York City. He went on to complete a residency program in interventional radiology and is now part of a distinguished group of radiologists in New Haven, Connecticut.

Perhaps inspired to some degree by his father's skill in photography, Robert's hobby is astronomy and he spends whatever spare time he has shooting incredible pictures of the heavens with professional equipment. His talent and techniques have produced unbelievable vistas and NASA has even featured his work on their website. Dr. Robert Gendler is world famous and his published books have been translated into multiple languages. Since photos can say a thousand words, one can check out his website at www.robgendlerastropics.com

Unfortunately, his sister Susan developed breast cancer in her early thirties and, after a long battle which included fund raising, she succumbed to that disease. Mindy too passed away, albeit in her first year of life due to a pulmonary infection.

Along Came Etta

Living in Brownsville, Brooklyn with my parents and working for the Precision Apparatus Corporation, my wages crept up as the US got into defense work supporting the war effort overseas. My leisure time was spent with my friends, Bernie and Bob (Barbanel) as well as several others; Walter, Weffie, Montie, Herbie, and two-chinned Mike, who got his name from his obesity.

The girls were the other half of our group whom we paired off with. I was attracted to sixteen-year-old Etta Futernick, who was easily the prettiest. Etta looked a younger replica of the famous movie star, Hedy Lamarr, with black hair and brown eyes, a slim figure and shapely legs.

I was eighteen then and I had just gotten over chronic shyness around the opposite sex. Having been raised in a family of two brothers and no sisters, I flushed bright red whenever I would talk to a girl. Aside from getting fired up by looking at the underwear and stocking ads in catalogs and magazines, I had no sexual experience with the opposite sex except in my imagination. That is, if you do not count my rather curious fourteen year old cousin. When I was about ten, we were sometimes visited by my aunt Rachel and her daughter. During the visit, my cousin and I would go to the bathroom to play It, an experimental, anatomic game of our own invention. We had to pass our parents on the way to the bathroom but they were too old to know what was going on. All I can say is that the game was interesting to me, but I was too young to make it very interesting for my cousin.

When I got a little older, my friends and I would, occasionally, get together at night with girls. Once, I wound up with a pretty girl who was visiting our hostess's home with her sister. They were from Canada and my companion was very obliging. There was lots of kissing in a dark room and while there was very little resistance to my further exploration, there was no assistance from her in trying to get under her fortress-like undergarments. After several hours, I waddled home in extreme discomfort.

There were similar experiences with a girl that I visited several times while she was babysitting. My mother had met her and was delighted by her honey blonde looks and generous curves. In those days, I guess mothers fitted their daughters with corsets which not only slimmed the figure but served as body length chastity belts. In retrospect, I should have equipped myself with specially designed extraction tools. Listening to my friends, they boasted that they had far greater success with their encounters than I had. I was terribly jealous and feared that I would remain a virgin forever. Even the condom that I carried around yellowed with age.

Bernie paired up with Roz or Rozzie, nicknames for Roslyn. Bob and Hilda made up a pair and Walter, a couple of years older than the rest of us, matched up with Sophie. Herbie joined up with Claire - but then went to war and came back with a piece of shrapnel in his brain, which caused permanent paralysis on his right side. Monty, a heavy smoker, married Evie but he died young of Buerger's disease, which causes the legs to go into a tight spasm especially when exacerbated by smoking, a bad habit he could never give up.

Etta was quite attracted to me when we were in our mid-teens, and I to her. We figured that one day we were going to be married. We all married our matches, except Weffie who had no mate in our group. All of the marriages lasted until the death of one of the partners, which is something quite rare for marriages these days.

As you may have noted, our nicknames were formed by attaching "y" or "ie" to the root of the given name. Weffie's given name was William. Although we could have shortened it to Bill, it somehow became Weffie.

Years earlier, when Walter was eighteen, we pooled about twenty-five dollars each to buy a used Auburn, a cloth-topped sedan with a long hood. It had an incredible thirst for gasoline which cost about fifteen cents a gallon then. We bought a black chauffeur's hat for Walter as he was the only one old enough for a driver's license. We coordinated our vacations to get away together and our destination was always a rented bungalow in the Catskill Mountains. Every summer, when my parents could put a few dollars together, they would rent a place to get their three sons out of the city where polio was rampant. (If they couldn't manage that, it meant sleeping out on the fire escape or on the roof due the hot humid weather.) In the summer of 1937, for some reason, my mother had to go back to the city with my younger brothers and the bungalow was available.

So off we went. On our way to the Catskills, however, we passed through Kingston, New York. At a construction site in an intersection, Walter detoured around the excavation. All of a sudden, our massive Auburn ran into a brand new car driven by a Kingston insurance broker who turned out to be very influential in that city. A motorcycle officer showed us how our car should have maneuvered the detour by squeezing around the site on his motorcycle. We all had to accompany him to the police station where it looked like we might have to spend the night in jail. But they quickly found a judge who made us promise that we would pay the damages when we got back to the city.

Our vacation was great after that and we returned safe and without further incident. Though we never got enough money together to pay the damages and Walter would often show us the threatening notices he received from the Kingston Police Department. They threatened to come to the New York area and arrest us. It never happened. But I have avoided Kingston ever since.

Pranksters Bernie and Sam

We never avoided a good joke or prank, especially Bernie and I. I remember one such golden opportunity when Walter's niece was getting married in a large hall. We called it the Russian Dummy, based on our mispronunciation of the true Russian name. Walter's parents were from that country and we all curried favor with him since he owned a small pool room where we played billiards whenever we could afford the twenty-five cents charge.

The hall consisted of a dance floor surrounded by chairs that lined the walls. There were two gaps in the line of chairs, one for a bar and the other for the bandstand that seated four musicians.

Our group was given the job of filming the entire ceremony and the reception that followed. During a break, the musicians and the bartender went outside for a smoke. The floor cleared as everyone sought their seats. One of our buddies started filming the guests with Walter's

8 mm camera. He panned the seated guests and reached the two seats where Bernie and I were sitting. He paused and we waved at the camera.

As he resumed panning, we ran behind him and plunked ourselves down in the next pair of empty seats, and so on. By the end, we were miraculously in all the scenes. When Walter's brother, Nicky, picked up the developed film from the neighborhood pharmacy, he hurried it home to show to the waiting family, including the newlyweds. Quoting Walter, Nicky's narration ran something like this:

"There is Aunt Tasha, Uncle Boris, Cousin Ivana, Bernie and Sam, our neighbor Ruth, her husband Joe, their son Phil, Bernie and Sam, Grandma Sasha, friend Joan, our coworker Francie, Bernie and Sam," over and over again.

Towards the end, the panning reached the bar and there were none other than Bernie and Sam mixing and shaking the drinks. A few moments later the film of the bandstand showed Bernie and Sam beating the drum and tooting the trumpet. Long before that scene, everyone was rolling on the floor, laughing hysterically.

Growing Up and Getting Serious

As happens all too often, laughter ends far too soon. Even pranksters like Bernie and me have to settle down. As the war effort went into high gear, I began to earn much more money at wiring tube testers. I was the fastest of their wiremen in the company but they never moved me up to the test department. My pay, which included overtime, reached about sixty dollars per week. The big money jobs, eighty dollars to ninety dollars per week, were further up the knowledge scale.

At this point, I was regretting that I had to drop out of college. I took a competitive exam for admission to Cooper Union's night school. I was admitted but lasted only one year. This was mostly due to fatigue as I was working long hours at the Precision Apparatus Company in Williamsburg, Brooklyn. I had to hike across the Brooklyn Bridge to get to the school. Three of the four classroom walls were covered with blackboards. As I followed the math being written on the blackboard at the front of the room, my eyelids would droop. When I opened them, the professor was already at the back of the room writing up a storm. The homework was another story as I was also working weekends. I had to drop out after one year due to sheer exhaustion.

Later on, and without a college degree, I earned the title of assistant engineer but had a limited salary due to my lack of formal education. Finally I switched to a small company in Long Island City, Queens. The company name was Fada Radio. Their regular products consisted of small radios of five vacuum tubes, nicknamed the All-American Five. Fada Radio derived its name from the initials of FAD Andrea, who was a pioneer in the early days of electronics. The king of the All-American Five was Emerson radio, a name that has since been adopted by others.

Production of such non-essential products was limited due to the demands of war production. Government contracts were easy to obtain from the military even without bidding. Fada Radio took on several contracts and the one that I worked on as a project engineer was for an audio signal generator that the US Government needed in vast quantities. The sole producer, up to that time, was a tiny company in the Pacific North-west that was started up by two engineers in a home garage. The Government was afraid that this tiny company could not handle the demand. They needed a second source. The prime source was named Hewlett-Packard, after the two engineers that founded it. A $100 invested in the Hewlett-Packard Company then, would probably be worth over $1,000,000 now - but who had such a vast sum back then? Its survival at that time was doubtful. I was given the job of matching and improving the product which was a marvel of performance despite the primitive materials available.

Another contract which Fada was working on was for Loran Equipment which was an advanced, ship-positioning system based on several shore-based transmitters. Since satellites were far off into future, the US Navy was setting up a Global Positioning System using a fleet of ships. This was around the 1940s and was a version of the modern day GPS mechanism that employs satellites today. I believe that Loran was short for Long Range Navigation.

The team working on the Loran project had few engineering degrees within the group. This was also true of my project competing with Hewlett-Packard. In fact, I believe that the only engineering degree in the organization was held by the chief engineer. Each morning he arrived with a mysterious bottle in a brown paper bag which he placed in his desk drawer. By the end of the day the empty bottle and paper bag had been discarded into a waste basket.

On one occasion, while passing through the Loran project area, I took a moment to join the project team there to look at the instrument screen which held the Loran display. The obvious problem that they were studying was the jiggling of the display, slowly moving up and down. After quickly assessing the problem, I went to the machine shop where I fashioned a steel case of certain dimensions. Later, I found the opportunity to revisit the Loran team, which was still working on the jiggle in the display. I slipped the steel case over the power transformer which converted the power line voltage to the various voltages needed by the vacuum tubes doing the work. The jiggle disappeared instantly. It had been caused by the magnetic field at the power line frequency, which had been escaping from the power transformer through its thin metal case.

A far more difficult problem was the distortions in the wave shapes of the audio signal generator on which we were working. When we went to the chief engineer with the problem, he stated, that he didn't give a damn about the distorted wave shapes just as long as we meet the harmonic level specifications. I looked at him incredulously as the distorted wave shapes were due to the presence of the excessive harmonic signals. This was another fork in the road for me. As I walked away I promised myself that I would work harder, so that one day I wouldn't have to report to bosses, particularly ignorant ones.

Courting Etta

Etta and I had been a pair for several years and it was understood by everyone that someday we would get married - understood by all but her parents. She was a beautiful young lady and often spent some summer vacations at her oldest sister's home in Buffalo, New York.

I was just out of my teens, from a poor family, and not on my way to a real profession. A sorry sight. Etta reminded me later on that I would often show up after work in a sweater with my elbow poking through the worn sleeve.

A telephone was a rare finding in the average home in those days. If I wanted to place a call to Etta, I would have to call the landlord's apartment just below her family's apartment. The landlord's wife would shout Etta's name into the air-shaft common to both apartments. Etta would then go down one flight of stairs to answer my call.

Such calls were placed from the local candy store, which acted as a communication center of sorts. Cashing in on the arrangement were several youngsters who were waiting for incoming calls so that they could earn a few coins by running to fetch the person called.

During the work week, I would pick up Etta at her home in the evening and we would go for a ride in my father's 1939 Pontiac. I had helped my dad buy the used car which cost about $250 and probably had about forty-thousand miles on the odometer. In those days that was close to the lifetime of the automobile as metallurgy was still primitive. The motor would become troublesome at around that mileage point with the crankshaft bearings and the piston rings wearing down. This would manifest itself by a bearing knock and heavy oil consumption.

The larger part of the cost of the car was paid off in installments, much like today's car loan. Etta wasn't impressed. In fact, she was surprised that our car was not purchased for cash. Her father would never purchase anything that he couldn't pay for immediately. Though it was the installment plan that allowed us to have nice furniture and a large radio console, the installment payments were almost impossible to pay off due to the high rate of interest.

After my workday we would sometimes wind up in Lovers' Lane in Canarsie, located about five miles from her home. Our love affair progressed from boyfriend-girlfriend to an engagement. Marriage was still off in the distance due to her parents' reluctance to have their beautiful daughter marry such a poor groom.

Etta's oldest sister, Becky, had married a man that she had known from her younger days in Russia where they both grew up. His name was Isadore and he had arrived in the US essentially penniless. He wound up in Buffalo where he got a job as an electrician's helper with hard work and low pay. With tenacity and ambition, he learned the trade and branched out on his own in Buffalo. He made frequent trips to Brooklyn to woo Becky, bringing gifts for the entire family. Back in Russia, it had been a dim hope of his to somehow win the apple of his eye. After all, he was also a poor youngster, and she was the daughter of the owner of the village general store.

Izzie gradually met Becky's parents' requirements in that he was affluent and fairly orthodox in his religious beliefs. They slowly swallowed their reluctance to have their oldest daughter move four hundred miles away. Becky and Izzie married. They raised four children and numerous grandchildren, as well as great grandchildren.

As a married couple they would occasionally drive down to Brooklyn. One day they invited Etta to spend her summer vacation with them in Buffalo. She was about sixteen years old when they picked her up and drove her to Buffalo. She spent that summer in the couple's vacation cottage in nearby Canada. They expressed their desire to have Etta meet a dental student from an affluent family in Buffalo. The idea behind this was to spark a romance, and that she might want to remain in Buffalo to help raise Becky's growing family. Little did they know that when she returned to Brooklyn in early fall, all she would want to do was to see that poor bushy-haired boy with the elbow sticking out of the threadbare sweater and the twenty five cents an hour job. The one without any strong religious fervor.

Early Years of Marriage

Etta's parents' reluctance flipped when Etta and I were alone in their apartment one Sunday. Her parents arrived in the late afternoon to find us asleep in each other's arms. This shocked them. In that instant, they started planning for an elaborate wedding. The custom was that the bride's parents would pay for most of the wedding, which was good for my parents who could only make a tiny contribution. The wedding day was set for January 1, 1942. My mother was especially delighted as there were war-clouds on the horizon and married men were being excused from the draft which had just begun. That didn't last long, as the war involved many millions of men from various countries.

One month before the wedding, we were visiting one of Etta's brothers when her twin brother Joe arrived with an announcement that the Japanese had just bombed Pearl Harbor. The date was December 7, 1941. Almost every one of my generation remembers what they were doing when they heard the news.

The next month we were married, which was scary. Etta continued to work at a dry cleaning store, from opening to closing, for a few more months. I urged her to quit as I never liked my former hectic home life with both parents working.

The next adjustment revolved around the fact that my in-laws were religious. It was not the way I grew up. I adapted quickly although not willingly. Before the major religious holiday of Rosh Hashanah, which was followed ten days later by Yom Kippur, I was expected to buy a new suit, a couple of shirts, and a fedora hat, all of which were worn during the entire three days of the holidays.

As required by the orthodox customs, Etta's entire family sat all day long during those three days with the women separated from the men. All of the sons and son-in-laws sat on a long hard bench with my father-in-law parked solidly at the end. To go to the men's room in the synagogue, we had to work our way to the end. That is my father-in-law had to get up, sit down and then repeat the scenario upon our return. It made you think twice about whether or not you really had to go.

The synagogues were in small buildings without air-conditioning. It seemed to me that the holidays in early fall always landed during what we knew as an Indian summer. The temperature and humidity seemed to reach levels found in a sauna. Any attempt to open windows was greeted with shouts of "draft, draft," because people were afraid of catching pneumonia if the windows were not hermetically sealed.

Since I had no childhood training, my reading of Hebrew Scripture was complicated by sweat rolling down from under my hat brim and into my eyes and shirt collar. The time dragged on. To make matters worse, we had to stand up and sit down every few minutes.

The last of the three days was Yom Kippur. It was particularly rough as we had to fast from sundown the night before until the first star appeared at the end of the next day. It was roughly a twenty four hour period. We couldn't even have a glass of water. This was meant to help us repent for all of the sins we incurred during the year and to persuade the Lord to forgive us. The holy day ends with three recitals, of the Hebrew equivalent, "Hear O' Israel, The Lord our God, The Lord is One, Blessed is the glory of His Kingdom, forever." Then seven recitals of "The Lord, He is God." The final statement, "Next year in Jerusalem," triggers the blowing of the Shofar, the Ram's Horn. Only then were we allowed to eat and drink. Whew. What a relief.

After one or two moves between rental apartments, we moved into an attic apartment in Flatbush, Brooklyn, which was a short trolley trip to the Williamsburg section of Brooklyn where I worked. I met up with the same conductor each weekday morning and at the same time. I would sit close to his position up front and we would chat. I can't imagine about what, but it made for a pleasant trip.

One day, I woke up later than usual. Despite my haste, I arrived at the trolley stop about twelve minutes too late. To my surprise, my regular trolley car was half a block away crawling along and my conductor-buddy was watching for me in his rear view mirror. Although the next trolley was already in sight, I ran for my regular trolley. I thanked my buddy for his kind consideration. I didn't dare face the other passengers in the trolley car. Small kindnesses like that just don't happen today.

And Baby Makes Three

When Etta became pregnant, we moved to a larger apartment in East Flatbush on the second floor of a two-family house. The house was also occupied by the landlord who lived in a single room carved out of the first floor. The rent was about $40 a month, a large part of my salary. Back then a hot dog cost 10 cents and a Hershey bar cost a nickel, as did a telephone call and a subway ride to anywhere in the metropolitan area that the subway system traversed. We stayed there for some years.

In 1945, Etta gave birth to our first born, Jeff. He was an irritable baby and we spent hours trying to put him to sleep at night. We scratched his back, rocked him, and sang him to sleep, sometimes all at the same time. His favorite song, which only sometimes worked, was Heartaches, popularized by Ted Weems and his orchestra in 1947. Heartaches was written a lot earlier by John Klenner and Al Hoffman. As I recall, it went like this:

Heart aches, heart aches,
My loving you meant only heart aches.
Your kiss was such a sacred thing to me,
I can't believe it's just a burning memory.

I didn't know much about heartaches at the time but both Etta and I knew about arm aches as we took turns at night getting up to hold Jeff whenever he cried. It took hours. When it was my turn, I would set up my Ham radio station, W2KEE, communicating only by keying in the Morse code so as not to disturb our newborn son.

When Jeff began to cry, I would warm up a bottle of formula (these days they don't bother with warming up the baby's bottle), prop it up for him to drink (they don't permit that these days as it causes ear infections) and move to the adjacent room. I would communicate with radio amateurs around the world to pass the time. In those days my hearing was so sharp that I could hear a pin drop. I could tell easily if

Jeff lost his bottle. These days I could hardly hear a bomb drop. Ham radio helped me pass the night hours as well as pen a nasty little poem:

A plaintive wail in dead of night
And, from my peaceful slumber, I am torn
To stagger forth with sleep dimmed sight
And wish that he was never born!

A Plea for Peace

If anything good came out of that poem, it was that it encouraged me to write others. Since World War II had just ended, I made a more serious attempt at poetry during those long nights while watching the baby. My brother Paul was so impressed that he presented my poetry to his students, as well as to the children in his summer camp newsletter where he was the chief counselor. My kid brother was a highly literate person. His approval of the poem made me proud.

When Paul published my poem for his summer camp, I jokingly objected to his placing his name at the end of it because it might signify that he was the author. His retort was that since he had to proofread the poem and make some corrections, this gave him the right to co-authorship.

The clouds of war have shortly flown;
The harvest reaped that Mars hath sown;
Now vanquished lies the Teuton host
And Yankee boots tread Nippon's coast.
The mighty fist with power bold
Attempts eternal peace to mold

Science tore the arid desert crust
And then two cities turned to dust.
A Goliath created for terror and woe
But yet no David to stem this foe.
When human struck
the atom asunder,
Did he not rob God's own thunder?

A peace by force of the mighty three
Who cannot among themselves agree
Cannot be eternal, cannot last.
War will win as in the past,
Once again to destroy our fairest youth
Eye for eye, tooth for tooth.

Peace forever, it must be had,
A world never in armor clad
For if ever Man is ruled by hate
And anew this great
globe conflagrate,
Then surely will the victor find
A world devoid of all Mankind

Though the storm be minutes past,
New events their shadows cast
Even now there is new strife
And once again the loss of life.
Millions dead, many more in pain,
Can all this be once again in vain?

- A Plea for Peace

The SEG Hy-Volter

I was more interested in numbers than words. One day, I noted a simple mathematical relationship between the spacing needed to have an electric spark jump between two metal balls and the voltage applied to them. I designed the SEG (my initials) Hy-Volter. It was made of a clear plastic tube with a red plastic cap and an attached wire which had to be clipped to a ground connection, usually the metal TV chassis.

The clear plastic base had a metal tip projecting which would touch the high voltage connection after the red cap was unscrewed to give maximum spacing between the two metal balls inside. The red cap was then slowly rotated to close the space between the balls. The rotation was stopped when a spark jumped between the balls. By looking at the bottom edge of the red cap, and adding the voltage reading indicated on the red cap to the first lower number indicated on the tube decal, the voltage was read.

There was a market then for an inexpensive device that could measure high voltage in thousands of volts with no need for precise measurements. TV repairmen could check the voltage supplied to the cathode ray picture tubes if the TV image was not bright enough.

I sold the SEG Hy-Volter to electronic distributors for a few dollars each but the sales never amounted to much. The concept of marketing and promotion was beyond me then. I assembled the SEG Hy-Volters each evening in a nearby one car garage, which I rented for about ten dollars a month. In the winter, I kept warm using a kerosene heater when I went to the garage after supper.

Once, the light that I had left on in the garage had an eerie glow as I approached. To my dismay, the kerosene heater had malfunctioned and the air was filled with long, oily flakes from incompletely burned kerosene. All of the components of the Hy-Volters were coated inside and out with the same messy stuff. I stayed up late that night cleaning up. That included the walls and floor.

I gave up production after realizing that I had priced it too low. Some of the customers also returned units which had been completely fried inside from having been connected to a high powered source. I had considered adding a high-voltage resistor as an extension to the projecting terminal but that would have increased the price of each unit by a few dollars and would have been the most expensive component of the Hy-Volter. It would have allowed the Hy-Volter to measure more powerful high voltage sources since the resistor would have limited the current required to a spark.

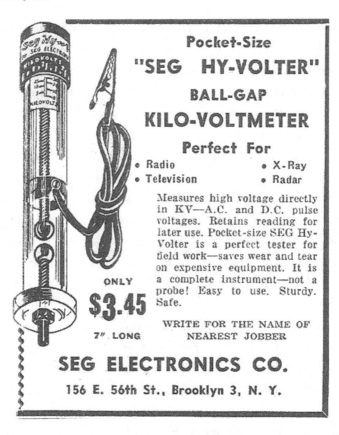

Illustration – Seg Hy-Volter (Over 60 years old)

Owing to my parents' political indoctrination when young, a profit was vulgar and so had to be kept small. Preferably invisible. Thankfully, I got out of the restriction on profit-taking, but not until much later in life.

Meanwhile, my employer, Precision Apparatus Corporation, prospered as World War II broke out in Europe and my pay rose a bit. We bought a used Hudson automobile, which we used for weekend rides with Jeffrey in Etta's arms. Seatbelts were unheard of at that time.

Since Precision Apparatus was a few blocks from the Brooklyn Navy Yard, we could see the intense preparations for war taking place. One day the air-raid sirens sounded off. We didn't know exactly what to do, but on looking out of the windows, we could see men on the roof of one of the nearby Navy Yard buildings. They were manning anti-aircraft guns aimed at the sky. It was scary, yet exciting. Of course, it turned out to be a false alarm. Work and life went on in a normal fashion and was, alas, quite boring.

Love for Music

During that time at work there was a distinct change in my personal tastes in life. The next production line to the wiring department was the testing department. The only tester was a sarcastic but bright fellow named Bennie who had a sharp retort for any question posed to him. His work station had the only radio permitted on the factory floor. Bennie had it tuned to WQXR, the New York classical music radio station, even though we all complained about it and asked him to tune to a station that had Swing and Jazz. He kept the same WQXR on all day long.

After months, I noticed that certain classical music selections sounded better than others. That is, they were more easily tolerated than others. Later on, I realized that I was actually looking forward to listening to them. Brahms's *1st Piano Concerto* became my favorite. I would study the schedule in the newspaper so as not to miss that particular piece, or other favorites. These included Bach's *Toccata & Fugue*, *Scheherazade*, and classical pieces by Rachmaninoff, Grieg, Beethoven, Tchaikovsky, Ravel, Grieg, and so on. They brightened my day on the production line.

While I had developed a distinct taste for the classics, I still enjoyed the love ballads that I listened to when I was not at work. I loved to dance and Swing was the most popular music style as played by Benny Goodman and his orchestra. Other bands were well known by their leaders such as Artie Shaw, Jimmy Dorsey, Tommie Dorsey. Harry James also, who, as a trumpeter, was well known as the husband of Betty Grable, the blonde heart throb and pin-up actress.

Artie Shaw had a spectacular career after Begin the Beguine became famous. At that time, the 45 RPM record player had its hey-day and I got mine as a gift. If you got tired of playing a song over and over again, you could play it backwards from the center of the record out to the edge by giving it a counter clockwise spin at its start. I loved so many of the songs from that era. I even memorized the words of some of them like Cole Porter's Begin the Beguine.

The Beginning of War

The romantic, idealistic verses of young love are a sharp contrast to the realities of life that were presenting themselves around the world. As the United States was moving closer to war, Precision Apparatus was getting more demands for their tube-testing products. Finally, Precision Apparatus moved to their own building in Elmhurst, Queens, as the old factory was bursting at the seams.

Later, I took on a part-time night job teaching electronics to Signal Corps enlistees during World War II. This meant leaving Precision Apparatus Company after working late and hustling to midtown Manhattan to the Radio Television Institute. The enlistees were permitted to hold their civilian jobs until the nine-month course was completed. Then they were inducted into the service.

Teaching was great. I had to keep learning to stay ahead of the class - some of whom were college graduates. Eventually, I dropped the wiring job and began to teach full-time. My teaching colleagues were mostly employed in large firms at high level jobs and interacting with them was rewarding. I began to feel much more comfortable with the teaching of highly technical material to a group that had been selected by a government agency for this special training. Nevertheless, after repeating the course many times to new groups, it became quite boring and I sought something more intellectual.

With World War II draining our available manpower, I was called up for military service. However, the company that I worked for got me deferred instead. I was necessary to a very important military project. The project consisted of the first of the remote-controlled guided missiles. That deferment would not last many more draft calls. I prepared all of my licenses and papers for duty as the radio officer on a Merchant Marine freighter. At that time, the US was shipping tremendous amounts of material to the embattled Soviet Union, in midwinter. Large convoys of freighters steamed around the Scandinavian countries escorted by American warships. About 40 percent of our ships were torpedoed before reaching Murmansk, the Soviet Union's only ice-free port. The freighters were sitting ducks for the German submarines.

Before I could complete my preparations for the Merchant Marine, I was called up for a draft board physical exam, which was the last step prior to induction into military service.

We all lined up facing the medical doctor examiner. Aside from briefly listening to the heart and lungs, the next step was to unzip or unbutton the fly of our pants for our private-parts exam. I was found to have a right inguinal hernia which disqualified me. I was given a 4F classification. It was a shocker. I had always wondered what that soft bulge was in my right groin. It turned hard and painful at times.

It had appeared when I was about sixteen years old. I had hitch-hiked rides to the Catskill Mountain resort area where I tried to get a summer job as a busboy at one of the large hotels that were located all over the area. The pay for that job was small, aside from the tips, but the free food and social life were great attractions. When I found that there were no jobs available and I was essentially penniless, I took a one-day job with one other teenager unloading a freight car full of bags of cement for two dollars. It was unbelievably difficult. The rough cement powder on the outside of the bags abraded my skin.

Although it wasn't my fault, I always felt the 4F classification was a badge of dishonor. I tried not to disclose it unless absolutely necessary. In that era, surgical repair of the hernia meant at least one week in the hospital followed by an extended period of convalescence at home. In addition, no heavy lifting was permitted for six months. As I got older and the hernia grew larger, as well as more uncomfortable, I never had the time or the money for the surgery, which meant I had to wear a hernia support much of the time. This consisted of a stiff band of spring steel covered with leather and cloth, which encircled my body at the hip level. The right side looped around my right hip and ended in a metal-backed pad. This pressed against the bulging hernia, forcing it back inside my body. The left side looped around my left hip and groin, ending in a leather strap, which had perforations that could snap over a pin on the back side of the pad over the right groin. I would give this contraption a high mark as an instrument of torture, one worthy of the Spanish Inquisition. I ruled out repair of the hernia to a date decades later.

Assistant Electrical Engineer

I was soon hired by the Federal Electric Corporation, a division of ITT, the International Telephone and Telegraph Corporation, as an assistant electrical engineer. I did not qualify for the position of Electrical Engineer as I lacked the education and resulting degree. The company was working on guided missile technology. The project involved setting up transmitting and receiving equipment to control the flight of drones or unmanned airplanes. I worked under a senior electrical engineer designing test equipment for the program. He laid out the plans and I built and tested the equipment. The transmitted impulses were brief, in the order of a microsecond, and difficult to capture on the screen.

When I finally captured a few of the impulses on the screen, I called the senior engineer over. He hurried over with the chief engineer of the project in tow to show him the huge success. In his enthusiasm, he brushed me aside at the work bench and started twiddling the dials. I had been preparing cables for the next step and I had a soldering iron on the bench with the hot tip facing front. A few minutes later, there was a distinct odor of burning wool as his jacket began to smolder. He glared at me as he put out the fire in the wool over his jacket pocket. Our working relationship cooled off after that.

At Long Last! It's a Girl

Later on, I befriended a stout gentleman named Paul Freidman. He lived in an upscale apartment building with his wife of similar proportions. The apartment building sported an elevator since the building was six stories high. It was in an excellent location near Eastern Parkway at 270 Crown St., Crown Heights, Brooklyn. The Freidmans were childless and they treated me as if I was their son. They were quite comfortable financially and related by family ties to management people at Consumers Union, publisher of Consumer Reports magazine.

As my own family grew with the birth of Howard, my second son, our Flatbush apartment was getting crowded. Paul Freidman offered to speak to his landlord, Arthur, about renting an apartment to me when a vacancy opened up. I welcomed the idea. Furthermore, Paul had a key to the basement workshop that was complete with a lathe, drill press, and other machines for wood and metal working. How great was that? Paul spoke to Arthur, who agreed, and we moved into a sixth floor apartment. We were grateful that there was an elevator in the building. The new and astronomical rental fee was about seventy-five dollars a month which put a strain on my salary. I kept busy paying for that big monthly hit. I felt it was worth it.

One complication in our move to 270 Crown Street was that the former tenant, a pharmacist who was moving out, had built a closet in one of the rooms as there was a shortage of closet space. He wanted to be reimbursed for his cost of sixty dollars or he was going to have it torn out. I was too naïve to call his bluff and I paid him the sixty dollars. I learned later that any structure added to the walls of a rented room becomes the property of the landlord.

Arthur owned two adjacent buildings as well. He was part of a wealthy family that had a semi-monopoly for bulk newspaper delivery to newsstands and candy stores in the New York metropolitan area. I had heard rumors of some of the rough ways such monopolies were established, but he was a warm person with whom I occasionally interacted with in the basement workshop.

All in all, life was good on Crown Street. Etta was pregnant for the third time. We hoped against hope that the third and last of Etta's pregnancies would result in a girl, contrary to my parents' pattern. The pregnancy continued through the first winter in the new apartment. Since she wore a heavy loose overcoat in the cold weather, the neighbors were shocked when she appeared in February wheeling a baby carriage. She had not told the neighbors that she was pregnant. This had been down to a superstition handed down through generations of her family that jealousy toward an expectant mother-to-be by a childless woman, or one with a deformed child, would be the source of an evil eye that could harm the new baby.

Etta was under the care of a Brooklyn obstetrician for our third child. One evening, she told me that she was feeling intermittent pelvic cramping. As with the two prior pregnancies, the cramping became stronger and more frequent. I called the obstetrician and he ordered her to the hospital. We were not new to this. I picked up the small suitcase that we kept ready for the occasion and we were off.

At the hospital, Etta was hustled away by the nurses and I paced the floor restlessly. An hour or two later, a worried nurse came into the waiting room and told us that the obstetrician hadn't arrived and he wasn't answering his telephone. Since his office was in his home and I had visited with Etta several times before, I was able to drive there, post-haste, and tooted my horn. He stuck his head out of his bedroom window with eyes half-closed. He assured me that he would be at the hospital right away. He got there, just in time too. Later, I was able to see Etta on a Gurney being wheeled to her room. She looked pale and tired but happy, as she told me that we have a daughter.

When she appeared in front of our apartment building wheeling the new baby carriage, the neighbors heaped praise on the new arrival, after getting over their initial surprise.

You Never Know Who You'll Run Into

Etta and I had our own surprises living at Crown Street.

One time, Etta was going up to the apartment with the baby in her carriage and there was an elderly woman on the elevator with her that looked familiar.

Etta boldly asked her, "Are you Eleanor Roosevelt?"

The answer was, "Yes, I am here to visit a friend in the building."

Etta was thrilled and could hardly wait to tell me about the exciting encounter.

As previously mentioned, I had supplemented my wireman job's modest pay with a teaching position in midtown Manhattan at the Radio Television Institute while World War II was still in progress. The student body was largely made up of men from all walks of life that were due to be drafted into the military. By choosing the Signal Corps, which was the communications branch of the US Army, they were allowed to remain out of the service for a period of time while they studied the new field of electronics. I had to stay ahead of the class, which kept me hopping as I had to be able to answer the students' questions. My Ham radio background came in handy and I did well at teaching, which had finally become a full-time better paying job.

At breaks between classes, I would go for walks in mid-town Manhattan not far from the Grand Central Station. I would occasionally see an elderly lady looking into the store windows. Passersby stopped to stare at her so I asked someone who she was. I was told that she was the great Greta Garbo, the storied movie actress of Ninotchka and other big-time hits. Although she was a fixture in the neighborhood, she paid no attention to those who stared at her nor was she ever seen with someone accompanying her.

World's First TV Geek?

The teaching curriculum included some very early work in television. It was deemed certain that, when the war ended, television would be the wave of the future. In fact, cathode ray tubes were part of a well-developed technology since they were used by the military extensively in oscilloscopes and radar as part of the war effort. They were later morphed into television picture tubes.

Generating high power radio waves led to the design of magnetrons. These were large vacuum tubes that were mounted in an assembly that produced a strong magnetic field. The heavy electron current flow through the magnetron was guided by the magnetic field and could be cut off almost instantly by varying the field. That would generate high frequency and high voltage impulses for radar. These pulses were then delivered to a directional antenna that aimed the high frequency radio waves at targets like planes and ships, illuminating them for the return signal. The radar apparatus would pick these returned signals up and paint them on the cathode ray tube screen.

After World War II ended, television became wildly popular. I continued teaching at the Radio Television Institute and earned extra money repairing early television sets, most of them having 10 inch screens. The RCA brand was popular and used the successful 630 chassis that RCA had developed. Most of the repairs involved finding which vacuum tube had failed as they were all based on electrons boiling off of a red-hot filament inside of a tiny metal tube, called a cathode. Like any electric light bulb, the filament burned out eventually and the vacuum tube needed replacement.

The vacuum tube could fail in other ways. While the filament would still light up, the vacuum tube needed to be replaced. The cathode ray tube, which produced the image on its coated screen, could also fail, while the circuitry producing the high voltage needed for accelerating the electron beam was also apt to fail.

Several manufacturers made television chassis very similar to the popular 630 chassis. One such television chassis was made by Techmaster in the early 1950s and the selling price began at about $120. There was no picture tube or cabinet included. This was left for the enterprising radio repair and television repair shops that bought the missing cabinets from various newly organized wood-working factories to match the customers' tastes. The picture tubes increased in size from 10 inches, to 12 inches, and then leaped upwards to 24 inches in diameter. Frequently, the TV shops would buy the complete TV set with the ten inch picture tube as the prices dropped. They would take out the TV chassis, discard the ten inch picture tube (or use it in a repair), and assemble the TV chassis into an elaborate cabinet with a larger picture tube.

The cabinets that had housed the smaller picture tubes and their chassis were thrown away. I took that opportunity to ask the TV shops that were converting the television sets to large screen to save the discarded cabinets for me. I would glue knobs into the empty spaces and do the same with a plastic frame over the picture tube opening. The new set looked the part, but was empty. I offered these to furniture stores at about seventy-five dollars each. Aside from the fact that I didn't get many cabinets to process, the extra money sure came in handy. An interesting fact is that having faux television sets in a furniture display is still being done and seems to be a substantial business when done nationally.

Next Job-Field Engineer

While we were still in the early days of television, production could not keep up with the demand. I left my teaching job at the Radio Television Institute and joined the staff of the Video Products Corporation in Red Bank, New Jersey, as their field engineer. They produced a television set using a chassis of their own manufacture similar to the popular RCA 630 chassis.

The production line workers that had saved their money during war-time rationing of goods, gasoline, and even staples like canned salmon and tuna fish, as well as the millions of veterans returned from the war, all wanted housing, cars, and television.

I assembled a 10-inch TV set from a kit, which took a few weeks of evening and weekend hours. This became the entertainment center for our family and friends. On the night that Milton Berle had his comedy show, Etta and I would set up rows of chairs for those special people we had invited. The popcorn and soda pop flowed and all had a good time. Television technology kept improving and eventually black and white TV gave way to color television, but only after a brief false start.

The FCC held a competition for the best system for color TV broadcasting and receiving. The two leading contenders were RCA (Radio Corporation of America), and a division of CBS (Columbia Broadcasting System). The CBS color TV system won the day, albeit marginally. Their system consisted of splitting up the broadcast picture into the red, blue and green segments and transmitting them sequentially.

At the viewers' end, there was a synchronized spinning disk in front of the picture tube. This was divided into red, blue, and green filter screens. It was cumbersome, expensive, and noisy. In the end, the all-electronic RCA system won the battle, which involved special tricolor picture tubes. That is, there were three kinds of phosphor dots printed onto the back of the glass screen. These glowed in red, blue, and green, respectively, when struck by the moving electron beam.

My job as a field engineer involved my visiting distributors and customers of the Video Products Corporation in the Greater New York Area, as well as New Jersey and occasionally Pennsylvania. I would make sure that they were pleased with the technical aspects of our products, which now included complete television sets under the new name of Sheraton Television. If there were any complaints, it was my responsibility to resolve them by reporting to the engineering department at the main plant in Red Bank. Unless it was something I could handle on my own.

I worked out of the company's sales office in Manhattan under the vice president, Mr. Harold Morrison, who was a handsome, debonair gentleman, about ten years my senior. He had numerous wealthy friends, many of whom wound up with Sheraton TVs. Aside from my engineering responsibilities, it was my job to take care of any TV problems that came up with our products in his friends' homes. As Mr. Harold Morrison was single, he had several attractive girlfriends and they all seemed to have Sheraton TVs. Later, Cupid caught up with Mr. Morrison and he fell in love with a pretty French woman, got married and raised a family.

Prior to his marriage, I would join him for the annual Chicago trade shows. The shows featured the latest TVs, record players, and, later, tape recorders. I was uneasy at first, what with the liberal use of call girls as a means for closing sales. It was more my style to invite potential clients to dinner at a fine restaurant. With Video Products paying the transportation, food, and lodging bills, I learned, at least temporarily, the nouveau riche way of life.

Never having flown by air, I went by rail from New York to Chicago and back for each annual show. Each trip lasted almost a whole day. Mr. Morrison did the trip by air, which was but a few hours. At one show, accompanied by a new, super salesman hired by Harold, I was persuaded to stay on later that night rather than catch the train, and then fly back. I felt bad when Harold told me how sorry he was that I had to endure the long train trip. That airplane trip home opened the door to many more such trips for me and my family.

In addition to the friends and family that were attached to Harold, I also met many of his executive friends such as Irving Schachtel, the president of Sonotone Corporation, in White Plains, NY. Sonotone was the leading manufacturer of hearing aids in the US. Back then, hearing aids were larger and clumsier due to the fact that they used vacuum tubes instead of transistors, which were just beginning to be manufactured. The first transistors were point-contact devices which were primitive, depending on a fine springy wire making contact with the internal surface of the transistor at exactly the right spot.

Sonotone had entered into the production of those point-contact transistors but the defect rate was very high. Prior to their first all-transistor hearing aid, they depended more on their skill in manufacturing. They used their own miniature vacuum tubes and so could make their hearing aids smaller than the competition. Since vacuum tubes needed their red-hot filaments, the hearing aid battery had a duration of hours rather than days.

During World War II, the US Government bought large quantities of especially rugged vacuum tubes, from Sonotone for use in anti-aircraft shells which would not explode until the shell reached the immediate vicinity of the enemy aircraft. The internal sensing electronics would trigger the firing mechanism. Up to that development, much more accuracy was needed in the detection of the enemy aircraft by radar or the shell had to be dialed for an estimated altitude before firing.

Many years later, I learned from Harold that Sonotone had been an unremarkable manufacturer of hearing aids and that they were having financial difficulties. The board of directors turned to their star salesman, Irving Schachtel, whose amazing sales success kept bringing in business. He was brought into the management of the company as vice-president. The company's fortunes improved with various new developments such as sintered nickel-cadmium batteries, bone-conduction hearing aids, tiny vacuum tubes for hearing aids, and UHF (Ultra High Frequency) TV tuners. He advanced to president of the company, which grew and prospered financially, becoming a leader in various fields.

I was also impressed with Sonotone's sales manager, an older man named Bob Lewis. If I was in the area of the Sonotone plant in White Plains I would make it a point to visit him. He and his wife treated me as though I was their son. I believe they were childless as they never mentioned their offspring. Bob became one of my mentors, offering me encouragement in my struggle to shape a career. Years later, he helped me enormously when I went into business for myself.

In our Manhattan sales office, there were several people that became my friends. One was Larry Freeman, age unknown, single, who lived in the same apartment that he was born in. His parents had passed away and he slept in their old bed, which sounded gross to me. He was always looking for the wonder-woman that would change his life and he was secretive about his age. I didn't quite agree with his method of selling, which sounded more like a desperate plea for an order, but he was successful anyway.

Bill Fine was another salesman. He was in his sixties and had made a long-term career of calling on customers and selling them anything from clothes to cars. His hallmark was a big cigar which I never saw him light up. Occasionally, I went along with him on his selling trips. As I was a young married man, I was shocked when he confided to me once that when his wife reached fifty years of age, she told him that was it and there would be no more sex. It turned out that she was never interested in love making ever again. I couldn't understand that at the time. I have learned a lot since then.

A less frequent visitor to our sales office was a young nephew of Harold's named Marshall Butler. Since the Morrison family was obviously quite well-to-do, I assumed that Marshall was a spoiled young brat. Later on I learned that he had joined up with a brilliant Asian scientist that had expertise in the field of growing crystals such as silicon and rare materials needed for transistors and integrated circuits. Marshall became quite famous as a young billionaire and became a generous benefactor of various charitable organizations.

Occasionally, I got to leave the Manhattan office and visit the plant in Red Bank, NJ in order to interface with the engineering staff about my findings out in the field. The company president, William Morrison, would call me into his office and put me through a little routine that I never quite understood. He would find reasons to criticize which would fluster me. At that point, he would suddenly switch gears, become very friendly and even flatter me. In retrospect, I am still dumbfounded about the logic behind his method of motivation.

Opportunity Knocks

As the television industry caught up with the demand for its products, the picture tube size grew substantially and sales of the custom products began to shrink. Video Products Corporation began to experience increased price competition and a smaller customer base. The subsidiary, Sheraton Television, never did get very popular and their advertising budget was miniscule compared to that of the bigger brands.

Their major competitor in the custom TV field was the Techmaster Corporation, which was still profitable. Their president, Leo Lazarus, ran his operation with a tight fist. After Video Products declared bankruptcy and headed for dissolution, I was contacted by Leo Lazarus who offered me a deal. He would attend the court-ordered auction of the inventory of Video Products Corporation and buy up all of the available parts to continue assembling the custom television chassis. His goal was to keep the parts and finished products flowing into his customer base. With one or two assistants, I would do the work and make a reasonable profit. He would provide the manufacturing space in his own Brooklyn factory.

The assembly of the Video Products inventory purchased by Leo Lazarus at auction took me a few months. It gave me my first taste of being in my own business. Eventually, Techmaster and I parted company. I continued on my own, repairing television sets for my customers, as well as for other TV servicemen.

TV servicemen either had their own shops from which they sold television sets and parts, or were part-timers repairing TVs for extra income. If they visited a home for a TV repair, or the TV was brought to their shop for repair, they would first try vacuum tube replacement. If that wasn't the problem they would take the non-functioning TV set to my shop, usually for a fixed price repair. It was hard work and the income was modest. My shop was in a low rent store in a residential area located on Flatbush Avenue, Brooklyn.

I derived the name of my fledgling business from my initials, Seg Electronics Company. I hadn't used that name since the days when I hand built the Seg Hy-Volter. In prior years, I had initialed all of the tube testers that I had wired with my name, "Seg." This signing was required by corporate management to be able to fix blame if the tube tester was returned for a defect, like an unsoldered or poorly soldered connection. That fact turned out to my advantage in my new venture.

Ever driven, I searched for additional income. One such source came from Paul Freidman, the same neighbor who helped us get our apartment on Crown Street. His brother-in-law was a vice president of

Consumers Union. He suggested to the administration of Consumers Union that I would be interested in purchasing the samples of various appliances they were testing after completing publication of the test results. They agreed. Over the next few years I sold the samples in my small shop. I kept some of the samples for possible use at home, such as a Husqvarna sewing machine and a Remington shotgun. This nice sideline helped me survive over the next few years while I continued with my wholesale TV repair business. I was helped by a full-time TV repairman named Fruiten Ackerman, an Afro-American. This left me free to enter into other lines of business with more potential.

Fruiten remained with me for several years until I was able to drop the TV repair business entirely. Along the way, Consumers Union ended the relationship with me. Their legal counsel had ordered our relationship stopped as the money received from me for the used samples might be construed as profiting from the sales. This profit might have jeopardized their status as a non-profit organization.

One of my customers for the Consumers Union samples was an interesting gentleman named Arthur Ritchie, a member of the Bible Christian Union. BCU's office was in a large building on the opposite side of Flatbush Avenue from my shop. Their main effort was in proselytizing their religious beliefs all over the world using banks of printing presses in the basement of their building to produce literature. They even had a machine shop in the basement to keep the printing presses in good shape.

Mr. Ritchie was skilled at all of the machines. He was even allowed by the Bible Christian Union to do some work for me, from time to time, later in my career. This came in very handy at times, although I wasn't quite sure if he was allowed to keep the money. If he was interested in a Consumers Union sample, he drove a hard bargain. He became a frequent visitor to my shop and a close friend of mine. In retrospect, I rate him one of my best mentors. He never tried to convert me. His honesty and straight-shooting ways were wonderful examples for me to follow. He rarely turned me down if I needed his help.

Recently, I looked over his correspondence with me including e-mails from his son after Arthur's demise. In his declining days, his family had moved to the Midwest and then to Spain where he passed away. His son let me know of Arthur's passing and his fondness for me and the friendship that we shared. I was shocked when his son confided in a recent e-mail that Arthur had saved every dollar that he ever earned from me over the years. When he retired, he was able to buy a surprisingly large house of several thousand square feet in the Midwest for his family. When they moved to Spain years later it was into a small five-hundred-square-foot house. His family had dwindled by then.

The Partnership of Marcus & Gendler

Once in my TV repairing career, there was an interesting project that turned up. One of the larger TV and electronic parts stores that I had called on for Video Products Corporation would ask me for help from time to time. They must have been impressed with my technical knowledge as the owner called me by telephone when I was struggling in my own business. He asked me if I would be interested in becoming a coauthor of an electronics book. When I immediately agreed, he arranged a meeting for me with Abraham Marcus who had been the very successful co-author of "Elements of Radio." It was a book that had become important to the US Military as communications had changed the face of military warfare.

Abe Marcus was a bright and dedicated individual who never believed in letting people step on him. I learned quite a bit about his life. One anecdote he related really impressed me. In the bitter days of the major depression, he had been employed as a school teacher. He watched for opportunities to improve his financial position and got a coveted position as a shop teacher at a major trade school. On his first day at the job, he was visited by two supervisors who were delineating his duties. It sounded quite acceptable until he was told that one of his assignments was to go to a neighboring coffee shop and buy lunch on Mondays and Wednesdays, which he was to deliver to the school Principal. He responded, "That sounds great. And, of course, he would buy and bring me lunch on Tuesdays and Thursdays." Interestingly, he didn't lose his job. I believe it was earned by taking a city sponsored Civil Service exam.

Now that television was popular, Abraham wanted to write a book to be named, "Elements of Television Servicing." He offered me 10 percent of the royalties that would be due to him from Prentice Hall, the publishers that produced his first book. I accepted as I was dazzled by the opportunity and impressed with his popularity.

I was responsible for all of the technical material in the book. He would drive from his home in Queens, New York, every Wednesday evening to my home in Brooklyn with his hand-written manuscript prepared from the technical information of the prior Wednesday meeting. He had meticulous handwriting and, as he was profitable for Prentice-Hall, was allowed to submit hand-written material for publication. I would review his prior week's submission and we would talk about the next week's work. The preparation took about two years of Wednesdays but it was finally over. A year later, I arrived home in the afternoon of that day. Etta and the children were waiting for me in front of the apartment building in which we lived. She was grinning from ear to ear as she handed me one of the six complimentary author's copies of "Elements of Television Servicing," by Abraham Marcus and Samuel E. Gendler. I joined her with my own ear-to-ear grin. We next worked on another project which was a book named, "Basic Electronics." The financial arrangement was similar. That book turned out to be quite popular as well. The commission that I received was welcomed revenue over the many years that the book was in print.

As for Abraham, he passed away while vacationing in Turkey with his wife, Rebecca. He had been suffering from angina pains but never paid much attention to them. In those days, the role of cholesterol in heart disease was essentially unknown. Cholesterol was believed to be in the normal range if the value measured was below three hundred.

Much later, the "Basic Electronics" book was due for revision as it was still popular. I set myself to the task of reviewing and revising "Basic Electronics." I spent quite a bit of time on the revision, which gave me a modest supplement to my income for a number of years. There was no interest by Prentice-Hall in a revision of "Elements of Television Servicing," as the material was considered obsolete. Transistors had replaced vacuum tubes. In turn, transistors had been replaced by integrated circuits. These were tiny blocks that were produced by complex machinery and contained entire circuits of which there could be up to millions of transistors incorporated.

A primitive early vacuum tube computer took up lots of large cabinets. Our present day compact tablets or desktop computers have hundreds of times the speed and memory.

First Big Deal

In my years of teaching at the Radio-Television Institute, I made friends with many of my colleagues that also taught there. Now that I was in business for myself, I was alert for any way to leap-frog my little business into a more substantial mode.

One of my colleagues at the institute, a part-timer named Paul Michelson, was also a full-time employee of the New York Telephone Company. Early in my struggles to stay in business, he told me about a project with which he and his colleagues at the phone company were experimenting. Since data transmission was a new field, their equipment seemed somewhat inadequate as it was designed purely for voice transmission. His colleagues had put together some equipment that was standard. With some modification this equipment could be used for data transmission. Over the next year or two he would bring some standard equipment to my shop. We would wire this and add some purchased equipment to produce a special configuration. He would report to me on its successes and failures but the project seemed to be moving ahead albeit very slowly. I continued to build the samples adding some components of my own.

A further explanation of the type of equipment needed for the new data transmission field could be described as follows:

Voice transmission through telephone lines was quite easy but there was a need for boosting the high and/or the low frequencies to allow more natural communication as needed for reproducing music. The telephone lines tended to limit the high and low frequencies and that made music sound quite flat. The sound system field had evolved into what was then known as high fidelity. There was a new kid on the block, which was transmission of data. For data to be transmitted with high accuracy, the high, low and mid frequencies of the signals had to be faithfully reproduced. There was the additional burden of having the frequency components arrive accurately in strength and in the time required in transmission, which was a new and tough requirement.

The public had become quite accustomed to the limitations of sound transmission through the telephone system and so the high and low frequencies which were decreased or attenuated had to be balanced against the middle range. This was done with the use of equalizers which were standard telephone boxes containing inductances, switches, and capacitors. Paul would supply me with the components on loan from the telephone company. We assembled these components into the telephone boxes. In practice the switches could be used to adjust the high and low frequencies for the highest fidelity or for better transmission of data.

A year or two later Paul advised me that the last sample submitted was a success. It looked like a production contract would be offered to me. This was wonderful news until one day when Paul arrived at my office agitated. He told me that the project had been approved but that Western Electric Company, which was also part of the American Telephone and Telegraph Company, was given the contract to manufacture the project.

I prepared a letter to the New York Telephone Company listing the work that I had performed over the past few years without compensation, and the fact that the contract was given elsewhere. There was no response for a few weeks. I learned from Paul that there was an intensive investigation in progress, one in which all of the employees of that division were asked about the relationship between Seg Electronics and the New York Telephone Company. The upper echelon specifically pointed out that they had placed the New York Telephone Company into a legally binding agreement with Seg Electronics Company by having their employees ask for samples to be produced with no provision for payment or any contract limiting their liability.

The company proceeded to impose severe penalties on their employees by demoting them from their desk jobs to outside activities, some of which involved climbing telephone poles. No one was very happy.

I was contacted and asked to appear before a vice president named Fred Reynolds at their headquarters in downtown Manhattan. I was asked to quote the production cost to the New York Telephone Company if I produced the entire project in my shop. I quoted $87,000. I was told by Reynolds that the job was mine if I agreed to hold New York Telephone Company harmless from any further damages. My answer was that I would have to consult with my attorney. That was the right answer as they offered me the full contract. I believe that they were relieved in that I was obviously honest and was not trying to take advantage of the company or the situation.

I rented another shop a block away from my regular place of business and hired some wiring and assembly personnel. The telephone company provided visiting inspectors to make sure that the work was consistent with their standards but it all went very well. The substantial chunk of money in my bank account gave my business a sorely needed lift - and an appetite for more. There was overhead, plus labor, and material expenses, but that was my first taste of monetary success.

Predators Circling

When all of the equalizer equipment had been delivered to the New York Telephone Company and paid for, there was a distinct vacuum in my business. Looking for leads for future business, I read all the periodicals printed for the electronic industry, which contained the latest news and trends.

One article caught my eye. It was a tiny news report about Ecuador extending its television network across the country from its major cities. I visualized a network of my custom-built transmitters. They would send the amplified TV signals from mountain peaks to mountain peaks, with a local cable company in each area distributing the signals to the surrounding communities. It sounded exciting, especially since I had money in the bank.

The article continued with the fact that a Mr. Piña of Ecuador was coming to the United States to purchase supplies for the project. The article listed the date of his visit and the hotel. I called and left a message for him. He called the next day and was interested in my sales pitch. He scheduled a visit for several days later.

Mr. Piña arrived on schedule accompanied by a tall American gentleman whom he introduced as a member of a prominent US stock brokerage company. After looking at my small and primitive production facilities, they suggested that I handle a big part of an ambitious project in Ecuador. Mr. Piña turned to his companion and told him that I should be interested in showing my good faith by making a substantial deposit into their Panamanian bank, whereupon his companion whipped out a thick receipt book. The invisible antennas at the base of my posterior skull began to send me warning signals. I declined, quoting other obligations.

I didn't realize it at that time but, after future successes, I noticed a pattern wherein there was almost always an accompanying offer made to me that was too good to be true. Sometimes it was simple and obvious, such as offers from my bank following up on my temporarily swollen bank balance. Other times, the responses came from more remote sources. I can't say that I avoided all of the traps that came my way whenever my bank account swelled, but my "antennas" saved me many times. The juicy offers obviously came from people with special talents in sniffing out substantial bank accounts and potential investors or clients.

The Minuteman Missile Program

As I had been phasing out of the television servicing business, one of my customers for television service repairs came to me with an interesting proposition. He was a technician for RCA. He explained that the equalizer equipment, that I had been providing to the New York Telephone Company, might help out with distortions in data transmission through the telephone lines. RCA was contracted with the Air Force regarding the Minuteman Missile Program, as the data transmission sent to program the missiles was arriving at the silos quite distorted.

The professional possibilities sounded attractive to me. I arranged a meeting with the engineers of RCA in lower Manhattan. I took with me one of the finished units from the New York Telephone Company's project. It was tested for the data transmission of the Minuteman missile and there were distinct improvements at certain switch positions. I prepared some samples for RCA using the values of inductance and capacitance at switch positions in much tinier sizes. This allowed my company to be listed as a supplier of equalizers for data transmission - there would be orders in the future.

Installing Sound Systems

Earlier, I wrote about my childhood friend, Sidney Barbanel, or Bob. He had learned drafting and engineering at the esteemed Brooklyn Technical High School. Now, as a New York State licensed engineer, he was helped by his uncle, Ruben Dankoff, who was building bowling alleys all over the Greater New York Area.

This was back when bowling was fast becoming a national fad that attracted tens of thousands of people all over the country. Bob drew up the plans and specifications for heating and air conditioning systems, as well as the entire electrical and plumbing systems for each of his uncle's bowling alleys.

This work launched his engineering career but he was astute enough to extend his efforts to other projects as well, including the construction field. Eventually, he had professional offices in Montreal and Paris, as well as the original Long Island office. Bob became quite wealthy at a young age and was able to engage in philanthropy, giving generous grants to worthy charities. He passed away at ninety one on Long Island. His immediate family consisted of his five daughters, some of whom became attorneys. He offered to help me by specifying electronic equipment and installations that I could furnish.

These mainly consisted of public address equipment with loudspeakers mounted in the ceiling, and electronic amplifying equipment at a central location. Background music was piped in and bowling alley personnel could make announcements by microphones. At its peak, I had several employees busy doing these installations. It helped my young business survive.

My business also included home and store installations of Hi-Fi sound systems for background music and announcements by store personnel. As Bob's professional engineering offices became busier, he was able to refer many small and large jobs to my business. Since my business consisted of many small and diverse operations, I was kept busy - although nothing approached the success that I had with the telephone company.

One of the largest of the sound systems I installed was at Prince George's Plaza in faraway Maryland. This involved many square miles of coverage for the large sound system which was temporarily used for special announcements to the construction workers. The foreman of the job insisted on having some of the loudspeakers placed behind the temporary toilets in the field. I tried to convince him that it would not be very comfortable for the workers. He stated that the idea was to limit the time they spent at their natural functions. The loud announcements would prompt their return to work.

No. 36865 at Your Service!

No one had to hasten me to work. I followed a popular publication called "Dodge Reports," which published lists of construction jobs in all parts of the country. I called the engineering people designing the work in my area to ask if their specifications called for any sound or public address system. One call had a surprising effect on me that I wouldn't realize until years later.

I called a certain professional engineer's office. I was able to reach him and in answer to my question he stated that yes, there was a sound system involved in his project. The troublesome part was that the specification was that the equipment had to be manufactured by RCA.

I tried to convince him that I used equipment on my jobs that was manufactured by the David Bogen Corporation and that it was my sincere belief that Bogen was manufacturing the equipment for RCA. He made a statement that influenced me greatly. He said, "I am the professional engineer responsible for this job and I say that equipment has to be made by RCA. Goodbye." He hung up on me.

I was furious but helpless. I swore to myself that one day I would become a professional engineer. Then I would call him back and give him what for, for the hard time that he gave me.

I looked up the New York State standards that were required to become an engineer-in-training. Over the next few months, I prepared an application for the state's Department of Education listing my experience and my teaching job. It took a few months to get an answer but I was accepted. I proceeded to study on my own for the professional engineers' examination. This was exciting for me. I had been so busy building a business that I felt I could never return to my university studies. I read up on the material needed which included all branches of engineering to pass the exam. Applicants taking the examination could bring books and written materials to the test. Unfortunately, there were no laptops at the time. For further reinforcement, I had taken a part-time course. I was pleased to notice that I could remember much of what I had learned without too much effort.

I prepared for the examination diligently and gathered several textbooks on the engineering fields that I had to master. On the day of the examination I arrived with a shopping cart containing my chosen texts with plenty of stickers on the critical pages. The exam took all day and I was far from sure that I had passed - but I did. Unfortunately, I had no opportunity to call, nor did I remember the name of, the professional engineer that had triggered my becoming New York State Professional Engineer License No. 36865.

Regardless of the unmade call to the unnamed engineer, I was proud of my accomplishment. At my next automobile license renewal, I purchased vanity plates PE 404, replacing my vanity plates W2KEE. My success fired up my desire to continue my education to a bachelor's degree. Now I could sign my letters, "Samuel E. Gendler, P.E.," accented by my professional engineer's stamp and seal.

Go East Young Man!

The business of raising a family is usually one of progression. As often happens with success, Etta and I decided to move the family to a better environment. Throughout my adventures Bernie Gold and I remained close friends but we moved apart, financially. His job as a "Galleta" sales and deliveryman had paid well but, when he actually took over the Tropical Cracker business, he really prospered. He moved his family to a new home in Jericho, Long Island, which is quite a distance from the city. As the Long Island Expressway did not extend into Long Island very far during the middle of the fifties, traveling into New York City was quite a chore.

My friend, Sidney Barbanel, had built his engineering business and moved his family to the North Shore of Long Island where he bought a boat. He would later trade upwards several times to larger boats.

The growing trend in my Brooklyn community in those early days of our country's expansion was to "Go east, Young man," contrary to author Horace Greeley's expression "Go West, Young Man." The burgeoning US economy after World War II had helped ambitious young people gather wealth. The rationing of certain foods, gasoline, and appliances, and the increasing need for production line employees, drew housewives into the work force and bid up the hourly pay. The soldiers who returned from war added to the need for more of everything depleted by the dedication to war effort.

Although I had achieved some success, my growing business threw off little extra money. I needed more space and good schools for my three children that were growing rapidly. My brother, Paul, advancing in the field of education had married a school teacher and they had a young son and daughter. Etta and I discussed with Paul and his wife, Rochelle, the drive toward the bustling new communities of nearby Long Island. Farmland was being dug up to make way for housing developments. The new communities needed shopping malls and good schools. The educational levels of the school systems soared in most areas of Long Island.

We decided to look for houses that were adequate for our respective families. I found a split-level house that was only a few years old in West Hempstead, Long Island. It had an excellent high school. It was only about ten miles from the Queens border on the Southern State Parkway, and the Belt Parkway continued to the Flatbush area where my business was located. It was perfect. The next-door neighbors showed us the property. The owner of the house next door was Bentley Loeb, a famous basketball coach. They had two children, a girl entering her teens and a boy about ten years old.

The interior was bare. There was a folded towel draped over the rim of the bathtub. We commented on how nice a gesture that was. Later, when we revisited the house, we lifted the towel and there was a big chip in the enamel of the tub rim. It was dishonest but not bad enough to foul up the deal or spoil our friendship.

Paul and Rochelle opted for a house in Bellmore, Long Island, about fifteen miles further west. Paul was determined to change his employment to the Bellmore School System which worked out quite well for him.

There were several problems during the move. Since my business was in a growth phase, I was cash hungry. My father-in-law gave us $2,000 for the down payment toward the then enormous price of $19,000. The next problem was the $200 per month mortgage payment as I had been paying $75 a month rent for our Crown Heights, Brooklyn apartment (increased from the original $60 a month). I never asked Paul how he managed his down payment but I guess he had no problem with it as he never complained to me.

Somehow things worked out. My son, Jeff, started his education at the West Hempstead High School and did very well. The other two children went to the Eagle Avenue School, which was quite adequate. My business improved enough to make the $200 a month mortgage payment comfortable. There was also an additional charge I hadn't expected since we no longer were eligible for the free education that our children received in Brooklyn. The additional charge for the three children was $400 a month but the business handled that nicely.

Since there were only three bedrooms for the five of us, I constructed a bedroom and bathroom in the attic space with little help. I needed a plumber to do the plumbing work, but I did the bulk of it in the spare time I had and it made the house comfortable.

Our relationship with the Loebs next door was never warm, especially after one episode. Our daughter Leslie, who was approaching her teens, was getting excellent grades at the Eagle Avenue School which pleased us a great deal. We were really proud when we were visited by a member of the West Hempstead School Administration. They told us that Leslie was doing so well that it was decided that she would be transferred to the Cornwell Avenue School which was designated for honor students.

The great feeling that the transition generated was cut short when Bentley rang our doorbell and stormed into our home in a rage. He raved and ranted about how the transfer of Leslie into an honor program reflected on all of those kids who didn't make the transfer, especially his son. According to him, it would not only ruin his son's future career but would also damage his son emotionally. We were stunned. We didn't quite understand what we were supposed to do. Did he want us to pull Leslie out of the honors program?

We sympathized with Bentley and assured him that the transfer was not due to any special effort or connections on our part. From then on our relationship with him was strained. We just responded politely whenever we happened to meet. While it was an unfortunate situation, it was unfair of him to attack Leslie's success in such a manner, but that was life in the 'burbs.

The Great Libardo Vargas Cuellar

One day, our youngest son Howard, who was doing quite well in West Hempstead High School, came home one day with a surprise. He had signed up for us to host a foreign exchange student for his or her senior year. He told Etta and me that the probability of our being accepted was quite low. We were quite apprehensive about this new page in our lives. After reflection, we agreed.

We were interviewed and accepted by both the high school and American Field Service officials as the hosting family. Several months later we were at JFK airport with other expectant hosts, all waiting for the planeload of foreign exchange students to arrive. After the plane landed, dozens of excited students were welcomed by their host families for the next year. We almost gave up hope that our student was in the group. Finally, a somewhat older, slightly-chubby young man strolled down the corridor to us.

He let us know, in fair but accented English, that his name was Libardo Vargas Cuellar. He had enrolled in the AFS program in order to learn how and why the US had been functioning so well. He planned then to return to his native Colombia afterwards to straighten out the rogues that kept his country so poor.

We later found out Libardo came from an upper middle class family and had three brothers, Carlos, Denis and Gino. His father had passed away a few years earlier of a heart attack, which was endemic in his family history. His mother, Alicia, was handling the family business which consisted of several shops. He confided to us that he was a little above the maximum AFS age of eighteen and had already graduated from high school in Bogotá, Colombia.

He learned the routine of a Jewish household and got along well with the kids. Since telephone communications with Colombia was poor and expensive, I connected him with his family by Ham radio often. He did well in his senior year at West Hempstead High School where he got VIP treatment and, at graduation ceremonies, was given valedictorian honors. Etta and I were thrilled at that event, especially when we were introduced as the host parents.

We grew attached to our "hijo Colombiano" (Colombian son) and this attachment extended to both families. My sons and daughter often visited his family during vacations. The youngest Vargas brother, Gino, nine years old, also stayed with us for a year. He attended Eagle Avenue Elementary School. Gino enrolled speaking only a few words of English but by the end of the school year was speaking in excellent English.

At the end of his school year his mother came to pick him up. She visited with friends and family that had immigrated to the US. Etta and I had trouble communicating with Alicia during her brief stay with us. I once said, "Gino, please ask your mother if she wants to go shopping with us to Klein's Department Store." He turned to Alicia, grinned, and asked her in English. I had to point out to Gino that he had to switch back to Spanish.

Getting Acquainted with Colombia

Little did we know that this serendipitous relationship with Libardo would be a lasting one with far reaching consequences.

A few years later, I went with Etta and Leslie to Colombia for an extended visit. For the first part of the trip, we stayed at the Vargas apartment. For the second week, we had booked an airplane trip to the major cities surrounding the area. The fare covered all of a packaged trip of our choice; it was called Conozca Colombia, or Get to Know Colombia.

Etta and Leslie went ahead of me by a week as I had some pressing business matters to finish up. The day before my departure, Etta called me and asked me to purchase a gift for the young daughter of Alicia's relatives that we were to visit. I hustled out to Klein's Department Store in Hempstead, Long Island and went looking for a Barbie doll since it was popular at that time. The only Barbie dolls that were in stock at Klein's were those with brown skin. I hesitated for a minute or two but I recalled Libardo had once told me that there were no color barriers in Colombia. Skin colors ranged from the ethnic Spanish, with fair skin and blue eyes, to the dark-skinned Indios.

Upon my arrival, we were taken to dinner by Alicia at an elegant restaurant in Bogotá. The waiters wore tuxedos and the meat was tender and delicious. I was shocked to find that each meal cost only the equivalent of two to three dollars. The exchange rate was about fifty pesos to the dollar. We went to visit Alicia's relatives the next day. I gave the gift wrapped package to the daughter who promptly unwrapped the Barbie doll. The family was shocked when they saw the dark skin color, although they tried to hide it. So much for Colombian color blindness.

We were served a delicious lunch of Colombian food. After, we were invited to watch a film of the family on vacation. The dark room was small. I was dismayed to hear my stomach growling and bubbling. The sounds were so loud, deafening to me. I never felt as embarrassed in my entire life.

The three of us boarded an Avianca airplane to Medellin a few days later. Near the airport, the pilot banked the plane sharply to pass between two mountains. The city was quiet but I didn't feel comfortable. Medellin had a bad reputation as the home of Colombia's mafia. Regardless, our stay there was uneventful and without incident.

Our next stop was Barranquilla. On the way there Etta felt quite ill with digestive problems. She was nauseous and vomiting. We checked into our hotel and Etta went right to bed. In the morning, the nausea was still active but the vomiting had stopped. Leslie and I went downstairs to the restaurant for breakfast. There had been a torrential rainstorm the night before and the restaurant was flooded. The central level was knee deep in water. Leslie and I sat at a table on a raised ring of tables 5 ft above the flooded level.

While sitting there, we were entertained by an employee. In an attempt to clean up the water with a mop, he would slosh his way to the center of the flooded lower level, dip his mop into the pool of water that had accumulated, and walk to the perimeter where there was a large pail. Almost no water reached the pail as the wet mop would drip most of it on the way back.

Shaking Hands With El Presidente

The next day, Etta felt better. We took our next plane trip to Cartagena, which is an ancient coastal city with fortifications. We noticed that the passenger entry and exit door was tied in place with wire. By now we were used to unusual situations. Upon landing at the airport, we made a deal with a friendly taxi driver, who spoke some English. He was to take us to all of the important sights for no more than the equivalent of ten dollars and get us back in time for a flight back to Bogotá. It was a wonderful arrangement that kept us fascinated as we explored the fortifications and ancient dungeons.

We got to the airport with ample time but were informed that our plane would be delayed because El Presidente Carlos Restrepo was due to land at the airport. We were packed into the elevated viewing area surrounding the landing strip and guarded by soldiers facing us from the railing with weapons drawn. Surrounded by a crowd, Etta and I suddenly realized that Leslie wasn't with us. We were panicked. We figured that she was somewhere in the crowd.

The president's airplane landed and a red carpet runner was rolled out from the landing stairs. A military orchestra started playing martial music. A single file of plainly dressed locals marched onto the air strip. They held hand painted signs welcoming El Presidente. They stopped as President Restrepo walked along the line shaking hands with the marchers. Halfway along the line, he shook hands with a young girl that was taller than the short President. It was Leslie. We never did learn how she got into that lineup.

Apparently, it wasn't big news to anyone else. The next day in Bogotá, we looked at *El Tiempo*, the most prominent newspaper in Colombia. Their feature didn't show the tall "gringa" shaking hands with the short Presidente.

The Tragic Airline Collision of 1960

In February, 1960, there was a mid-air collision between United Airlines Flight 826 and Flight 266, known as the Park Slope plane crash. Flight 266 crashed into Staten Island and Flight 826 crashed into Park Slope, Brooklyn. Over a hundred people aboard the two airliners perished, along with six more on the ground.[1]

In the investigation that followed the crash, it was pointed out that the communication between the airplanes and the ground control had substantial problems. Prior to the crash, there had been complaints by aircraft personnel that the communications over New York City were hampered. The source of that interference was from electronic equipment used below by factories in the heat-sealing of vinyl, which was used in large sheets as a cheap replacement for leather goods, usually purses, luggage, and even tablecloths.

The equipment for the heat-sealing process was basically a radio transmitter emitting a strong signal on frequencies close to the air navigation frequencies. The signals came through as powerful, buzzing noises. There were instructions by the manufacturers to have the equipment enclosed within wire screening enclosures. The wire had to be of conductive material such as copper or steel, but not plastic. The enclosure also had to be large enough to surround the employees, as well as the equipment and the vinyl material. The electric cables that powered the equipment within the enclosure had to pass through electronic filters. This was to ensure that the high-frequency, interfering signals generated by the heat-sealing equipment did not escape from the enclosure through power lines.

Since the floor and ceiling also had to be part of the wire screen enclosure, and any gaps in it would act like a lens allowing the interfering signals to escape, its construction was a nuisance to the factory owners. I got involved in all this when I was contacted by the FCC's New York City office. They asked for permission to list my name as a consulting engineer available to test and certify that an installation was not permitting interfering signals to escape. I had been recommended since I was already listed as a professional engineer in electronics, and had a registered radio amateur license. In order to certify that such an installation met FCC standards, a series of measurements would have to be made in all of the streets encircling the installation. A number of calculations would have to show that the signal strength at each measurement location did not exceed FCC limitations.

I agreed to have my name listed as a professional consultant on this problem. Consequently, I received many telephone calls during the next few years from companies in the heat-sealing business. I purchased equipment to help with the measurements. When my regular business was not very active, I would do the measurements myself. At first my equipment slowed down the procedure, particularly in the crowded streets of Manhattan. Searching for the buzzing signals by twisting a knob was time-consuming. The signals had a brief pulse length only when the sealer was brought down on the vinyl fabric. Even worse, the frequency shifted as the sealer was heating the vinyl fabric. The knob had to be twirled to pursue the shifting signal while measuring the signal simultaneously.

I kept looking for suitable equipment to continue certifying the heat-sealing equipment in a simpler and more rapid manner. Several years later, I was fortunate enough to have the opportunity to purchase a used spectrum analyzer. It displayed the signal, as transmitted, by a vertical line whose length above a horizontal base gave the strength of the signal.

The horizontal baseline had markings that indicated the frequency, while the shifting signal frequency appeared as a vertical line moving along the horizontal base line. The height of the vertical line was a measure of the signal strength. The shifting of this line along the horizontal base line showed the frequencies of the interfering signals.

There was no twirling of knobs to follow the shifting signal. The measurement at a single location took less than a minute or two. There also had to be numerous measurements along the four blocks surrounding the location of the installation. I was helped by the fact that my sons, Jeff and Howard, were going to college by then and were available to do the measurements. I would do the calculations later. That enabled them to earn extra money for their part-time work during their summer vacations. Jeff had been admitted to Rensselaer Polytechnic Institute and Howard to Cornell University. The timing was excellent as their summer vacations coincided with the hot summer weather. It was the favorite season for the FCC inspectors to get out of their non-air conditioned offices, a building formerly a Federal military building.

Soon after I started to do the certifications I began to install the screen rooms using my staff. I arranged with a contractor to do the work under my plans as a professional engineer. I would do the calculations based on the measurements at home, prepare the graphs, and place the completed certifications in a binder with my PE seal proudly displayed on the outside.

As my business went on to bigger things and the bowling alleys were mostly all built, my employees had been merged into other work. We moved into larger quarters. I was kept busy managing different product lines. The sound system work and the TV range extenders slipped into a minor role, mostly a sideline business. I didn't want to turn down old customers that had depended on me in the past. These sidelines could not be handled by my new personnel who were now involved in management and production of electronic equipment.

I was getting better known around Long Island and the New York Metropolitan area. I would get called in on consulting work, some of which was interesting and needed some quick thinking. The extra money came in handy especially with my three teenagers heading into higher education.

As an example, I was visited by a wealthy gentleman who owned a large estate further east on Long Island. He invested relatively small amounts of money in new ventures. He had the expectations of today's venture capitalists, that the investment would make it big. He wanted my help on evaluating an invention of a secure door lock. I headed out to his mansion one evening and he took me into his workshop where the two inventors had assembled their supposedly impregnable lock into a doorway set up in the workshop. I studied the mechanism and noted that it depended on the attraction of two powerful magnets. I called in the investor. Using a small square of sheet metal I had fashioned in his workshop, I pushed it between the door mechanism and the door frame. This interfered with the magnetic field. The door opened easily. I was thanked, invited to stay for dinner, and given a nice check in payment.

My listing by the FCC led to a consultation invitation from the manufacturer of equipment similar to the powerful transmitters that heat sealed plastic. This application was different. It seems that storage potatoes, when sliced and fried, don't have the fresh look of harvested potatoes. That is unless they use powerful radio wave transmitters for the cooking process. I was asked to go to their installation in Fort Wayne, Indiana. I was to solve the problem that the city's television reception was being wiped out by the powerful signals of the transmitters cooking the French-fried potatoes.

I flew to Fort Wayne and met with an electronic technician that had been assigned to me. When the transmitter was turned on, a large area around the installation had their television reception drowned out by buzzing signals. I inspected the installation and noted that some screening had been installed to shield the area from the powerful generation of interference. The metal door to the steel cabinet housing the transmitter was suspicious. It had been spray painted at the cabinet factory. We used abrasive emery cloth to clean the metal door edges of paint as well as the adjacent edges of the cabinet surrounding the door. My helper had some brass stripping that went over the areas that were stripped of paint. When the metal door was closed the brass stripping closed off the cleaned space between it and the cabinet. The interference dropped to a faint shadow of its former level. We went over the installation for other gaps and fixed the few that we found. The results were almost perfect. I took off that afternoon for home.

The company called me a few months later for a similar problem in California. I flew there on a Sunday. The installers had paid attention to the details of shielding but had missed a screened door into the equipment, mainly because it was close to the wall and inaccessible. I was able to shield it by stuffing screening into the space between the wall and door, to demonstrate that it was the problem. I called the company and learned that they expected me as the head of the project was awaiting word. I explained the problem and gave him my idea about to how to improve the shielding. He was delighted. He told me not to concern myself with it. They would have the original team move the equipment with a rented fork-lift to expose and shield the door.

You Little Stinker!

Busy with my career, I never got that hernia that the army doctors had diagnosed repaired until many years later. The story of the repair began when I was at a Men's Club meeting at the West Hempstead Community Center. A member arrived late to the meeting. He was immediately greeted by many of the other members. He was asked about a recent operation that he had just had and replied enthusiastically.

The man explained that he had suffered from an inguinal hernia. He had it surgically treated at the small, but famous, Shouldice Hospital in Thornhill, Canada. The hospital was named after a doctor who had built a practice of treating hernias with a hospital stay of three days. No lifting restrictions were placed on the patient after the procedure. They could even exercise shortly after the surgery and go home on the third day, carrying the luggage with which they arrived.

It was so popular that patients came from all over the world. Naturally, there was a long waiting list for an appointment. I bided my time about the hernia. One day, I had to go to Ontario on business and I decided it was time to take action.

I begged the admission person at Shouldice Hospital to admit me for the surgery. I told her how many years I had suffered with the hernia and about the barbaric hernia support that I had to wear and how torturous it was for me. She smiled. She told me that I was in luck as they had just received a cancellation. The normal waiting time was several months. I called Etta and told her a white lie that my business trip was prolonged. I said I was going to stay in Canada over the weekend.

The next morning I had the surgery in a beautiful operating room under local anesthetic. Next to the operating table there was a stand with a roll of gleaming wire that was used to close the internal incision. I was in a dreamy state during the whole process. It seemed to me that I had stopped breathing. I forced myself to breathe again. This happened several times during the forty-five minute procedure. I'm sure that I never stopped breathing.

At the end, the surgeon leaned over me. In a delightful British accent, he told me to put my arm around his shoulders. With his help, I stood up with my legs shaking.

I went back to my room and slept until lunchtime. I found that I was able to walk but with a distinct curve to the right due to an ache in the right groin. When I mixed with the other patients, it was difficult conversing with a first or second day patients that had had the same side operated on. Our right slanting curves leaned our torsos in opposite directions when we tried to face each other. The food wasn't bad. I slept well with a mild sedative offered by the nurses. The next day I was visited by the surgeon who removed alternate staples from the outer skin incision. That day I did some light exercises like stretching side-to-side and bending forward and backward.

That evening I called home and spoke to Etta. She surprised me by reminding me that my business appointment was close to the hospital where our acquaintance had his operation. She asked me why I didn't visit and get more details about the operation. I could hold the truth no longer. I told her that not only had I had visited the Shouldice Hospital, but I liked what I saw and had the operation performed. She was surprised. She expressed it lovingly by saying, "You little stinker."

The next day, the remaining staples were removed and I was ready to go home. I asked the nurses if there was anyone to help me with my two suitcases. They told me that since it was Sunday there was no auxiliary staff on duty. If I didn't feel up to carrying my own bags they would be glad to carry them for me. I opted to carry my own bags. It turned out to be a surprisingly easy task.

Etta met me at JFK Airport. She was shocked when she saw me carrying my own bags. I told her that Shouldice Hospital would allow their surgical patients only a few days off work for disability unless the patient had a very demanding job, like lifting pianos, or installing loud speakers between the ceiling and ceiling tiles of a bowling alley or carpet store. In that case they allowed a week or two.

Many years later, as a medical student, I visited Canadian hospitals during a brief vacation from medical school. I made it a point to visit Shouldice Hospital. It was as beautiful as ever. I was even allowed to assist one of their surgeons in the early morning of the next day, as well as accompanying him on patient rounds. That was quite a thrilling experience for me.

True to their word, Shouldice sent a brief questionnaire to me each year for the next ten years, asking about how well the hernia repair had held up. My hernia never recurred and despite the use of wire as a suture material, the airport metal detectors never triggered an alarm when I passed through either.

The "Hustling Hubby Through" Award

When I earned my professional engineer's license, despite the lack of a degree, I became enthusiastic about finishing my college education. I had geared myself up to study lots of material and had qualified for the much esteemed license, which opened the door to large projects and enormous responsibility. Upon receipt, the license cautioned me to care for the document carefully as it would probably be the most important document I would ever receive.

I thought over my elementary school education, notable for my skip over the second half of my fifth year. My junior high school years were shorter too, as I had been promoted into the Rapid Advance classes.

At sixteen, I had entered CCNY but I was ill-prepared for it. At the time the world was in the throes of the Great Depression. The unemployment rate was high. CCNY was attractive since tuition was free. There were no grade advisors. I had no way of learning the ins-and-outs of free education since I was so young. I wound up with early morning classes and a free afternoon but, had another class at 5 p.m. I dropped out after one year with miserable grades. Years later I took the entrance exam for Cooper Union and passed against heavy odds. This also lasted one year as I was entering engineering night school but working lots of overtime in defense work. I felt discouraged but I decided to try for admission to Brooklyn Polytechnic Institute, which was considered number six of the top ten US engineering schools.

With a tremendous stroke of luck, I was interviewed by the kindly Professor Canavaciol. He saw beyond my earlier college disasters. He gave me credit generously wherever he could. I estimated that it would take me about seven years of evening classes to graduate. This took a lot of deliberation. On one hand there would be the advantage of more doors open to me and my struggling business. On the other hand, the time for school and homework would be demanding on me and my family.

Most classes took place twice a week. This gave me more time at home with family. I was encouraged by my wife, who would have to bear the brunt of the upbringing of my three teenagers. Having my own business was helpful in that I could arrange my own hours.

After much thought, I decided to go for it. I signed up for the first semester with trepidation and anticipation. I learned that the school was going through a revision of its engineering programs. The teaching staff was top notch. They had published some notable textbooks.

The college campus left a lot to be desired. Classes were in an old building. This changed to a larger building attached to another that had once been the American Safety Razor factory. Polytech, as the college was often called, had started in Brooklyn and remained there with an annex in Long Island. (Recently, they affiliated with New York University and changed their name to the Polytechnic Institute of NYU.)

The first class that I took affected my life greatly. It dealt with Laplace Transforms which enabled linear differential equations to be solved easily and depicted graphically with ease. They were first invented by Simon Pierre Laplace several hundred years ago. From my self-taught background in electronics, the information was dazzling. Laplace Transforms had been used by mathematicians ever since. I had admired the history of self-taught Oliver Heaviside, an Englishman who applied them to telegraphy and other electrical circuits in the mid-1800s. He applied complex numbers, which was quite a novelty in those years, to solving the equations for electronic circuitry. He used his own variations to Laplace's work, which are still in use.

Laplace was also influenced by the genius of James Clerk Maxwell who had written a two-volume treatise proving that electromagnetic waves must exist. They had not been discovered at that time. For me, the most remarkable Maxwell discovery was that these theoretical waves would travel at the same speed as light through space. He calculated that speed from the measured characteristics of ordinary materials and his number was amazingly accurate.

The existence of these waves was later proven by people like Guillermo Marconi by transmitting raspy signals generated by electric spark-driven transmitters. He started with the detector close by. As his detectors improved he was able to transmit and receive the buzzing signals over greater distances, even across the Atlantic Ocean. This invention was a godsend to ship traffic. In an emergency, before electromagnetic waves were discovered and utilized, a boat in distress could only send up flares or signal with semaphore flags. Little could they foresee that radio, television, lasers, and interplanetary communication were the future as a result of this technology.

My first instructor was a young Korean-American scientist, Sang Youn Whang, who was a brilliant man. I was able to master the new concepts quite easily and scored an A. Another class that I was taking that semester was Integral Calculus. It was difficult but I believe that I got the top grade there also. The homework in that class was daunting. Etta bore the load of handling the kids without a complaint.

Sang Whang and I became friendly. After finishing the semester, our friendship continued outside school. My business had been growing slowly and he helped me with advice whenever I had questions. Our families mixed quite well and we visited each other from time to time.

Sang confided that his earnings from teaching were not sufficient to raise his family and give his three children an equivalent education in South Korea. Sang's father was a Christian Minister with strong ties to the Korean government. His son, Sang, was fourteen years old when he had a miraculous experience. His family lived in Seoul, the capital city. One day, when Sang was alone at home, he heard that the North Koreans surprised the world by invading South Korea. Seoul was essentially defenseless. The North Korean soldiers had sent a team to find and capture Sang's father since he was an important government figure. They arrived to search the house. Sang was hiding in a closet and one of the North Korean soldiers opened the door to look inside.

He spotted Sang but closed the door. He loudly reported that there was no one inside. Talk about a guiding force in life.

Over seven years of evening studies I did well. I achieved mostly As and an occasional B. Not all the material was easy. For example, transistor circuitry proved tricky due to having to work more with current flow-controlling transistors. I had more experience in voltage controlling transistors due to my work on vacuum tubes and my teaching.

I particularly enjoyed a complex field of study in an electromagnetic fields and waves class. The young instructor gave the class a quiz about material that he had taught in the prior session. He returned the papers the next class meeting following the quiz. The students looked over their papers silently. Finally, one of the students raised his hand and complained that the results were poor, with grades of thirty to forty. The contention was that the material had been taught ambiguously. The teacher responded by saying that it couldn't have been that difficult because there was one student with a grade of eighty five. I stared straight ahead minding my own business. All the students glared at me.

The usual pattern of my learning was that, in the various classes, I would start the class without much of a prior background. My initial grades were not particularly high but as the semester progressed, my grades would soar. In several classes, where there was a mixture of the new Laplace Transform approach and the classic teaching, some of the older professors were not keeping up with the new concepts. The students would ask them tough questions that left these professors floundering. In several of these classes, the professors would look anxiously at me for answers when the going got tough for them. It was flattering but I would have preferred that they had known their stuff.

I got accustomed to mostly A grades with an occasional B+ or even a B at times. The years passed by. The growth of Seg Electronics, night school, homework, all while raising a family was becoming a drag.

Seven years after entering Polytech, I checked the school catalog to see which classes I still needed for my Bachelor of Electrical Engineering degree. I was surprised to find that there were no more classes left for me to take. I applied for the diploma and the response was that I was eligible for graduation. A small note at the bottom of the letter read magna cum laude. I looked up the meaning. I learned that extra awards were added to the title for outstanding performance. These started at cum laude, moved to magna cum laude, then, at the top, summa cum laude.

While the full time students had one graduate with a summa cum laude rating, my magna cum laude was the highest honor for Brooklyn Polytechnic's night school graduates that year.

At the graduation exercises, Etta and I brought our oldest son, Jeffrey. He was about to enroll in Rensselear Polytechnic Institute, a top engineering school in Troy, New York. We trusted that the ceremony would inspire him. I'm sure that he was impressed. After the speeches, the graduating class was called to stand up. They marched in single file up to the podium to shake the dean's hand and receive their diplomas. The honor students were called up to the podium individually to receive their honor diplomas.

Brooklyn Polytechnic had a social organization that held a dinner meeting for the new graduates shortly after the graduation ceremonies. While some might argue that engineers lack a sense of humor, they don't. The wives received fancy "Hustling Hubby Through" diplomas, as well. Etta was thrilled, but it was a tiny reward for all those years handling the children and household problems with little participation from her hubby.

Dr. Krauss Takes Revenge & Vice Versa

As I mentioned earlier, when I enrolled in Brooklyn Polytechnic Institute (now Polytechnic Institute of NYU), my first instructor was Sang Youn Whang. He had confided to me that he was planning to leave Polytech because the salary was not adequate for his growing family as they would need financial support soon for their advanced education.

While Sang was still at school, I did ask him to help me with some electronic design work for several projects I was working on. The results were excellent and led to more work for my company. When he resigned from Polytech, I made him an offer to be the vice president of my little company and accept a minority interest. He accepted. This worked out well for both of us.

That was about the time that I was in my last year of studies. One of my classes was in an advanced electronics curriculum under Professor Krauss. He knew quite a bit about me. I asked a question once and his curt response was that he would not answer it. The question dealt with my business and I would have to ask it outside of class and pay him.

I managed to learn that he was a friend of Sang Whang. The professor believed that I had lured Sang out of the school. He was convinced that I had taken advantage of Sang and that I was becoming a millionaire on his hard work and efforts. So Professor Krauss continued to give me a hard time, as well as awarding me a C grade which I felt was spiteful. It was the only C grade I ever received at Brooklyn Polytechnic Institute.

After I graduated, I decided to take a post-graduate course in the filter network field in which my company was becoming well known. I filled out a request form and took it to the graduate grade adviser for approval. The grade adviser was no less than Doctor Krauss himself. He recognized me and I greeted him with my request form.

He responded by starting to flip through a file of index cards. He said he had to make sure I had no deficiencies. I responded quietly that I had graduated magna cum laude, that there shouldn't be any deficiencies.

His fingers stopped flipping the index cards. He resumed, but much more rapidly. He said he had to look anyway.

I was certain that he was considering how my C in his class would look among all of the A grades I had accumulated. It might possibly even affect his reputation as a teacher and professor if someone ever reviewed my record.

That was one of life's sweetest moments. I have never forgotten. It taught me to be patient in difficult times. Just like the time the professional engineer, whose name I could never remember, told me that it was his way or the highway. It taught me to hope that the wheel of justice would turn and bring satisfaction instead of disappointment.

The Gemini Space Project

Over the years, Seg Electronics employed representatives that were engaged in identifying potential customers. They were mostly paid on a commission basis of about 5 percent. This led us down strange pathways but we usually came out with a whole skin. We were very responsive and innovative. I had kept track of contacts that could help us if things got heavy. I had become confident in my ability to work my way out of tight spots. When Sang Whang joined us, we made a powerful team.

One of our reps had his own former business in the closed-circuit television field. He brought to my attention a Request for Proposal by the US Air Force for a closed-circuit television set-up for the first Gemini space flight. It was for five TV cameras around the launch pad and one on the launch pad at Cape Canaveral, Florida. Within the blockhouse, one of the consoles would be devoted to the control equipment for the cameras. A bank of TV monitors was to be suspended over racks of the TV equipment.

My rep even knew where we could purchase the TV equipment for a reasonable price as there was no special requirement for full military specifications. The TV project was for this one flight. The TV cameras had to be in encasements that would protect them from the torrential rains that were frequent at the Cape.

My bid turned out to be the low bid, super low. Our bid was about $30,000. I learned later that the other bids were about $80,000 for more expensive equipment. The Air Force sent a team to evaluate Seg Electronics for the job. We looked competent since we had been manufacturing filter networks for the US Air Force. The team leader, Major Queras, told me that they would approve our bid, which they did.

The Gemini Space Launch program was the next step after the Mercury program with one astronaut. Gemini was to start with an unmanned flight in low-earth orbit and advance to high-earth orbit flights. Then they would start manned flights by two astronauts. While preparing for the Gemini I flight, NASA was preparing a larger launch pad for the future Apollo flights. With three astronauts, those flights would lead to the moon landings.

I reserved a room at a motel near Cape Canaveral. When all the arrangements were complete I flew down to Orlando, Florida, where I picked up a rental car. I drove sixty miles to Patrick Air Force Base. I checked in with Major Queras, who was the project manager, and then onto Cape Canaveral and Pan American, the managing company.

After I was given a Gemini hard hat and an identification badge, I was taken for a tour around Complex 19. The Gemini launch vehicle had been assembled and mounted upright on the launch pad. In the blockhouse I was shown the racks for my equipment and the console for the remote controls for the TV cameras. There were sturdy stanchions around the perimeter of Complex 19 and one stanchion on the launch pad for my TV cameras. During my tour, the guide pointed to some men passing by us and pointed out Gus Grissom. Several years later, I learned it was the same Gus Grissom, who died in a fire with two other astronauts in the first Command Capsule atop Apollo1. The incident delayed the Apollo program by about eighteen months.

There were no windows in the blockhouse which was very strongly built in order to withstand a disaster. The takeoff might be aborted and the space craft crash back onto the blockhouse. The complex around the blockhouse could only be viewed through a periscope at the top center of the blockhouse. There was a long tunnel of several hundred feet that connected the blockhouse to the launch pad. That tunnel contained many heavy cables which carried enormous A/C currents. Those cables gave me lots of problems. My much weaker TV signals had to pass through by them.

The Gemini was due to take off in late 1963 and there were only a few months for me to complete my installation. It was the hardest work I have ever done in my life. I typically worked from 7 a.m. until after midnight at which time I would head to my motel room for a few hours of sleep. Most of the time I worked alone, except for a brief visit by Sang Whang. He couldn't stay long as he needed to get back to SEG Electronics to manage the rest of our workload.

Back at the launch pad a friend of mine, Warren Esterly, volunteered to help me out. He had extensive experience in closed circuit TV. He pooped out at about 3 p.m. or 4 p.m. each day. For the long cables through the cable tunnel, I engaged local electricians that had clearance to work in the complex.

There were frequent inspections of my progress by Major Queras, as well as by RCA Corporation staff that was responsible for the electronics at the cape. Their chief engineer and various members of their administration and technicians would visit me as well. Major Queras was friendly and encouraging at his inspections. I welcomed his visits.

I had depended on my sales representative to carefully review the US Air Force specifications for the job. They were quite complex and in a field that was alien to me. While I had taught television theory and practice, and worked as a field engineer for a television receiver company, I had little experience in television cameras and generating the images. I was learning fast on the job. It helped having just completed my Bachelor of Electrical Engineering at the Brooklyn Polytechnic Institute. Several events alerted me to emerging complications. The RCA inspectors questioned me about a clause in the overall specifications that I and my sales rep had missed. The clause stated that the system had to be compatible with national television. This was so that the images of the spacecraft, which would be viewed inside the blockhouse console, could also be shown to TV viewers in the US and around the world. This was a horse of a different color.

Another problem woke me up to political involvement. I had to fly back to my facility in New York a few times during the several months of work on the project. One time, I got back to Florida after a heavy rain at the cape. To my horror, the water-resistant TV camera enclosures had leaked. Some of the cameras were in several inches of water. I called the manufacturer in California to complain. I was told that the job should have been done with waterproof enclosures. In fact, they still had the waterproof enclosures that were scheduled for the job at their factory. I was shocked since I realized that the project was supposed to go to some other company at a much higher price.

I adapted my enclosures to be more rain proofed by adding some better seals and we had no further problem in that department. The compatibility issue was tougher. I located an adapter, expensive at $1,000, and made it work well by adding extra components.

In retrospect, I realized that I had better be watchful. I had upset someone's slam-dunk deal with the possibility that payoffs were not going to materialize. On review, not everyone was as friendly as Major Queras and the RCA chief engineer. In the prior inspections, several members of the entourage were silent and grim.

One Sunday, I got to the complex at the usual hour and found it closed. I was told that Pan American, managing company of Complex 19, was reworking the electrical system. I had a brainstorm and looked up Major Queras' telephone number since he had told me that he lived nearby. He answered the phone and I told him of the halt to the work. I also knew that he was an avid fisherman. I commented that it would be an ideal day for fishing. He agreed. Half an hour later he arrived with his motor boat in tow. We had a great day fishing off the cape. Tiny fish were leaping out of the water and splashing back down. I don't think we caught any, but I enjoyed his company and the forced break in my drastic routine.

The work was finally completed but not before bugs showed up. It was late November, 1963, and we received a notice. President and Mrs. John Kennedy were going to tour the cape the next day. The blockhouses would all be in lockdown. This was strange because we all held Secret Security clearance. I watched through my blockhouse periscope as the president's entourage drove by without stopping. President Kennedy went on to the airport and then on to Dallas for that fatal day in an unprotected open car.

I called for the final inspection of my project and the RCA chief engineer with his team showed up when scheduled. The TV pictures looked good but the RCA chief and I debated whether the fan-shaped test pattern's stripes were distinct enough. The concern was that the stripes were not blending into each other at the tightest crowding. In the end he agreed that it was adequate. Major Queras arrived and the

RCA chief told him that he approved the project. The major told me to meet him the next day at Patrick AFB for the signoff. I was delighted that this tremendous effort had been completed.

After everyone left, I got busy preparing to pack my tools and leave. The phone at my console rang. I picked it up and the caller said that his name was Bob Smith. He wanted to speak to the RCA chief. I told him that they all had left after approving the job. His response was, "Oh." This shocked me. It sounded as though he was surprised. Bob Smith had been introduced to me at one of the early inspections. I didn't know his title or specific role but he always stayed at the perimeter of any group doing the inspection. He never commented or smiled. He closed with the request to have the RCA chief call him should he come back or call.

I immediately called Major Queras at his Patrick AFB office and told him of the suspicious call. He told me not to worry and that he would look into it. The major called me back an hour later to tell me that I was right. He said he, "Put out the fire." The next day, I met with him and signed off. I headed to the Orlando Airport that day with a feeling of tremendous relief.

Although the Gemini 1 Space Flight was delayed, it was launched successfully in April, 1964. It was scheduled for an unmanned flight with a duration of four days. The propulsion did not cut off promptly. The flight lasted about eight days before burning up in descent as designed. I followed up with Major Queras by phone after the flight and he reported that my equipment worked as expected.

I learned a lot on that project, technically and politically, about how to watch my butt.

Minuteman Missile Program

Sang Youn Whang had done a few successful consulting jobs for me prior to his leaving Brooklyn Polytechnic. I stayed in touch with him as I believed that we had the potential for a future together. As I said before, having Sang join me in Seg Electronics was one of the most beneficial moves I made for both of us.

The opportunity presented itself when RCA contacted me. They had run into trouble with data transmission for the Minuteman Missile Program. To prevent the possibility of sabotage of the signal from Air Force Control Center to the Minuteman missile silo, a filter network had been installed to prevent extraneous transmissions from being introduced by outside sources. These sources included power line buzz or high-frequency interference from transmitters.

The filters handled this problem easily but distorted the data transmission signal. This data transmission signal was of the type called diphase. The distortion caused by the filters also caused errors in the information transmitted. RCA had received samples of filter networks from companies that were skilled in designing filters but none of them functioned properly. It was assumed that the group time delay of the filter networks, which increased at the low and high frequencies, affected the wave shape of the diphase data signal.

Since my equalizer was incorporated into the design, I was invited to quote such a filter. I invited Sang Youn Whang to consult for me in that matter. He studied the problem. When he was satisfied with his results, we scheduled a meeting with the RCA engineers.

Sang and I arrived at the RCA offices in lower Manhattan where we had to present our findings to a team of about fifteen engineers seated at a table. Sang lectured to the engineers using a blackboard that was provided. He explained that their diphase signals were mostly affected by the phase delay and the phase intercept rather than the group delay, which the competition had been using in their design.

When Sang finished his presentation, there was a hubbub of loud conversation from the engineers debating the findings. An older engineer, who had been silent the whole time, cleared his throat and all conversation stopped. Sang and the engineer engaged in a dialogue. They were the only people that understood the problem. The end result was that Seg Electronics Corporation was awarded a contract to build a sample filter network for the project.

Since computers were being used only in large corporations, Sang spent a few weeks designing the corrected filter using a Friden calculator. The calculations involved day and night work. He would punch out entries and wait out the buzzing and clacking by the carriage to finish each calculation. After the design was completed, we assembled the parts in the RCA specified package and delivered it. The filter was a huge success.

The diphase data transmission came through undistorted and adequately filtered. I was encouraged to set up production facilities for the huge production run expected for the filters and the formerly approved equalizers. No competitors were approved as suppliers.

Production began about six months later. I set up a credit line with the Franklin National Bank, Long Island, to move to larger quarters and purchase production equipment.

Production of that filter continued for several years and Seg Electronics thrived. We became a well-known supplier of filter networks to the electronics industry. Other production runs were small compared to the Minuteman filter that was in demand by the Air Force. I made many trips to RCA's purchasing department in Camden, New Jersey, to meet with the various buyers of our products. During one visit, the filter buyer showed me one of the Minuteman filters sawed in half. He laughed when I looked at it on his desk and said it had accidentally fallen off his desk and that's why it was broken in two. I held it in my hands and noted that it was not ours. The number of components was far greater than in our filter.

The filter buyer realized that he had made a mistake by showing it to me. I realized that we were way ahead of the competition.

Members of the Air Force inspecting our production facilities had warned me that the production runs were bound to increase in the future and that I would need a larger production facility. I moved Seg Electronics to a factory building in East New York, Brooklyn, to prepare for the increased production. This meant tapping into the credit line deeply.

We had an excellent team of production workers and testers including a production manager who had been rejected by the Navy for being underage. He was seventeen and bright. He became a great tester and moved up to production manager. His name was Joe Hills and he married one of the wiring women. He was the only Afro-American in the company.

We progressed from the Friden calculator to a typewriter-sized Olivetti computer that used magnetic cards to store the data. For complex jobs we rented time on a GE large frame computer. After a few years, computers more sophisticated and compact became available at lower prices which made our design work easier.

We experimented with a special filter that could simulate any characteristic for filtering, as well as group time delay. In those days miniaturization was in its infancy so the finished product, which involved delay lines, occupied most of a desktop.

The software for this computer filter was written by a new employee of ours who was a Chassidic Jew. He was extremely orthodox and so was not available at the many holidays practiced by his sect. At our first test of the software-controlled filter, we ran the complex software on the giant GE computer via our local telephone line. The computer signaled us by beeping that it was calculating. After about fifteen minutes we were convinced that there was an error in the software that had the software program running in a loop. It was an expensive error that cost more than five-hundred dollars to fix. I pleaded with GE for some forgiveness and got the price reduced by a couple of hundred dollars. Our Chassid eventually left us to join Bell telephone laboratories which had a reputation of being reluctant to employ people of the Jewish religion. His brilliance obviously impressed them, but he must have been a rather unusual sight at Bell Labs, wearing his yarmulke.

The first and only model of the software controlled filter was purchased by IBM and shipped to their facility in France. When Etta and I spent our next vacation on the Riviera, we visited the surrounding area and one of the stops was at the IBM plant. It had a novel use for this filter. Since their company was experimenting with the international data transmission, their people could ask personnel in the field to measure the overall characteristics if there were any problems with the transmission lines. They could reproduce those characteristics at their French facility with our filter and troubleshoot their equipment to make it work with those characteristics. It was quite a feather in our cap that my little company wrote software for such a leader in the field like IBM.

Data transmission was steadily increasing in popularity and the predominant method of transmission was through telephone lines. Modems were being developed at an increasing rate. They took the signal that was generated and converted it into signals that the transmission line could carry reliably. At the receiving end there was another modem that converted the data signal back into the original source signal. The usual way of testing such a circuit, and the modems, was to rent a line from the telephone company, from one side of the United States to the other, and a reverse line as well. A signal would be transmitted by modem into the line and carried back by the other line to the source. As the telephone company had published specifications for their standard lines, what was not realized was that the telephone company equipment rerouted lines automatically if the signal got weak or noisy.

I carefully reviewed the telephone line specifications and designed a telephone line simulator. It electronically duplicated the noise and telephone line characteristics of frequency range and phase jitter. This was done in a rather interesting way. I wrote down the mathematical equations for the overall simulator and reproduced that equation electronically with specific components.

I used trigonometric formulas such as:

$$sin\ (A + B) = sinA\ cosB + cosA\ sinB$$

Where A was the signal coming through the telephone line and B was an adjustable signal generated in the simulator for phase jitter. Sine was shifted to cosine by a 90 degree phase shifter. Multiplication was accomplished by active devices sold by electronic parts dealers. Addition was done by adders bought in the same way.

It worked very well and sold at the rate of one or two a month at a few thousand dollars each. I expected to sell a total of a hundred over the years. In actuality, it has sold for well over the thirty-five years after I sold the company.

While we were busy producing the Minuteman filters, our long-term future did not look bright. Electronic equipment was shrinking in size. Printed circuits began to capture the field. Transistors and integrated circuits were making tremendous inroads in size and price. Entire filter circuits, which involved large numbers of good-sized components, could be replaced by small integrated active circuits. This meant the use of transistors printed onto tiny circuit boards. At first only very simple filters could be built that way. Over time the complexity increased. We felt that we had to change direction and get involved in digital active filters.

Clem and Becky and the Hollywood Star

As the years had passed, my father gave up his grueling career as a bakery truck driver and deliveryman. My mother had long since stopped working as a seamstress. They finally owned a car which didn't need monthly payments. They had a big responsibility babysitting for their three sets of grandchildren, which they enjoyed very much. At time, my mom, Becky, would have them move to Miami Beach, Florida, and then back to the New York area.

They loved to help out in my growing business when they moved back up North. It gave them great pleasure to be part of their oldest son's business. My dad would drop off small deliveries or documents that had to be done in a hurry. They also picked up urgent production items that were running short.

I am using the word they instead of he since Becky always accompanied him. In a rather unusual arrangement, Clem drove the car but Becky navigated from the back seat. Since he was far from being the speediest driver, impatient drivers would swing out from behind Dad's car and cut in front. Mom would shake her fist at the aggressive driver calling him a "bandit," or "killer."

On one of my quick airplane trips, I landed at LaGuardia airport and picked up my car at the parking lot to head to my office in Brooklyn. I took the Interboro Parkway, now named the Jackie Robinson Highway. Traffic was creeping along in the right lane but going faster in the left. I got into the left lane and passed the car that was slowing traffic in the right lane. There was the driver, Clem, and the back seat navigator, Becky. I waved to them as I went by. I later greeted them as they reached my building.

Once, I hustled into my plant through the delivery entrance, and there was Becky and Clem. They were waiting to pick up some papers that needed urgent delivery. My mom beamed at me. She exclaimed, "My Hollywood Star." My entire production line was within earshot. I blushed fiercely. I avoided looking at my employees but I knew that they were all trying to hide their grins.

If my dad complained of feeling sleepy, my mom would insist that he park the car to catch a little nap. She once confided in me a great invention. I listened as she described adding roll-up wire screens to the car windows to keep out mosquitos and flies. She emphasized that she thought of this since my father took frequent catnaps when he felt sleepy. These days, some of our expensive cars sport such wire screens.

Wall Street

It was obvious that the filters that we were producing would become obsolete. We knew we had to invest in the future. We were too small to be a factor in the growing field without any financial backing. Many competing companies were going in for IPOs (initial public offerings) and these were popular with investors as well.

Since our balance sheet was looking good, I went shopping for an underwriter for a public offering. We had numerous solicitations from finders that had received commissions from companies for arranging the financing through their underwriters. In an effort to develop other markets, we undertook government contracts for diverse products. These included power supplies for the Sidewinder missile, telegraph keys, transceivers, and, in my own field of filters, filter networks duplicating the characteristics of the telephone lines as specified by AT&T. One set of those networks supplied to the government of Israel. None of these fields turned into decent production runs, which was disappointing.

I negotiated with various underwriters directly, or through finders, but nothing materialized. Our financial position stopped its upward growth as the Minuteman filter production quantities had not reached its projected peak. Without that growth most underwriters backed away from the deal. We were also having problems with cash flow. Underwriters usually required a substantial investment for the paperwork and legal requirements of going public. We abandoned that approach and sought direct negotiations with investment funds. The only positive response that proved worthwhile was with Value Line, a respected publisher and investment fund. That connection was made by me. It moved towards a contract at $250,000 for a 25 percent interest in Seg Electronics Corporation. Note that while $250,000 represents a substantial sum today, in the 1960s it was huge.

It was at that time a disturbing event took place. We were served with a law suit from one of the finders who had brought us an underwriter. He claimed that we had negotiated with that underwriter, and had accepted his terms for a public offering, but that we had reneged on the deal. That was far from the truth. That underwriter and I had both agreed that his expertise was not suited for my type of initial public offering. The amount claimed in the suit was $60,000. It was a mythical sum since his finder's fee would have been less than half that amount.

My legal representation was from an attorney friend and neighbor of mine in West Hempstead. The plaintiff's attorney was aggressive in interrogating me but he was not able to poke holes in my testimony. On the other hand, the plaintiff being questioned by my attorney for details of the transaction became rattled. He made obvious errors in amounts, details of meetings, and was generally confused.

I did much better on the stand but the plaintiff's attorney chipped away at my advantage whenever he had the opportunity. He compared us using different standards. Addressing the jury, he stated that the plaintiff had become confused when testifying as any reasonable human being would. On the other hand, my calmer statement was proof of a rehearsed lie.

After the lunch break, my attorney and I went to the basement of the Superior Court and he did some research. He looked up the name of the plaintiff and found several lawsuits of a similar nature that were active. We returned from lunch and my attorney opened a new line of interrogation as the plaintiff was still on the stand.

It went like this (and I used fictional names here):

He asked, "Have you heard of Mr. John Smith?"

The Plaintiff answered, "Yes."

His attorney leaned forward in his chair.

My attorney asked, "Do you have a similar action against Mr. John Smith?"

He answered in the affirmative and his attorney jumped up and objected, stating that this was not a proper question. The judge denied the objection.

My attorney then asked a similar question about the XYZ Corporation and received the same affirmative answer. He enumerated all of the officers of that corporation, one at a time, with the same question and received the same affirmative answer. This destroyed the plaintiff's case. It may not have been the case, but it appeared that the plaintiff was in the business of suing almost all the people he had ever dealt with. His poor performance on the witness stand stacked the cards against him as well. The jury returned a verdict in my favor.

With that suit out of the way, I felt free to continue my negotiations with Value Line. A closing date was set and I made plans to move the company into the field of the future. We would move into active filters as well as marketing and promoting the telephone line simulators. In these later areas we seemed to have a monopoly although the requirements were still modest. The bulk of our production was still the Minuteman filters but the projected vast quantities were not showing up. The closing date with Value Line was only a few weeks away and we received some bad news. We learned that Congress had closed the Minuteman missile program. We still had a substantial backlog for the next few months of production but the future looked bleak. This was conveyed to Value Line. They elected to continue the deal with the expectation that we had the brains and production capabilities to make their investment a success.

Seg Electronics Corporation struggled for the next two years, continuing with the same Minuteman filters in small quantities while trying to develop expertise in the active filter field. The telephone line simulators continued but in the same small quantities of one or two a month. We were also hindered by the fact that an engineer employee that we had to lay off went to work for a large competitor. He had taken the telephone line simulator plans with him since his new company marketed a similar device, but I believe it bore the same minimal sales results.

We also received a small production run order from Phillips Petroleum for our filters, which were used for petroleum exploration. As I understand it, Phillips Petroleum engineers would set off a small explosion in a potential oil field. Receivers were placed around the area where future oil wells were predicted. The receivers would pick up the reflections of the explosion which would be passed through our filter networks and some of the extraneous signals eliminated. The desired signals would then be processed in their equipment, which allowed them to start to excavate for the oil wells.

On our first production run for the company, the shipment was sent by air to Phillips. At the landing field cases were literally dropped off the back of the plane and onto the tarmac. The filters were heavy and so the packages took some heavy damage. They had to be returned to our factory. We were able to rework them and recheck the filters before packing them more securely. Fortunately, the transporting airline paid for the rework.

I received a fairly tempting offer from an acquaintance of mine, Juan Wicher, who was a brilliant engineer that had immigrated to the United States from Argentina. He had done some excellent work for the military establishment there. He had set up a production facility but the rules covering employment made managing his workforce almost impossible.

As an example, Juan had a very expensive precision lathe that he had imported from Europe. The operator of the lathe showed no inclination of trying to meet production schedules. When he was pressured by Juan, he "accidentally" permitted the cutting tool to continue to cut past the spinning metal and start cutting into the lathe itself.

In those days, Argentina was run by a military dictatorship. It would imprison people at will. Juan had somehow fallen into the bad graces of the military establishment. He had had to leave the country. Since my filter networks were used in the data transmission field, he approached me and described the work that he had been doing in Argentina on the new field of data transmission. He explained that he had been working on a data transmission modem in Argentina that was more advanced than the modems in use in the United States. I was susceptible to the concept of a new improved data modem. I made him an offer to sponsor his development in return for a majority interest in the invention. I provided him with a special section in my factory that would work to develop the new data modem. He had his own office where he drew the circuit diagrams and gave instructions to two newly hired assistants. The work progressed over the next few months but never reached the completed stage where it would have been packaged and marketed.

Juan came to me and said that he was finished with the preliminary design and that he was moving on to another project somewhere else. It turned out that he and his wife had opened a shop to make and sell fur coats in his neighborhood of Queens, New York.

He showed me what he described as a fine piece of work. It consisted of plastic boards with components hanging off in all directions and a crude schematic diagram.

I was embarrassed at being so naïve. This was a costly lesson. I closed that section of my company immediately. Sometimes in life, you've got to know when to walk away and cut your losses. This was one such time.

Enter the IRS

With two years of disappointing results and continuing losses, the future that once looked so promising now looked grim for Seg Electronics Corporation.

It was during that hiatus that we took the project of installing closed-circuit television for the Gemini1 launch. While we made a reasonable profit on that project and it was a feather in our cap, it did not reward us enough for the three months of my time away from my core business. The active filter field had been inching along with small developments from many sources. It did not turn into big business until long after we had to drop that line after producing some primitive filters. The field had not advanced sufficiently to allow development of more sophisticated filters and miniaturization had not shrunken the packages sufficiently.

At one point, we could not pay our employees' withholding taxes to the IRS. Consequently, an IRS agent arrived one day without notice and with authority to lock the doors and shut the business down. He was a kind person and I tried out various alternatives with him.

One alternative was a fledgling company we had purchased earlier for a few thousand dollars. It was called Corona and made transceivers. With the purchase of the company that had no employees, we also owned the company name. I pointed out to the IRS agent that they would be closing both companies and that the tiny one had no assets and no debts. That was enough for him to avoid locking the doors.

We had burned through $250,000 of the Value Line investment and still faced an $86,000 balance in the Franklin National Bank credit line secured by personal guarantees from Sang Whang and myself, as well as our wives. We still had a backlog of the Minuteman filters but in smaller quantities.

I was anxious about my next visit to the Franklin National Bank. I had to tell them that I could make no further payments on the credit line balance at this time. Due to the personal guarantees, we might have to forfeit our homes, our cars and our wives' jewelry (like wedding rings). In desperation, I went to my cousin by marriage, Dr. Ben Futernick, not for money but for something to calm my nerves. Dr. Ben gave me a few Valium pills of 2 mg each which is a tiny dose. I tried one pill and it gave me a tranquil feeling that lasted for a few hours.

Dr. Ben and I had a friendly relationship and we respected each other professionally. His patients seemed to adore him. He had trained as a general practitioner, before the days of specialization. That involved functioning as a surgeon, removing gall bladders, kids' tonsils, cancerous growths, and all the so-called mysterious things a medical doctor does. I had been a subscriber to *Scientific American* magazine since I was a teenager, and I was as interested in the medical discoveries as much as I was about the latest electronics.

The next morning I took another 2 mg pill, and went to a meeting at the bank. My investment advisor there greeted me and I gave him the bad news that I could not make any payments for the foreseeable future on my credit line. To my surprise, he took the news peacefully. He commented that what I owed the bank was small in comparison to a builder that had gone into bankruptcy on Long Island for well over $1,000,000. He did ask me what my intentions for the future were. I said we were going to continue to struggle with the expectation of turning around the fortunes of the company. He requested that I stay in touch with him every few months and let him know whatever progress there was to report. I left the bank much reassured as I had expected the worst.

The struggle continued over the next few months, at which time I was contacted by the bank and they suggested that we meet with the head of an electronics company that manufactured powerful transmitters. Their products were not particularly advanced but they had good marketing techniques. One of their techniques was to have their vice president/sales manager take prospective customers to a golf course and then to a fine restaurant for dinner, during which time they discussed what the company had to offer over wines and liquors.

We had barely started in our relationship with them, when they realized that we did not fit well in their plans. They opted, with the approval of the Franklin National Bank, to have Seg Electronics Corporation go through bankruptcy proceedings. After so many years, Seg Electronics Corporation closed its doors and the bankruptcy sale was scheduled.

I visited the Franklin National Bank and sat down with the investment officer to discuss a payout plan. I told him that I would sell enough of my personal belongings to raise a few thousand dollars to start all over again. They referred me to their firm of attorneys and I met with them. Sang Whang and I agreed, to pay a small amount each month with a balance payment or a lump sum due at the end of five years. The attorneys were not difficult to deal with since they realized they couldn't get blood out of a stone.

The sale took place as scheduled but it was not attractive to the buyers of equipment and parts as our parts were very specially prepared for certain pieces of equipment. With money that I raised from my family, I bought certain pieces of equipment that could get me started again in the filter field and parts that were in preparation for the Minuteman filters.

As for my good friend Sang Whang, he got an attractive offer for engineering design from Milgo Electronics in Miami, Florida. They produced modems in large quantities and could afford to pay Sang a substantial wage. He lived there for many years although he passed away a few years ago after a long illness.

The Making of E.J. Howles, Inc.

I named the new parent company E J Howles, Inc. by assigning "E" for my wife Etta, "J" for my older son Jeffrey, "How" was for my younger son Howard, and "Les" was for my daughter Leslie. I had also bid a hundred dollars for the name *Seg Electronics* with no other opposing bidders.

The first filter production that the new company produced was for the Minuteman filters for which orders had still been dribbling down. They were assembled in the basement of my home in West Hempstead by myself and Joe Hills, my Afro-American backup man. The government inspectors visited us and were cooperative in accepting our tiny production. Without a heavy debt structure and high overhead hanging over our heads, we were able to pick up enough business to open a small facility and employ a few people. Within a year, we had a profitable operation going and I was able to make the modest payments required by the attorneys for Franklin National bank.

We had an interesting proposition going on with Litton Industries. They had a project, which could reach a large production volume and it required time delay correction filters that had to meet very exacting specifications. We had the advantage of having met similar specifications in other equipment in the past. Litton Industries sent their chief engineer, Walter Neuser, as well as their quality control chief to check out our facility before giving us the order for the sample filters. They gave us a clear path to continue with the sample project at that meeting. I took both of these chiefs to lunch not too far from my factory. They sat in the back seat of my station wagon and I was the driver. The quality control engineer was commenting on the then recent war between Israel and its Arab neighbors by expressing amazement at the small country defeating the bulk of the Arab armies.

Walter Neuser, who had been in the German military as director of communications during World War II, commented that the Arabs were a "decadent people." I smiled inwardly. Not too long before it had been the Jews that were the decadent people.

After providing the samples that met their requirements, we received a substantial production order amounting to several hundred thousand dollars. That substantial order was granted to us after a meeting at Litton Industries headquarters in Westchester County, New York. Their offices were on a steep rise above the road leading to their plant. There was a large parking area between the offices and the road. Several engineers and administrators were present at the meeting and the negotiations were quite active and noisy. One of the engineers was standing at the window facing the road below and listening to the conversations without comment. He shouted, "There goes John's little Volkswagen down the hill without a driver." And then, "There's John running after it."

We all rushed to the windows to watch the Volkswagen heading down the hill, across the road and into the garden of the small private house across the road. John caught up with his Volkswagen, quite undamaged but it had made a big mess in the garden. After the drama of the day, our negotiations resumed and we got the order, which turned profitable.

As we accumulated a favorable bank balance, we were ready to expand modestly, but this time I took a different tack. I searched for a property in Queens to serve as our factory and still bring in some income to me, and my family, rather than support a landlord and face rising rents over the years, I found such a property in a one-story brick building with a large basement on Jamaica Avenue in Richmond Hill, Queens. One detriment to the property was the presence of the Jamaica Avenue subway line which was elevated along much of Jamaica Avenue. Needless to say, it was fairly noisy. Although New York City had a program in place to eliminate such subway structures, they very noisy and they blocked sunlight from housing and industries along their line.

The property had been vacant for quite some time and there was a lot of debris in the basement. When I took possession, I hired some laborers to help clean up. Much of it was in old fifty-gallon oil drums. When these were brought up to street level, there was a general exodus of rats that went hopping down the street to God knows where.

Finally, the basement was cleaned up and we housed our small machine shop, which helped us a great deal. We had moved quite a distance from Arthur Ritchie and his machine shop that kept his printing presses in top-notch shape. He did visit us from time to time but more for social reasons. Many years later, I learned from his family that he never spent any of the money I paid him for his help. He was a wonderful friend and he helped me substantially at a critical time in my life. The timing of his friendship could not have been better. As I learned much later in life, he also treasured my friendship greatly.

As business conditions improved, my staff increased in size and Etta and I were able to get away for short vacations. We were quite comfortable with doing so as the plant was under the watchful control of Joe Hills, our production manager. On one of our winter trips, we arrived in Miami Beach for a one-week stay. On the first evening following our arrival, I received a telephone call from Jeff, my older son, who said that he was calling me from inside the plant. He had been called by the alarm system company to report that there was a fire in the building.

The alarm system people had also called the Queens Fire Department and they were busy spraying the fire. Later, we learned that the fire had spread from the roof of a brick-and-concrete annex of our building. We had cleaned up that annex to use as part of our plant. Since my employees were going to be working there, we had installed a ceiling-mounted gas heater to keep the annex warm in winter. The installers had passed an exhaust pipe for the heater through the ceiling and roof without paying attention to the need for an extra layer of installation between the roof and the exhaust pipe. When the temperature dropped sharply that night, the exhaust pipe heated to the point of setting the roof on fire.

Fortunately, the damage was mostly caused by the water and we only lost a day or two of production. We had enough insurance to cover any damages. The incident didn't discourage my wife and I from taking our year-end vacations. But, as the years progressed, our three children grew increasingly less interested in vacationing with us as they developed their own clique of friends.

The Union Guys

When there would be dips in the production of our filters, I occasionally brought in a colleague that was skilled in an allied field of electronics, such as closed-circuit television. The hope was that he might bring in some interesting leads on a sales commission basis, since he had no production line of his own. If a sale resulted in a production run, I might need his help in running his product through our production line.

One such episode happened before Joe Hills became production manager and it had a surprise result. With one of our production runs, a colleague of mine that I will call Bill O. was guiding my production line people in running the production of an item that he had introduced to us. The next morning, no production line worker showed up to work. I received a phone call from a man that said, "I am a representative of the Cabinet Makers Union (fictitious name). I am in a nearby coffee shop with all of your production line workers. They all signed papers that they want the Cabinet Makers Union to represent them in negotiations with your company. Are you prepared to enter into such negotiations?" I responded, "Show me the signed papers before I agree to negotiate." The voice responded that he would come to our plant right away.

About fifteen minutes later, a tiny man appeared at our plant. He was dressed elegantly in a shiny black suit and snow white shirt accented by an elegant tie. He was accompanied by a tall individual who was burly and crudely dressed. I met with the tiny spokesman who showed me a packet of papers signed by my production workers. I looked at my colleague, Bill, who was fairly tall and strongly built. He took the tough guy approach and said to the spokesman, "You have no right to do this. Get out of here."

The little guy flew into a fury screaming, "Don't you dare talk to me like that or you'll be found in a wooden box six feet under." Bill backed away. I spoke to the little man more softly and asked him for more details as to whom I would have to negotiate. He gave me some details about the head of that branch of the Cabinet Makers Union whom I will call Tony. I responded that I would call Tony and make an appointment to see him. The two union men left and my production staff started dribbling in. At closing time, my senior team and I left together and we looked around. Half a block away, the gorilla-sized man and the tiny one were engaged in an intense conversation, ignoring us.

I called Tony the next day and we had a reasonably friendly conversation. I met him at his elegant office, a few days later. Tony was a handsome young man with a smooth style. His elegant suit was obviously custom-made and the shelves around his office wall were lined with beautifully bound books in various languages. I commented on one book, which was in Hebrew script. He told me that it was given to him by his girlfriend.

Getting down to business, he reassured me that he knew that we were a small company and it was his goal to get my employees a small raise in pay on a per hour basis, which should not be burdensome to us, as well as have them contribute to the Union's Health and Welfare Plan. According to Tony, this would get the employees a better deal than their present health plan with us. It all sounded great to me and not at all the horror that I had often heard about with encounters of this type. We parted with the understanding that his attorney would prepare the contract, which I told him would have to be reviewed by my attorney. He told me that was fine with him.

After we shook hands, I left his private office. Before reaching the exit I encountered the gorilla type that I had met earlier who said, in a gruff voice, "Hey, Tony is offering you a very good deal that he will have trouble getting approved by the guys above him – so don't forget to take very good care of him on Christmas, which is coming up soon."

I felt a shock wave. I had heard accounts of "taking very good care" amounting to very big payoffs of cash.

When I got back to my office, I called my friend, Bernie Gold, whom I remembered as having had similar problems with his Tropical Cracker business in the past. He had entered into a much more benevolent relationship with a different union whose chief was Vince B. He said that he had never been asked for a payoff. He volunteered to ask Vince B. if he would consider taking Seg Electronics into his organization. I replied affirmatively. Bernie called me back to tell me that Vince had checked with the guys above him and they agreed.

Vince sent some organizers to persuade my employees that his deal was better and less dangerous to the company's survival. My employees agreed and signed new slips. I sent a letter to Tony telling him that my people had changed over to a different union that had solicited them, and had gotten a majority to sign up with them. Of course, I was a little nervous. I kept remembering the wooden box remark with great dismay. A few days later, I got my response and was faced with an office full of gorillas led by the now not-so-suave Tony who threatened me, furiously, that he would get the other union to back off and then I would get a deal from him that would put me out of business.

As it turned out, however, Vince's guys were higher than Tony's guys. Tony was the one to back off, stating that Vince B. had promised him a bigger company than mine as an exchange. He called me a week later and asked me to reimburse him for the few hundred dollars for his organizing costs. I pleaded that we were a small company and offered to reimburse him half of those costs, which he accepted.

Vince and Tony were true to their word and I never had another battle with them. This did not reassure me completely. I kept checking the undersides of my station wagon and raising the hood for a quick inspection every time that I parked my car for the next few months. Just once, as I was approaching my parked station wagon, a shabbily dressed man walking ahead of me stopped at the curb next to my parked vehicle. He stopped to light a cigarette. While lighting up, he inspected the equipment that I usually carried in the station wagon. As I approached the vehicle, he casually blew out the lighted match and ambled away.

I glared at him, which didn't disturb him at all – after all, he was just an innocent bystander that needed protection from the wind, to light his cigarette. Back then, even innocent actions like that seemed highly suspicious. That was the climate of fear we operated in for quite a while.

Part II

While Vacationing on the Riviera...

It was the early seventies. I was about to reach my fiftieth birthday – a good excuse to celebrate. A vacation on the Riviera sounded nice and exotic, and expensive. Regardless, Etta and I chose the world-class destination for our year-end, two-week getaway. While the weather is cool there at that time of year, there is almost never any snow. This allows for ample sunbathing but not swimming. There, in the south of France at the edge of the Mediterranean Sea, destiny called. Little did we realize what a far-reaching impact this vacation would have on our future.

The vacation package came with a Fiat rental. It was the tiniest car I had ever driven. From the front I could reach behind me and retrieve a road map next to the rear windshield above the back seat.

Our hotel was in Cannes, which was our home base. After a couple of days of sun bathing beneath cloudy days and some rain, we decided to visit nearby areas. We headed east until we reached Nice where we stopped for lunch at a picturesque little inn.

The menu gave us a hard time since it went beyond my high school French. The patrons having lunch there tried to help us make a choice. While they knew their French, they were not very proficient in English. We all enjoyed the effort and the lunch, whatever it was, and we went on from there.

The next stop was at the IBM plant in La Gaude, France. The scenery was great and the building was dignified and impressive. I met one of the engineers who spoke English. I explained that we had made a piece of equipment for them several years before. I described it as a universal filter network that could be programmed to match any transfer function. He knew what I was talking about. He told us that the universal filter there was still in constant use. It had served its purpose admirably. It was gratifying that my little company had designed an active state- of -the-art filter and accompanying software that my people wrote for the giant IBM. The filter was bulky as the basic components could not be miniaturized. It was early in the active filter game. Over the next few decades we would see incredible shrinking of the active components. Now, even the entire contents of the Library of Congress could be stored on a tiny chip. Feeling warmth within my chest, I thanked him and we continued on our way.

Our next stop was at St. Paul de Vence, which was a charming little city with lots of nooks and crannies. It was crowded with galleries. We explored for an hour or two and went on to our next stop which was the principality of Monaco. The casino there was magnificent. I looked forward to gambling some trivial amounts of money but, when I went to the tables, the minimum bets were enormous. We quickly left and went to on to Italy.

At the border there were rows of cars being checked over by the customs inspectors. We got our passports ready but, after one glance at the tiny Fiat, we were waved through. The first city that we reached was San Remo. We drove through and continued to Ventimiglia, which means twenty miles in Italian. Twenty miles was the distance to the border – how charming.

In late afternoon we headed back along the coast of the Mediterranean Sea. The weather was gorgeous and the going rapid. When we reached Nice, we sought out the same inn at which we had lunch. It was busier for supper and there were several English speakers. We had a jolly time. There was much laughter and many questions about our trip and where we came from. We were asked to look for and contact relatives in the US with special messages. When we got back home, I did contact a few of the leads that were given to me. In fact, we were visited by one of them.

Lightning Strikes!

The next day in Cannes, the weather was better and we went sunbathing. I obtained a copy of the international edition of the *New York Herald Tribune* to learn what was going on back home. An article on the front page struck me. It described the great difficulties that medical students studying abroad were having in getting accepted into the US medical profession. American medical students who had been studying at the University of Guadalajara, Mexico, had formed a committee to explore the various options open to them. They were trying to gain entrance into the US medical profession.

A photograph on the front page showed several American medical students who had founded the committee. Of particular interest to me was the fact that the head of the committee was a former dentist who was forty years old. As I had just turned fifty, I was fascinated. I had always been interested in scientific matters, mostly electronics, but medicine was a close second.

In a flash, I had an epiphany. I decided right there and then, while vacationing on the Riviera at the edge of the Mediterranean Sea with Etta, and while celebrating turning fifty, what I wanted to do for the rest of my life. I wanted to become a medical doctor.

While other wives might have said, "Honey, turn the page," my wife sighed and asked if I was certain about this. I said that it needed more investigation, but I was going to look into it. All of the years that I spent in electronics were interesting, sometimes rewarding, but they had also been disappointing. While my business had grown, it had not progressed smoothly. We would fight for the chance to make the prototype filters or other electronic devices. If we succeeded in making the device practical, a much larger company would take the production run from us. This happened not just because of price, but because of connections. I had enjoyed a fair number of successes but had also endured many disappointments.

Although I didn't speak Spanish, after Libardo Vargas had lived with us for a year, my children had gone to Colombia on vacations over the summer. They had stayed with the Vargas family and had come back speaking a decent amount of Spanish. As on other occasions in my life, I had thought if others could learn these things then so could I. If my children could learn Spanish that quickly, I should be able to do it as well. If the American medical schools turned me down, Colombia would be an excellent destination for the next chapter in my life. Libardo was a junior executive with the Avianca Airlines of Colombia, which was their national airline. I contacted him and discussed my wild plan with him. He not only liked the idea but got enthusiastic about the concept. I told him that I still had a lot of things to work over in my mind before committing myself to the project.

I day dreamed over the exciting possibilities of studying medicine in the US or abroad. Although I was not sure what free time I might have available if I was accepted into medical school, it occurred to me that I might be able to benefit Colombia itself. My knowledge of electronics, specifically in data transmission, might help launch Colombia into that burgeoning field. I knew that Libardo had a friend, Gonzalo Gomez, who owned a small electronics company. He was intelligent and ambitious, which could open doors. Yet all of this was conjecture. I might not even get accepted into medical school, anywhere.

The Clock is Ticking...

On my return to the US, I checked through my address book. I came up with the name of an old friend that had connections with the Albert Einstein School of Medicine in the Bronx, New York. He introduced me to an official at the school whom I contacted. We discussed the possibility of someone who was fifty years old, and counting, studying medicine in the US. The results were discouraging. It was pointed out that the American medical schools rarely accepted any students over the age of twenty five. I read avidly about medical school admissions. Only exceptional candidates were accepted unless they were both young and of high academic ranking.

In addition, to be accepted into an American medical school I would have to take a pre-med curriculum for several years. The cost of medical school in the States was daunting. Students often ran up a few hundred thousand dollars in debt. My prospects seemed to be shrinking but I was far from throwing in the towel.

Instead, I contacted the University of Guadalajara, in Mexico. I asked them to supply me with their brochure for admission to medical school. That was the school described in the news article that got me started in the first place. According to the brochure, I would have to study Spanish for one year in Mexico and then enter their medical school for a six-year curriculum. The prospect of seven years of preparation, plus residency training, would make me more than sixty years of age by the time I was able to start my practice. While most of the Mexican medical schools did not accept 'Gringos' at all, the majority of them did accept some American students. I looked into the possibility of entering medical school in France or Italy, but it was much the same story.

I should have been so disappointed that I might drop the whole idea, but I became doggedly insistent in continuing. My emphasis had shifted to Colombia where I had family ties. I called Libardo Vargas by phone and discussed the possibility of going for interviews at the Colombian medical schools. He thought that would be an excellent idea. He promised to work on it. Several months elapsed with no further news from Libardo but I kept busy preparing for those interviews. I approached this new ambition of mine from a marketing viewpoint and spent quite a lot of time writing a Curriculum Vitae that described what I had accomplished in my life. My CV was added to copies of my two text books on electronics and several letters of recommendation.

As Seg Electronics had been doing well and was stable, I had to question what I would do with my business. Around that time, I had received several offers from interested parties about buying my company. I had not considered that possibility. I had no idea of what amount would be offered or if I would accept. One buyer consisted of two partners, Phil Basse and Ron Juels. They had founded a startup company named Comstron Corporation. They were long-time friends and I admired them. Over the years, I had used them several times for consulting work in active circuitry. They had designed a line of digital signal generators, which needed a manufacturing and marketing facility for the next step in their plans. The two partners of Comstron Corporation offered to put together their personal funds for a down payment on my corporation. The offer was a total of $500,000. The balance would be paid out over the next five years. This price was disappointing, but there were no better offers on the table.

One attraction of the offer was that the buyers would continue production in the same building. They would use the same personnel. I had a lot of confidence that the two partners would be successful in the combined enterprise.

In anticipation of my trip to Colombia, I had begun to study Spanish by taking some classes in the evenings at the local high school. I struggled with the popular local Spanish language newspaper, *El Tiempo*, and it would take me hours to read even one article. I also tried to watch television shows in Spanish, but they were incomprehensible. It was a very serious matter with so little time. As they say: The clock is ticking.

Now that I had done my homework, I called Libardo by telephone and told him that Etta and I were planning to go to Bogotá for a two-week vacation. I asked him to contact various medical schools in the city to arrange interviews for me. His contacts were well established as he was a junior executive with the national airline, Avianca. He excitedly promised to make all the necessary arrangements and even offered his apartment as a home base. I thanked him for his generous offer, although I realized that we would be sharing space with his three brothers and his mother, Alicia.

We arrived in Bogotá as scheduled, and were picked up at the airport by Libardo. On the way to his home, he told me that he had arranged five interviews over the next two weeks. Arriving at the apartment, we learned we would only be sharing with Libardo and Alicia. His brothers had made arrangements to stay with friends.

At each interview, Libardo translated for me. The first interview was with the Hospital Nuestra Señora Del Rosario where the interviewer was polite but not impressed. The second was at the Universidad Nacional de Colombia where the results were much the same. Neither of the two interviews had conceded outright rejection, but neither showed much enthusiasm.

Etta and I took the family to dinner several times that week to thank them for their hospitality. But, at the end of the first week, Etta had to leave for home since she sang at the choir of the West Hempstead Jewish Center which had an important singing engagement the following week. Libardo and I took her to Eldorado airport for the flight to New York City. She kissed us both goodbye and wished me luck with my next three interviews the following week.

Early the next week, we had an appointment at the Javeriana Medical School (Escuela de Medicina de la Pontificia Universidad Javeriana). The dean spoke excellent English and showed lots of interest. He said that the medical school had quite a few American students, but that their achievements were not very notable.

During the interview, he explained that I would have to take special courses in pre-med and Castellano (a Romance language very similar to Spanish that had originated in Castile, a region of Spain) in order to prepare me for entry into the medical school. As a giant step forward, he had me shown around the campus and I was introduced to various heads of departments. I met with him again after the tour. He asked me what I thought of the school. I told him that I was impressed with the facility and the professors. He asked me if I had met the head of the Pathology Department. I answered that I was not sure and he prompted me with, "You know, the Black Man." This surprised me since Libardo had once told me that Colombians, whose skin colors range from pinkish white to various shades of brown, did not rate people according to their skin color. The unexpected comment seemed out of place to me.

While that interview was much more interesting than the prior two, the dean (Decano) had said that I would need at least two more years of preparation. Then I would have to take the national medical exam in competition with Colombian high school graduates. As I was 51 at that time, and the medical school program was of four years duration at Javeriana, I wondered how many years I would be able to practice medicine after graduation.

Lightning Strikes Again

The next day, I had an appointment with the dean of a medical school named the Escuela de Medicina Juan N. Corpas. Libardo explained to me that this was a new school that had been started several years ago and had not graduated any of its students yet. The dean (and founder) of the school was a famous educator and eminent physician, Dr. Jorge Piñeros Corpas. The trouble was that the Escuela de Medicina Juan N. Corpas was not yet approved by the government of Colombia, nor was it listed with the World Health Organization. The school was named after one of Colombia's most famous physicians, Dr. Juan N. Corpas, an uncle of the dean, now deceased. Libardo was convinced that there would be no problem in the school eventually obtaining approval, due to the eminence of the dean and faculty. This made sense to me at the time.

The curriculum of the Escuela de Medicina Juan N. Corpas was rather unusual. It was established to provide family practitioners, which were in short supply in Colombia, to serve the vast population, which was mostly impoverished. The program had a duration of six years, the first four of which were academic years while the last two years made up an internship.

At the interview, I met Dr. Piñeros Corpas and the registrar of the school, Dr. Manuel Forero. Libardo again served as my translator. Fortunately, my interviewers understood English quite well. They started off by explaining that the curriculum was difficult and that, while the first-year class consisted of 110 of the smartest students of Colombia, only the better half of students moved on to the second semester. Of the few students from other countries that had enrolled, only one or two had ever succeeded in moving onto the second semester. None of these were from English-speaking countries. So we moved onto the second part of what seemed to be a rather discouraging interview.

Dr. Piñeros Corpas read my curriculum vitae very carefully. He commented on the fact that my company had supplied equipment to NASA and that I had worked on the space project. It had not occurred to me that the Apollo 11 space mission, with the whole world watching, would have had such an impact on my curriculum vitae. He also commented on the copy of my book, *Basic Electronics*, which he browsed through and declared a fine piece of work. Although I had difficulty following the course of the conversation, I could see that my interviewers were impressed with my credentials. At that point, Dr. Piñeros Corpas launched into a carefully worded statement, with Libardo translating slowly to me. Dr. Piñeros questioned why, at the peak of my career in the US, do I want to enroll in such a difficult curriculum, at the risk of losing everything. I painfully pieced together enough Spanish (really Castellano) to state that I was a big boy and I had made up my mind to follow this course for better or worse. And, if they did not accept me, I would go on with the same goal in mind.

The dean quietly commented that they would be honored to accept me. I was speechless. We all shook hands. It was communicated to me that I was to appear at the faculty the next day to receive the necessary paperwork and a list of books that I would need for the first semester, which was about eight months away. When we left the interview site, Libardo and I got into his car. We just sat there looking at each other in disbelief. It went so beautifully after the earlier, discouraging interviews. Maybe it was all a dream? I didn't want to pinch myself or it all may have ended in a flash. My mind explored the future and the danger of the 110 aspiring members of the first semester turning into the surviving 55 for the second semester. What would I do then? Would I move back to the US? Would I try again? I forced myself to stop the mental furor. This was my destiny and I was not going to blow it.

The next day at the administration offices, I was given a lot of information and a list of books to prepare for the beginning of my studies. In the package, there was an odd slip of paper that was addressed to the Director of the Public Cemetery in Bogotá, instructing him to supply me with a set of bones from one of the cadavers that they were always digging up to make room for the new ones. I learned that I would be expected to clean the bones and polish them, if necessary, to use for my first semester studies. This was a hard one to follow up on, so I decided to leave worrying about it until my return in five or six months.

Using the list of books that I had received, I went to the Salvat Book store and bought four giant textbooks on anatomy, all by Testut Latarjet. They were translated from French at the beginning of that century, and it represented a line of teaching that was obsolete in the US. In most of the world, anatomy books deal with the entire body right from the start. My Colombian books began with "Nosología," which dealt with the anatomy of the bones, then the blood vessels, nervous system, glands, and so on.

I told Libardo to cancel the one remaining interview.

Since I had been staying at Libardo's home, I left three of the giant texts there and took the first textbook with me to start studying. This was going to be a difficult project as I could not translate the Spanish.

The North American Horseman

The rest of the week went by in a flash. Although I spoke to Etta by telephone, the connection was weak. I elected not to break the news to her just yet. She, on the other hand, told me all the latest news about the kids and her choir recital, wishing me a safe trip.

Libardo dropped me off at El Dorado airport, also wishing me a safe trip and telling me that was looking forward to our families getting together in Colombia. Although the Avianca plane took off on time, the flight seemed to last forever. To help pass the time, I found a copy of *Reader's Digest* on board. Coincidentally, the condensed novel at the back of the periodical was about the trials and tribulations of a medical student struggling to become a neurosurgeon, which took about nine years. I read it with excitement. I fantasized that I could do the same thing, if I so dared. I stopped fantasizing since the goal of becoming a family doctor was my immediate and future goal.

The flight to New York passed close to the island of Cuba which was scary as relations between the US and Cuba were strained. I finally touched down at JFK airport in Queens in the evening. Etta picked me up and I remained silent through most of the drive home while Etta was telling me all about the events of the week such as her choir recital and the day-to-day activities of my family.

As we pulled up into the driveway of my home in West Hempstead, Etta turned to me and asked, "How did your interviews go?" I said, "The first one was interesting but it was the second one that was the winner. They accepted me. In six months, we will travel to live in Colombia." She stared at me incredulously. We both remained silent as we realized the impact that such a proclamation would have on the rest of our lives.

In tribute to my wife, she never expressed any reluctance about making the trip to a new land and a new life. This was helped by our prior trips to Colombia and our close relationship with the Vargas family. She had also visited the Jewish congregation there and enjoyed their choir, which would help smooth her transition into a new environment. There was ready availability of kosher foods too, which was important to her since she was raised in an orthodox Jewish home.

Over the next few weeks, we shocked our friends and family by telling them that we would be moving out of West Hempstead, and that I was going to study medicine in Colombia. This was a total surprise but they all wished us good luck. Some claimed that they were envious since they had been anchored in the same routines for many years. I had to break the news of my wild adventure to my business associates, including the two future purchasers of Seg Electronics. They all wished me the best of luck and success at my change of career. I was particularly impressed by the purchasing agent of Litton Industries who had treated me in a very business-like manner but had given us some excellent orders. He gave me a going-away gift of gold cuff links with G, the first letter of my family name. He genuinely seemed sorry to see me leave.

Over the next few months I negotiated and finally sold the shares of E.J. Howles's division of Seg Electronics Corporation to Phil Basse and Ron Juels. Before the final closing of the sale, I still directed the company full-time. In whatever time I could spare, I studied Spanish.

A lot of time was devoted to filling out forms and getting the right signatures to become residents of Colombia. This involved dealing with the Colombian consul whose office was in midtown Manhattan. Obtaining the right papers and signatures went more smoothly when I hired the son of the consul to work on my production line as he was on summer vacation from school.

One minor obstacle that I encountered was with my radio amateur license. It had been my hobby from the age of fourteen to communicate with other radio amateurs around the world. Setting up a station in Colombia would enable us to keep in communication with our family and friends in the US. Obtaining the permission of the Communication Ministry in Columbia to operate my amateur radio station would be slow and difficult. The consul helped substantially by writing a letter to the Minister of Communications on my behalf. He described me in a rather flowery term as a "Norte Americano Caballero," meaning North American Horseman. Oddly enough, this implies nobility. I thought back to my father's original Eastern European family name, Paniecki, which also implies nobility. It was a sign that I just might be moving in the right direction.

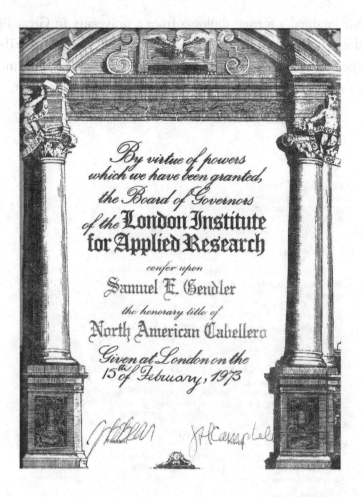

By virtue of powers
which we have been granted,
the Board of Governors
of the **London Institute
for Applied Research**
confer upon
Samuel E. Gendler
the honorary title of
North American Caballero
Given at London on the
15th of February, 1973

I received a carbon copy of the letter. It received immediate permission upon arrival in Colombia to set up my radio amateur station. An interesting variation of the rules and regulations for radio amateurs in Colombia is that the licensee is allowed to have an associate radio operator, who can operate the radio amateur station. That would enable Etta to communicate with friends and family when I was in school or elsewhere. This was not permitted in the US.

I explained this to Phil Basse and Ron Jules when I showed them the copy of the letter to the minister. They enjoyed it and laughed over the title, "Norte Americano Caballero." I thought that was the end of the story. A few weeks later, the post office delivered to me a mailing tube which contained a formal diploma from a university in Great Britain awarding me the title of "Norte Americano Caballero." Despite the fact that the university receives much of its income from selling unusual titles, I treasured the diploma. To this day, I have a replica of it:

Octubre 13 de 1972

Señor Doctor
JUAN B. FERNANDEZ
Ministro de Comunicaciones
BOGOTA, D.E., Colombia

Muy distinguido señor Ministro y amigo:

El caballero norteamericano señor Samuel E. Gendler, destacado ingeniero y técnico en materia de computadoras y cerebros electrónicos, viaja a Colombia con la misión de vincular a la Universidad Javeriana, Facultad de Medicina, su autorizada y muy calificada preparación profesional, reservada a aplicar a las disciplinas de la medicina su excepcional versación sobre la muy compleja materia en la que es realmente autoridad de reconocido prestigio en esta ciudad.

Por conocimiento que tengo de este importante caballero, quien, además de exhibir las condiciones precedentemente descritas, auna cualidades de señorío, las que permiten al suscrito, recomendarlo ante ese Despacho para que - previo el lleno de la totalidad de las formalidades oficiales al respecto, se le expida su licencia como radio aficionado, pues esta inquietud, según sus comentarios, constituye su más entusiasta afición.

Expreso al señor Ministro mi reconocimiento por la amable atención que prestará al señor Gendler, quien sabrá corresponder a la hospitalidad que le brinda Colombia y la Universidad Javeriana, a donde proyecta vincular su versación especializada.

Cónsul General

(Diploma Norte Americano Caballero
Illustration + Consul's letter) 1pages

A Microscope on the Cheap, A Plastic Female Torso & the Renault 6

My tuition at the Escuela de Medicina Juan N. Corpas cost the incredibly low price of about $200 a year. Living in Colombia was inexpensive since the exchange rate was 55 pesos to the dollar. At that time, a dinner at a fine restaurant cost a few dollars. Rental of a large apartment in a good neighborhood cost about 5,000 pesos a month which was less than $100 a month in the US. Live-in housemaids were paid the equivalent of about $30 a month and the standard time-off was one day off every two weeks.

To show my gratitude, I sought ways of enhancing their teaching program with audio tapes and films from the agencies of the US government. I sent a catalog to the Escuela de Medicina Juan N. Corpas to choose whichever films might be helpful to their curriculum. They chose quite a few which I ordered for them.

At my company, I received offers of surplus items that were available at bargain prices. One such item was a projection microscope which would enable the lecturer to magnify microscopic items like bacteria and project them onto a large screen. It must have cost the Veterans Administration Hospital in Buffalo, New York, many thousands of dollars when new but now received little use. No price was quoted. Firm bids were requested. I entered a bid of $125, and was awarded the projection microscope.

I also came across an advertisement that offered to medical schools and hospitals a plastic model of a woman's pelvic region. It was made of smooth pink plastic. It was quite lifelike but various additions, such as tumors, or abnormal ovaries, and uterus, could be substituted from the open-waisted side. This would enable the medical student to learn how to palpate the genitalia for various abnormalities. It was supplied on a small stand and encased in an attractive cardboard box which resembled a large hat box.

I packed the projection microscope into the container with my household equipment. The 16 mm films and the open-waisted, gynecological model were to go with us upon our return to Colombia.

During our preparations to move to Colombia, I received a phone call from Libardo. Several years ago, he had put in an offer to buy a Renault 6 automobile that was being made in Columbia. There was a long waiting list for this car and he had just received notice that it would be available within a few weeks. Since he knew that I would want to own a car in Colombia, he offered me the opportunity to buy it. The Renault factory in Colombia had been building the Renault 4 version for years, which was far inferior to this new model. Colombians preferred imported cars from the US or Europe. Colombia added a 250 percent import tax, which made imports extremely expensive. I accepted the offer and sent him a check in the amount of two thousand dollars, which was the full price of the car.

While that price sounds quite reasonable, the Renault 6 was not much of a car. It was cramped, even for four average weight passengers. There was no radio, air conditioner, or automatic transmission. The stick shift for the manual transmission came straight through the dash-board and projected about a foot into the car with a 90 degree, straight-up bend.

A few months later in Colombia, I had to stamp down on the brakes for a panic stop. Pressing down that hard resulted in my body putting a strong backward pressure on the back of my seat. The seat popped out of its track and I wound up, still in my seat, in the rear passenger compartment. Fortunately, there were no other vehicles close. I was able to reposition the front seat to its correct spot.

Our Kids – The Rocker, the Adventurer, & the Budding Doctor

As the housing market was depressed at that time, we decided not to attempt to sell our house until the market improved.

Our older son, Jeff, would live there. After four years of electrical engineering studies at Rensselaer Polytechnic Institute for his bachelor's degree, and another year for his master's degree, he had worked as an engineer in the electronics field. His enthusiasm had waned however. He did not want to continue in that field.

Jeff kept busy playing in a band and going through a hippie lifestyle so prevalent among young people at the time. When practicing his drums, he would lock himself in his room. We were treated to smells alike to a burning haystack, as well as sounds which seemed to rock the house.

Howard, our younger son, had completed four years of education at Cornell University in Ithaca, New York, in their school of Industrial and Labor Relations. The graduates of the school most frequently went into law school or worked in government organizations. During his studies in the program, Cornell had gone through some troubled times. One parents' weekend when we were visiting, the Afro-American students went on strike. They had occupied offices and the administration building. Catching the fervor of the time, Howard decided not to go to his own graduation nor sit for the government examinations. His determination was that the establishment should not profit by his high level of intelligence and training. When he did some student teaching in Pennsylvania, for some unknown reason, the administration asked him to leave. I was given to believe that some of his new principles in life were being passed along to his students, something of which the administration might have had zero tolerance.

At any rate, Howard had an adventurous trip hitch-hiking home. A state trooper in Pennsylvania tried to arrest him for hitch-hiking, but he hid in a wheat field and the state trooper soon gave up the chase. Somewhat later, he joined a group of friends and took up farming in a remote area of West Virginia. Etta and I were always quite suspicious as to the exact nature of the crop.

Howard came close to being drafted. He was called up by the draft board for his pre-induction physical exam. Since childhood, he was terrified of blood being drawn from him. He often passed out from the experience. At the draft board physical exam, a blood test was taken from all the pre-inductees. Howard passed out as soon as the needle was placed in his vein. The doctor in charge accused him of faking the fainting spell. Howard argued back. He pointed out that this has been going on since his childhood. He convinced them that he was not pretending and so they declared him unfit for military service with a classification of 4F.

Leslie, our youngest, was studying at Syracuse University in Northern New York State. Her major study was in Spanish literature, which normally led to a teaching career. Her minor studies seemed to include oddities like winetasting and skiing. She too had graduated West Hempstead High School with high grades. With the help of her summer vacations in Colombia, she spoke excellent Spanish or, to be more exact, Castellano.

In retrospect, Etta and I realized that they were floundering and seeking to 'find themselves,' the battle cry of the times in which we lived. They shared their angst with many young people in those days. That was disappointing to us but made it easier to think about leaving, and without many regrets. We knew that we would miss them from the bottom of our hearts. Yet we trusted that, while they were in the process of finding themselves, they would indeed one day find themselves. We were sure that that they would want to visit us in our new life. In fact, we hoped that our great adventure would inspire them to be more ambitious and set tougher goals for themselves.

The Mysterious $4,000,000 Donor

I was looking forward to moving to Colombia, a poor country. I was like the young Libardo Vargas who first came to us in the US in the hope of helping his own country. I wanted to help Colombia with the knowledge that I had accumulated from my formal and not-so-formal education, teaching experience, and proven business methods. The world was moving into information technology, or IT, and with my experience in modems, simulators, and active filters, I had a lot to offer the Colombians. Meanwhile, they were offering me a medical education. It would be I had hoped, what is called today, a win-win situation.

In preparation for our move, we had to be careful with household appliances since there was a heavy surcharge by the Colombian Government for importation of new appliances However, there was no surcharge for used appliances. We arranged to move our refrigerator, microwave oven, and my stationary bicycle, but we did purchase a slightly-used washing machine, on casters. There was no surcharge on the Renault 6 car that Libardo had purchased on our behalf in Colombia. We left much of our bulky furniture for Jeff to sell when he was ready to sell the house.

A large moving firm packed our belongings into a steel container which was sealed for the trip. It was scheduled to arrive in Colombia in about a month. We prepared for the plane flight, taking with us the essentials for the few weeks that would precede the arrival of our household goods. That included a variety of 16mm medical films, the projection microscope, and the plastic gynecological female torso with moveable parts.

Our children Jeff, Howard and Leslie, had no such qualms as they were making plans to visit us promptly. It was something that was reassuring to us.

Upon arriving at Bogotá's El Dorado International Airport in September, 1972, we were met by Libardo's family who were traveling in two cars, and then driven back to their apartment. We spent about one week in their home attending to various matters like immigration papers, resident identification visas (cédulas), and enrollment in the medical school. I did not exercise my written permission to obtain bones from the cemetery as I hoped I could purchase them elsewhere in a more finished condition. I was helped considerably by having the Renault 6 to drive around to the various agencies. Fortunately, I had obtained an international driving license before leaving for Colombia and that was adequate for about two years.

At my first day in Colombia, I had to drive the Renault 6 to the dealership in the south of Bogotá as it had been driven by Libardo for almost 1,000 miles before I arrived. The car was due at the dealership for an adjustment at 1,000 miles on the speedometer. South Bogotá was a rough area but I had to be patient and wait for him outside the dealership so that he could translate for me.

As I sat there, I was struck by the unusual heat of the day as Bogotá usually enjoys spring-like weather. The wide boulevard alongside the dealership was filled with ancient buses and cars, emitting diesel smoke and roaring noises. Earlier, I had noticed that climbing up stairs made me much shorter of breath than at home due to the high altitude (8,600 ft). I sulked a bit and wondered if I had made a wrong move. While pondering, Libardo arrived and, as he was as cheerful as ever, put an end to my downward spiral. I just shrugged and dropped that line of thought as we went inside the dealership.

Back at the apartment, I picked up the three big volumes on anatomy by the French Anatomist Testut Letarjet. As the reader may recall, I took the first volume covering nosología (the bone structure) home with me in order to prepare for the opening semester. The last volume of the three had a section that was wrinkled and discolored - as though it had been inspected many, many times. It was no coincidence. That section covered female genitalia. It was no mystery given that the four Vargas brothers had access to the books for several months.

During that first week with the Vargas family in Bogotá, we learned a lot about the family routine and enjoyed some great Colombian cooking. I took advantage of the opportunity to invite the family out for dinner. At that time, the meals were economical and the service superb. One evening, Alicia Vargas invited us out to dinner at a restaurant that was popular with foreigners. I enjoyed the Colombian-frequented restaurants better since these restaurants tried to capture the foreigner's taste for the food of their own country. At the end of the meal, Alicia paid the bill over my objections. She added a tip in pesos, which caused the waiters to show some unhappy faces. That did not seem to bother Alicia at all.

Prior to starting classes, I delivered the projection microscope, the 16 mm films, and the plastic female gynecological torso with removable parts to the school. The dean and rector looked over the donations and were very pleased. The entire donation was locked in a private room and used only to impress visiting dignitaries. Since I had spent about $1,000 for the whole lot, and the exchange rate then was 50 pesos to the dollar, the entire price was about 50,000 Colombian pesos. After a year or two, the 50,000 pesos somehow became $50,000, which later changed to many more pesos.

At the end of the week with the Vargas family, their maid was scheduled to go home to a distant part of Colombia for a one-month vacation over the Christmas holiday. Since I had the Renault, I drove Alicia and the maid that evening to the bus depot which was in a rough-looking part of Bogotá. The bus station was very crowded with passengers and buses coming and going. Alicia put her arm around her maid and hustled her off to find her bus. She had cautioned me to keep the windows closed and to pay special attention to everything around me. Aside from the hubbub, I was curious about young men walking through the crowd carrying something wrapped in newspaper under their arms. From the shape of those packages, I fancied that it might be a wooden club or a metal bar. I began to recognize several of the young men as they had passed by my car several times.

Not far from where I was parked, I also noticed an elderly couple getting off a bus. They were short, heavy, and slow-moving. Each one carried a battered piece of heavy luggage. They made their way to the curb in search of a taxi. It was dark by then. While the old couple was trying to signal a taxi, two of those young men joined them on each side. They engaged the couple in conversation and looked like they were offering directions because they pointed off to the right. With both husband and wife following the direction of the pointing, one of the young men grabbed the wife's bag but she turned and grabbed it firmly. The taxi had stopped by that time and the door was opened by the driver. The husband threw the bag into the taxi and pushed his wife in, right behind it. He entered head first. With only his rear end projecting from the taxi, one of the young men grabbed the seat of his pants. This trapped the elderly man so that he could not get in or out, while the young man used his other hand to explore the rear pockets. At that moment the other young man signaled an alarm as a policeman was walking down the street towards them. They both took off without their victims' luggage.

This scenario really impressed me. I had never seen anything like it but it seemed to be endemic to Colombia.

When in Rome… or Bogotá

Now that I had wheels, we went looking for an apartment. We wound up renting a house in Santa Ana, in the north of Bogotá. By one of many of life's coincidences, Santa Ana is the same name as the city where I lived in California. It was a two-story house. The owner was somewhat unhappy with the size of my radio amateur antenna which was eventually mounted on the chimney without any problem at all.

Santa Ana sloped upwards from the main street which gave my amateur radio station a higher altitude relative to most of Bogotá. This helped the transmission of our radio signal to other countries, which enabled us to communicate nicely to our family and friends in the US.

The neighbors had a large house and began a renovation project on their second floor. I watched the progress curiously. I was somewhat amused when the construction workers had to improvise ladders to reach the second floor, having broken up the staircase between the ground and upper floors. They also had large dogs so we had to tolerate loud barking.

Later, when I was going to classes, one of my professors, who was quite friendly with me, gave me a young duckling that had been given to him in exchange for medical services. We called the duckling "Don Sucio" ("Lord Dirty"). He waddled all over our property, watched over by all the maids in the area. One day, Don Sucio vanished. I looked all over the neighborhood with no success. When I went to the next-door neighbors, I asked a caretaker there if he had seen the duckling. To my horror, he took me to his trashcans to show me poor Don Sucio torn to bits by the dogs. It was a sad day and night after that.

Santa Ana had some other problems too. Several times when I walked up the hill to my home, I noticed water squirting out of a crack in the sidewalk or garden. When that happened, the city would turn off all the water to Santa Ana to fix leaks in the water system. Unfortunately, that repair may take one to two weeks to complete. Whenever I noticed that type of leak, I ran to my house to fill the bathtub and all the pots and pans, so that we had water to drink and wash until the repair was completed. Just some of the little things you learn to do to survive in an unfamiliar country.

Part of getting settled in an unfamiliar country included setting up accounts for electricity, water, and income tax, especially since I spoke poor Spanish. It was quite an experience. As I walked up to the electric company, I noted that they had a large front lawn which had an implanted sign. The sign read, "No Pise en el Prado," the Spanish equivalent of "Do Not Walk on the Grass." This made me laugh since prado means meadow or lawn in English, while pise means step in English but urinate in the English vernacular.

I had to get used to having to buy stamps which were needed for every legal transaction. They were bought from street vendors that displayed large sheets of them. They were needed for paying taxes, transacting government business, or getting licenses. Important contracts and other legal papers that required a notary seal were handled from storefronts and had more significance than just notarizing papers here in the US. The notarized papers in Colombia are stored in the notary's office and an interested party, when given permission, could examine them at those offices and request an official copy at any time.

To try to guard against corruption, which seems to be an impossibility in Colombia, many transactions such as paying taxes were repetitive. They required that the person making the payment had to go from one booth to another, just to get his papers properly stamped. Citizens or alien residents desiring to leave the country, whether temporarily or permanently, had to get a series of permissions from the police and tax authorities before being given the exit visa. Colombia did have a unique way for making things more complicated than they had to be.

From the conditions noted above, one could assume that there would be long lines at most times. While most people patiently waited in line, individuals with a lot of nerve would rush up to the window thrusting papers through the opening in the glass window. The people waiting in a line would shout, "Cola, cola," which means "Tail, tail," roughly translating into, "Queue, queue," or "Get in line." During my years in Colombia, these hustlers became less and less frequent.

Also during my years in Colombia, I couldn't help but notice the overall poverty of the country. Part of the reason is that the average pay for an ordinary worker, and even for an electrician or plumber, was a few dollars a day. That pay scale left most people impoverished. The government subsidized certain foods such as flour, cereal, and sugary syrup similar to molasses. Gasoline was also subsidized. House maids had a fairly standard wage of about $30 a month but their meals and living quarters were covered by the employer.

There were so many cultural customs to learn, as insignificant as they might first appear to a newcomer. For instance, when in friendly conversations with a Colombian, there were some niceties that had to be observed. If you were asked how big your children were and you tried to indicate height with your hand, palm facing down, that was a shocker. This was because that gesture was only used when referring to the height of animals. For human beings, the hand had to be held with the thumb pointed up. The height was indicated by how high the little finger side of the hand was.

In addition, the drivers were generally lawless. The wildest ones drove up onto, and along, the sidewalks if traffic jammed up. Bus drivers were the worst. If one bus, buses old and decorated with fringes and tassels, bumped or scratched another, both drivers came out with clubs or metal bars swing away at each other.

To make the business of being a passenger less enjoyable, fleas (pulgas) were endemic in buses or taxis. I dusted my socks with flea powder to avoid itchy bumps around the ankles.

Petty theft was also frequent and windshield wipers, as well as spare tires, were fair game. Often when driving past a ragged youngster, he would whip open one side of his jacket to show a row of windshield wipers for sale. Everyone had an angle.

That's not to say there weren't any delightful customs in Bogota. One observed every Christmas Eve was that the sky would be filled with colorful paper balloons in the shape of cows, pigs, small elephants, etc. These floating holiday ornaments are constructed with open bottoms with several filaments of fine wire attached around the opening. The wires are connected to a metal cup below with a piece of cotton cloth inside. Several people are needed to hold the balloon upright while floor wax is poured onto the piece of cotton cloth and ignited. This generated hot air and inflated the balloon fully while the weight of metal cup and its contents prevents the balloon from tilting. Needless to say, the Firemen (Bomberos) were kept busy that evening.

Automobile theft was common and it was said that it was well organized. One anecdote relates that a man had his car stolen which he reported to his insurance company. He was contacted by telephone, by an individual, who told him that he had his car and that it was in perfect condition. He named a site at which he would invite the victim to check over his car. If agreeable, he would release the car to the victim at a price.

The victim checked with his insurance company and was told that the price was very agreeable, and gave him permission to inspect the car. The caller reached him again and gave him an address for a meeting. He arrived at that address and met the man. The victim inspected the car and complained that the radio was missing. The caller used some curse words and complained that there are no honest people any longer in Bogotá. He said that he would drop off the radio at the victim's office at which time he would expect to get paid. That is exactly what took place but the victim then asked him what he would have done if the victim had called the police. The man answered that he knew the name and address of the victim and his children, whom the victim would certainly want to keep safe. That was the trigger that closed the deal and got his car back, as well as his radio in return for the agreed-upon lump sum in cash.

Alicia Vargas took Etta and me to visit some friends of the family one evening. Their name was Señor and Señora Morris Goldstein, and they lived in the penthouse of a fine apartment building. Morris had come to Colombia with his family as a youngster, studied hard, and developed important business connections. He and his brother opened their own import-export company, which prospered over the years.

As we entered his building for the visit, there was a doorman who interrogated us as to where we were going in the building. I'm sure he was quite well armed. Maurice showed me around his apartment, which was decorated with luxurious tapestries and elegant furniture. He asked me how I liked Colombia. My answer was that I liked it very much for the opportunity to achieve my goal. I added that I found it difficult to get accustomed to the incredible poverty all around. Wherever I parked my car, I stated there was always some poor little lady carrying her baby in her arms, well wrapped against the evening chill, and with her hand outstretched, offering to watch my car during my stay. I always gave the poor lady a few pesos for which she was grateful but as they were the value of about two cents each it was a pitiful amount. In fact, I had no idea what she would do if someone tried to break into the car other than scream loudly.

Listening to all of this, Morris smiled broadly and responded, "Look around. Do you see any poverty? I don't." This was said as he was scanning the elegant surroundings of his apartment. I realized the lack of sensitivity that existed in Columbia towards the poor. I felt Morris's remark callous and unwelcome.

Since I was aware of his business connections, I asked him if there was a more favorable exchange rate for dollars to pesos than what the bank was offering. He responded that Sr. Gurevich, who also was one of our Jewish brethren, was in that business in a downtown office building. He told me that he would call Señor Gurevich the next day and alert him that I was okay so that he would accept my check.

Morris also related an anecdote which, in retrospect, was a warning for me to watch my step with Colombian law. He said that on a Friday night, years back, he was working in his office later than usual when a stranger entered and asked him if he was Morris Goldstein. He acknowledged that he was that person. The stranger told him that he was an officer of DAS (Departmento Administrativo de Seguridad) and was placing him under arrest. The officer said he would have to take him to prison directly rather than to a judge since it was late on a Friday and, therefore, past court hours.

Morris asked loudly as to what was the crime he was being charged. The officer stated that he could not tell him and that he would learn when he got before the judge next week. Maurice argued back, mentioning names of high government officials that knew him well but all to no avail. He used a loud voice since his brother's office was next to his.

Morris's brother overheard all. He called some high government officials that they knew well. One of them called the officer back on Morris's phone and spoke to him, authoritatively, telling the officer that he would be down there within the next half hour. He arrived and they arranged a document stating that the government official would be responsible for Señor Goldstein's appearance the following week at the court.

Early the next week, Morris and his lawyer appeared before the judge who stated the charges, which would be deemed ridiculous in the US. It seemed that a customer of Morris bought some merchandise and paid for it several years ago. A short while ago, he went through his papers and claimed that he had overpaid by about 5,000 pesos against the invoice. So the charges demanded that Morris refund the 5,000 pesos.

Morris attested that he needed a delay in the proceedings to check his records and that, if the claim was correct, he would refund the money at that time. A new court date was set for a few weeks later during which time Morris checked his records and determined that he owed nothing. He arrived at the court as scheduled but the plaintiff did not show. The judge, who Morris had determined was a friend of the plaintiff, reset the trial date for a few weeks later to allow the friend time to show up. The situation was the same at the next trial date but the judge allowed another chance later. It was a no-show at that time too.

Finally the judge threw the case out of court. I was horrified at this narrative. I was firmly convinced that, as an American citizen, this could not happen to me – ha, ha to that one.

About a week later, I went downtown to Señor Gurevich's office in a tall office building. At the entrance to his office on an upper floor, a neatly dressed Colombian was leaning against the wall and didn't seem to pay much attention to me but I'm sure he did. There were no obvious bulges that were visible but I am sure that he was armed. I went inside and met Señor Gurevich, a stout gentleman. We shook hands and chatted a bit. I wrote a check in the amount of $5,000 and handed it to Señor Gurevich. He counted out about 250,000 pesos at an excellent exchange rate compared to the bank rate. I shook hands with him. As I left, I commented that Morris Goldstein must have given me a good recommendation when he called since Señor Gurevich exchanged the money with few questions. He said, "Morris never called me but we have to have faith in each other." I interpreted this as meaning that we shared the same religion. I needed that substantial sum as I was moving into my new residence and had to buy furniture and put down deposits at the utility companies as well. Over the next few years, I changed dollars to pesos many times with him. A few years after I had met him, he passed away, probably from a heart attack brought on by obesity.

A Short-Lived Venture

Libardo Vargas introduced me to his close friend, Gonzalo Gomez. Gonzalo was a cheerful, bright young man with an electrical engineering education. Accordingly, he had formed a company that was eager and ready to do anything electronic or electrical. I explained to Gonzalo how my former company, Seg Electronics, had gotten involved with data transmission and modem testing equipment. He was enthusiastic about the future of data transmission in Colombia.

I offered to contact my former junior partner, Sang Youn Whang, who had moved to Miami, Florida, to work for a modem manufacturer called Milgo Electronics. He was now a vice president of the company. I said that I would talk to him about having Gonzalo represent Milgo Electronics in Colombia. Gonzalo Gomez agreed and I joined him in representing Milgo Electronics.

Gonzalo arranged a conference at the Javeriana University (Pontificia Universidad Javeriana) and I addressed the conference using my limited Spanish. It was very well received and there were lots of questions from the audience. Unfortunately, the field was very young in Colombia but it certainly had a bright future.

SEMINARIO-SOBRE TRANSMISION DE DATOS

Meanwhile, Gonzalo arranged for a meeting with the Colombian Telephone Company that was the most likely, and immediate, customer. The meeting was set up at their engineering offices in Medellin, Colombia. Gonzalo drove there with me as the passenger. It was a long trip and we stopped at a hotel overnight, midway to Medellin. The hotel was built facing the town square which straddled the main road through the town. The windows of my room overlooked the town square. They consisted of horizontal slats of glass that could be cranked open or shut, or any angle in between. As I tried to sleep, a giant truck would come barreling through the square. The roar of the truck's engine and tires were amplified by the slat openings facing my bed. I jumped up each time with the full belief that the truck was bearing down on me. In the morning, we proceeded on our trip but I felt drained after an almost sleepless night.

In Medellin, we got a lackluster response by the telephone company engineers. They were polite but not enthusiastic. Somewhat later, we learned that IBM had been working with the telephone engineers on data communications. IBM had their eyes on the future as well.

I did some smaller projects with Gonzalo, but as an advisor and friend of the family. One of those projects was an electric blanket. On one of his visits to my home, Gonzalo became fascinated by the electric blanket that we had brought from the US. That's because the evenings in Bogotá were usually quite cool due to the extremely high altitude. He created an electric blanket. Upon testing it, the blanket burst into flame. He had not realized that the existing commercial electric blankets had tiny thermostats at various places inside the circuitry in order to prevent excessive temperatures.

A Great Set of Bones

Since medical school was scheduled to begin shortly at the beginning of February, 1973, I had a lot to learn to prepare for the opening day. Visiting the faculty a few times was one of them. I was given packages of mimeographed sheets from the faculty. This was done since many of the students were poor and textbooks of medicine costly. The students had to buy their own binders in order to protect the printed sheets but they were very inexpensive. I also asked for the name of a high-ranking, second-year medical student to help me review the first textbook of the four Testut texts that I had bought before leaving for the US.

Dr. Forero contacted the student, Arturo Cruz, who was willing to help me while earning sorely needed funds. I'm a little ashamed to say that I paid him only a dollar or two per hour to come to my home and work on the first book of the five-volume Testut series. By comparison, the average employee in Colombia was paid that amount for a whole day instead of one hour.

I read from the book slowly at first while he corrected my pronunciation. Since the text was in Spanish, or rather Castellano, I was learning the medical terms as well as the language. With the urgency of having to start school in a few months, Arturo was patient and helpful and we often worked until late.

Since we were working from my Nosología textbook, which is all about the bones of the body, Arturo brought parts of his set of bones with him. He had obtained the bones from the public cemetery and had cleaned and coated them with a clear tough plastic finish. Since he was now in the second semester, having completed his Nosología in the first semester, he offered me his great set of bones at an excellent price. I took him up on the deal.

Between the book and the actual set of bones, we had to learn about every anatomical feature of each bone. This included every name, every curve, every bump, and every groove of more than two-hundred adult bones and more than three-hundred baby bones.

I was amazed at the quantity of material that had to be learned. If I had access to the total requirements of the first semester before I enrolled in the program, I might have been frightened away. I used the same self-reassuring strategy that I employed regarding my need to learn the Spanish language. I said to myself, if my children could get fluent in Spanish then so could I. I didn't want to be negative about my circumstances, but I also recalled Dr. Piñeros sobering statement that only half of the first semester's 110 students will ever make it into the second semester.

I found that I could learn Spanish rapidly, especially out of necessity. In addition, I was immersed in the language since I was dealing with all of the local people with whom I came into contact. This included the household maid, a young girl (muchacha) who earned a dollar a day and received three meals, as well as her private bedroom and bathroom. Etta was also learning, but at a slower pace since she didn't have the wide range of contacts that I had. There was also no time pressure on her to do so. She interacted quite well with our maid and the various trades that delivered goods and services to our home.

We became members of one of the several synagogues in Bogotá. It was called the "German synagogue," probably because of the nationality of the immigrant founders. Etta enrolled in its excellent choir which sang for the congregation on high holidays. She adapted well, even understanding the commands by the choir leader at the weekly rehearsals too. However, I had to drive her to all those rehearsals as she had no interest in learning how to use a stick shift.

I learned that the three meals a day in our household were superior to the average Colombian household's menu. When Etta and I were visiting a family that had emigrated from England to Colombia, they complained that the household staff was developing intolerable habits. Their two maids were helping themselves to the same foods that the homeowners were eating. The lady of the house stated that the maids had ignored the fact that she had bought large bones with meat on them to be boiled into a soup with added greens. She said that this certainly should have been enough nutrition for the two maids that were working for them. We refrained from commenting on this delicate matter. We were not going to have a separate, sparse diet for our 'Muchacha,' although she was getting kind of chubby.

I believe the household cooking fuel was propane or some other liquefied gas. The gas company's open flat-bed trucks would come by weekly loaded with tall cylinders. All of the muchachas would rush out of their respective houses waving the correct number of pesos and besieged the truck. After all, if one missed the truck there was no way to cook food at home unless you jury rig the fireplace.

Etta and I had to get used to the unusual foods such as fruits like Tomate (pronounced tow-MAT-ay), with a taste between a tomato and a sweet fruit. We also had to get used to unusual spices. While we were not accustomed to drinking many alcoholic beverages, the national alcoholic drink was named "aguardiente" and it came with a high proof of alcohol. Translated, the name means "fire water" and just one sip quickly verifies the claim. It also has a distinct taste of anise, which tastes like licorice, and is very powerful.

First Semester – 1973

Much too soon, the first day of the first semester arrived. There we were. All 110 of us. I kept wondering who would comprise the 55 students that wouldn't make it the second semester. A large majority of the students were graduates of the Bacherillato, an extended Colombian high school program. The Juan N. Corpas School had chosen the best and brightest of those graduates for admission into its first semester. Now at fifty-one years of age, I was the oldest student. There were a few girls who were barely over sixteen. The oldest students between those two ages were two women in their late twenties with children. One of the two, Jennifer Lewis de Uribe, was born in England and had married the son of the Colombian Consul to England. They had two children when they moved back to Colombia, but they had gone through a divorce. The other woman, Gloria Fernandez, was born and married in Colombia. She also had two children. The three of us remained in competition for top ranking throughout all of the four years of the academic program.

I prepared anxiously for the first class at the beginning of February, 1973, feeling far from confident that I could compete successfully.

The Escuela de Medicina Juan N. Corpas had moved to larger quarters by the time my group began their first semester studies. Our first class was in anatomy and taught by Dr. Montaña. He was a short, stocky gentleman who was enthusiastic about his chosen field. He enjoyed working a few jokes into his teaching curriculum.

Dr. Montaña started his teaching session by reinforcing that 110 of us were starting but that only the top 55 would go on to the second semester. He then emphasized that the only acceptable dress allowed in his classroom was of conservative attire. He then discussed the trend among the younger male population in Bogotá to grow their hair longer, which he did not permit either. Jokingly, he hinted that men that let their hair grow long might find certain male appendages shrinking in size. We were all so apprehensive by then that most of us could just muster a weak smile. Still, he had a keen sense of humor at times.

Dr. Montaña related many of his personal experiences during breaks in the intense anatomy course. Many of them dealt with life in Colombia during La Violencia, about ten years earlier. That was a time when the country divided itself into the blue and the red. I never did figure out what the division was due to, but there was lots of violence at the time. One horrifying example, which was described by Dr. Montaña, involved an innocent man who stuck his head out of a window of his home to check the temperature outside. He was shot to death because he was wearing a red tie.

Dr. Montaña then launched into a rapid-fire teaching session in anatomy that had us all scribbling rapidly on our notepads. That session lasted several hours and we left completely dazed. One great worry of mine was resolved when I realized that, since Dr. Montaña spoke clearly and distinctly, I had very little problem understanding and following his monologue. The rapid-fire course kept us all studying well into the night reading our giant volumes of Testut Letarjet. We worked our way through every bump of the hundreds of bones in the human body. It appeared to be a superhuman task but the younger students were managing it so I knew it was possible. (After all, if they can do it, so can I.)

In one of his lighter moments, Dr. Montaña told us a joke about a medical student who was engaged by a Colombian husband to deliver the baby of his pregnant wife. When the labor pains presented, the husband called up the student who arrived promptly. With the husband observing, the student, in a surgical gown and gloves, prepared for the delivery. To his surprise, only the baby's hand popped out. The student tugged on the hand to no avail. He ran to the telephone and called his professor. The professor, on hearing the problem, ordered the student to quit and leave the delivery for the professor who would arrive right away.

The student turned to the husband and said, "This birth is too complicated for a student. My professor will be here right away to take over. Adios, Señor." Turning to the wife he added, "Adios, Señora." As he turned to leave, he reached for the baby's projecting hand and said, "Adios, BeBe."

It was quite a relief when the first week ended, but we had to go to a Saturday class which was labeled "Ciclo Cultural" ("Cultural Cycle"). We entered an auditorium which had a stage illuminated by overhead beam lights. Dr. Piñeros greeted us and introduced Profesora Lidia Sanchez, who would teach us the material for the first semester. He told us sternly that no one would graduate from the school that did not speak and write Castellano perfectly with one exception. He did not elaborate on who that exception was but I blushed inwardly. The profesora then took center stage and Dr. Piñeros left.

She emphasized the importance of representing the school with dignity and culture in order to impress the community with the stature of the student body. She also pointed out that the students came from a variety of educational backgrounds. She would attempt to determine the relative levels of preparation prior to admission to this medical school. She would do this by dictating eighty words which we were to spell out on a sheet of paper.

She spoke clearly and slowly but I had lots of trouble keeping up with the pace and the pronunciation. For example, one of the words "Higiene," which should be easily recognizable even in Spanish, was pronounced with a silent H and sounded like "ee-ch-YEN-eh." (The "ch" had the sound of clearing one's throat.) She announced that she would give us the results the next Saturday the class met again.

The second week went faster than the first. We took the bones that we were working with to class in order to help us follow the lecture. Around then, Doctor Montana began picking students at random to ask questions regarding the material that we had learned previously. This added another level of tension since we would listen to one of our classmates floundering in response to a question, realizing that we didn't know the answer either.

Saturday rolled around quickly and we were all seated in the auditorium when Profesora Lidia appeared at center stage with all of the dictation papers. She started by stating that the results were a disaster. There were as many as 125 mistakes in the eighty words of dictation and the class average was a horrible 35 mistakes.

She paused and said, "There was one surprising result." She looked out over the audience with her hands shielding her eyes from the overhead lights. She looked at me and called, "Samuel Gendler." I raised my hand and she questioned me in Castellano, "Which is your family name (apellido) and which is your given name (nombre)?" I responded giving her the correct order for my names, whereupon she announced to the class that I had made only 25 mistakes. I was thrilled. The students nearby congratulated me.

After the class was over, we filed out into the foyer. There were about five members of the faculty waiting outside. They saw me and smiled and applauded gently. I was even more thrilled and could hardly wait to get home and break the news of my unexpected success to Etta.

The class routine was consistently difficult but I became increasingly confident in my ability to handle the material. My confidence grew more rapidly as my total immersion in Spanish, or more exactly the Castilian version of Spanish, during the day in class, and outside of school, became the norm. My accent improved slowly over the next few years. Years later, when I thought my accent had improved sufficiently, I called a man by phone trying hard to trill my R's properly and use perfect pronunciation. I asked for, "Sr. Gonzalez, por favor" ("Mister Gonzalez, please"). His house maid removed the phone from her ear and called out, "Sr. Gonzalez, un gringo llama" ("Mister Gonzalez, a gringo is calling"). Gringo, pronounced GRREEN-go, is a derogatory term for an American man.

My inflated confidence crashed at the first exams in my first semester. The method they used was old-fashioned but brutally effective. It involved anywhere from one to six professors who sat behind a long table in a classroom while the students milled around outside. The students were questioned orally in alphabetical order. The first student entered and sat down in the single seat in front of the long table. The second student entered at the same time and sat down in a chair next to the entry door. The lead professor would start by asking a question and then each professor would ask his question in turn. If the student didn't answer a question correctly, the same professor would continue but with a barrage of additional questions.

I found that I could handle the quizzes and exams better if I began to prepare slowly and then more intensively as we got closer to the day of the questioning. The evening and night before were filled with tension and fear of impending doom, so each bit of information got stored rapidly and well.

After the first few weeks of class, we were led to the amphitheater where the cadavers were lined up on metal and canvas tables. We gingerly walked down the aisles between the cadavers taking care not to brush them with our clothing. The three or so very young girls in our class were apprehensive about handling their own cadaver, but that didn't last very long. A week later, as I walked past a certain cadaver, a girl student had her anatomy book open and propped against the cadaver's chest wall.

A more delightful custom at school was the observance of several important Colombian holidays. On those days, the students would dress their best and several would arrive with their guitars. At a break, the class would break into a musical interlude with guitar accompaniment. I found some of their songs delightful.

As the Escuela de Medicina Juan N. Corpas was in its second year and not approved as yet, I ran into a problem. Since I was a strange phenomenon, I would be introduced to strangers who were curious about me. They would ask me questions, which frequently included the name of the medical school at which I was studying. Was it the Javeriana? The Nacional? The Rosario? When I told them it was the Escuela de Medicina Juan N. Corpas, they looked puzzled.

I decided to correct the problem a bit. I went to the commercial center of the city and found a printer that did decals. I ordered about five hundred of them. They had 'Escuela De Medicina Juan N. Corpas' emblazoned on a bright red background. I also had the school custodial staff attach them to the rear window of each student's family car. They were very popular but we had to draw the line as the students were attaching them to their text books. The dean, at an assembly meeting of the student body, proudly described that he had driven along the Colombian coast several hundred kilometers away. Only one car was ahead of his and there was the decal 'Escuela de Medicina Juan N. Corpas' in the rear window. That was a rare treat for him.

Around that time, I had my first patient. Etta and I had made some new friends. They consisted of an American citizen, who was a military attaché to the US Consulate, and his wife. She was Iranian but spoke excellent English. They had met when he had the same job in Iran. They had a daughter who was about eight years old. We had visited them a few times and noted an odd behavior. If I asked anything about life under the Shah of Iran, who was in power at that time, and the eight-year-old daughter was nearby, they were effusive in their praise of the Shah. I learned that the Shah had an extensive spy system in Iran. Even the children were questioned about their parents' loyalty. In effect, they were terrified that the Shah might learn about anything negative in their attitude towards the Shah's rule through their young daughter.

One night, I was called by the attache's wife on a Friday night. She told me that her husband had some friends visiting for their Friday night poker game. The friends had left but her husband complained that his arms and hands were numb and that he was sitting up in a chair. As he relaxed, his numb arms would start to tingle whereupon he became increasingly frightened and they turned numb again. Inexperienced as I was, it sounded like hyperventilation. I still had a few Valium pills from the old Franklin National Bank affair so I went to their house. I gave a Valium to the wife, to give to her husband. I called in the morning to find out how he was feeling. She told me that he had gone to work so they had obviously helped. I was thrilled.

To broaden our horizons, we first-year students were taken on outings in the city of Bogotá to visit the public facilities. The first one was the morgue, which was crowded with new arrivals as the weekend had just passed. No wonder, the weekend was a time for fun and the national drink Aguardiente (burning water). Guns were ubiquitous, but if someone was too poor to own a gun then a machete would have to do. Getting drunk and starting fights was part of the scene. The loser (or the winner) would land in the public hospitals or the morgue. Since head wounds were the most likely site that was affected by the machete, it was nick-named the 'peinilla' ('the comb').

At the morgue, naked bodies were strewn all over. No blood was seen nor did there appear to be any refrigerators. I was impressed with the body of a strongly built young man lying face-up on the concrete floor. He had a tranquil appearance as though he was simply asleep. When I questioned one of the morgue employees as to what killed the victim, he nonchalantly turned the cadaver over and pointed to a tiny wound in the middle of the upper back. It was a bullet hole. We students filed out subdued and awed by what we had witnessed.

On another occasion, we visited a building that was strange to us. It was essentially a small prison that held people of both sexes (separated) involved in a crime unique to that part of the world.

If a young woman had a boyfriend, it was assumed by the girl's parents that there would be no sex between them until they were married (no comment). If the parents happened to catch them under suspicious conditions, like if the daughter went out with her boyfriend and didn't return until morning, it was assumed that sexual intercourse had taken place. The parents called the police and the young couple was taken to jail. Of course, they were placed in separate cells. Don't you dare think otherwise.

The next day at class, one such girl was taken out of her cell. She was strapped onto a table and her feet were fastened to stirrups. About ten of us at a time stood behind the gynecologist. We looked over her shoulders as she widely separated the vaginal labia so that she could observe the presence or absence of a hymen. If the hymen was present, they were both released from jail. If it was absent, the young man was given the option of marrying her right away or languishing in prison.

The case my group observed was that of a not-so-young woman. She was so embarrassed that she clapped her hands over her face and eyes during the procedure. The gynecologist was a giant Czechoslovakian woman that had immigrated to Colombia years earlier. There must have been a shortage of latex gloves at that time as she used a handful of shredded cotton waste to keep her hands from direct physical contact with the vagina. The poor victim was still a virgin. Everyone went home, including us. We learned a lot that day and it wasn't all medical. Class over.

There were better days and better classes. As I was the same age as many of my professors, they felt comfortable with my learning ability and often made some special accommodations for me. The pathology professor, Dr. Isaza, was an exceptionally heavy man and strict with his students. If they couldn't answer his questions, he berated them openly in class. He was not very popular with the student body.

He treated me like an old friend however. He proudly showed me the house that he had constructed with his own two hands. He had built it after marrying a considerably younger woman. I thought it unusual but did not comment when he showed me his bedroom. To reach that bedroom, one had to climb the steps to the second floor and creep along a catwalk about 15 ft long to the entrance of the bedroom. I marveled at his ability to do all that with his exceptionally heavy weight. The catwalk had to be quite strong to handle that load.

He invited me to join him at an autopsy in the tuberculosis hospital of Bogotá. We arrived early in the morning and entered a special room devoted to that purpose. We had to scrub up and put on gloves and surgical gowns as well as facemasks. The deceased patient had complained of trouble breathing and the doctor on duty had attempted to insert a breathing tube into his throat. The breathing tube was misdirected so that when the patient breathed, the inhaled air was pumped into the fatty tissue around the base of his throat. The lungs were cut off from the oxygen flow and gradually he choked to death.

As Dr. Isaza opened up the various areas of the deceased's body, he described what he was doing and I was able to follow him fairly well. As he removed certain organs for further study, he filled the void with sawdust and then closed the opening by suturing it. I felt it was crude but didn't comment. The room in which we worked had outside windows and, as the sunlight shifted, a medical assistant went to the windows to adjust the blinds. He called out that that most of the hospital's patients were watching the procedure through their windows at the other side of the courtyard. We were shocked and quickly closed the blinds of our room.

It was an effort for me to be so roughly exposed to death but I reasoned that there was much more to come. I could expect to become more calloused as time went by.

Dr. Isaza paid a heavy penalty for his weight because he suddenly passed away from a massive heart attack during my first year in medical school. There was no great concern about the role of lipids like cholesterol in those days, with the normal limits considered to be up to 300 mg/dl (deciliter).

My own total cholesterol was measured when I had a routine blood panel drawn by Dr. Isaza shortly before he passed away. It measured 280 mg/dl which, again, was considered healthy in those days. Later, I learned just how unhealthy it was.

The Thrill of It All

One day during the first year of school, Gloria Fernandez told Jennifer Lewis and myself that a great opportunity had opened for the three of us.

The medical school, Colegio Mayor de Nuestra Senora del Rosario (The Rosario) had its own teaching hospital for its medical students, the Hospital Infantil (Infants' Hospital). The hospital served women with gynecological problems but the top floor was devoted to labor and delivery of pregnant women. The Rosario, as a teaching institution, dates back more than 360 years and many famous people of Colombia were educated there.

Gloria told us that she had friends in the medical faculty of the Rosario and that the medical students had just left for a few weeks' vacation. Each day, one of us could spend time there in rotation and stay overnight with the on-call resident helping to deliver the babies.

With that incredible opportunity, we decided on a rotating timetable for us, given our school work and other obligations. I was asked to take the first rotation that afternoon and night, which I could do since my wife, Etta, was in the US. My two colleagues needed time to arrange babysitting for their offspring.

That afternoon, I assisted at surgery in one of their operating rooms. I had to don clean scrubs, wash up, and go into the operating room to get into the sterile surgical gown and sterile latex gloves. To learn how to do all of that, I stood next to the Rosario surgeon at the adjacent sink and did everything that he was doing. At the operating tablet, I was shown how to hold the retractors. It held the surgical incision wide open to give the surgeon more room to remove the Uterus for a Hysterectomy. It was dazzling to participate and wonderful to behold. Watching the surgeon deftly tie the knots, I promised myself that I was going to practice with them at home.

As the day passed and I encountered new situations, my fascination never waned for an instant. As night fell, I went to the top floor for labor and delivery. There was a young male resident on duty with several nurses standing by. There were three labor rooms with a woman in each. I sat down with the resident in a small room near the corridor to wait. He checked the women in labor from time to time. Suddenly, he shouted for the nurses to hurry in as the patient was ready. They wheeled the patient into the operating room and transferred her over to the surgical table while another surgical nurse placed a wrapped package onto the instrument table. That package contained the sterile gloves and the surgical instruments. She whipped it open and the resident gloved up, just as the baby's head emerged. I watched him tie the umbilical cord and I helped wash the baby. What a thrill!

Soon there was a repeat performance with the second pregnant woman and it was almost as thrilling as the first. By that time, it was almost midnight. I was still looking forward to the third and last delivery so I could go home and get some sleep. Yet, because it was so exciting, I couldn't imagine falling asleep. The resident told me to relax since the third pregnant woman had a long way to go in terms of dilation. The three women, all in labor, had been strangely silent even though no anesthetics were administered.

I sat down with the resident in the little rest area. I was too tense to relax. I walked over to the third labor room several times. The resident was half dozing. At about 1 a.m., I got up to run another check. To my surprise, the top of the baby's head was showing. That is, crowning. I shouted the alarm and the team came running. I held my hand firmly on top of the exposed crown of the baby's head to slow down the delivery (reminiscent of my own birth when the nurses did everything they could to get me back in the birth canal until the tardy doctor arrived).

As the nurse flipped open the sterile package, the resident shouted, in Castilian, "Glove up, Gendler, this is your baby!"

I exclaimed apprehension.

He shouted back, "Don't argue, the baby's coming fast."

I got into the gown and gloves in a flash. I was able to catch the baby, snap on the clamps, and clean up. What an opportunity. It was certainly one of the most powerful moments in my life. Even as exhausted as I was, I don't know how I was able to sleep that night.

The Limping Plumbing Assistant

It began to appear likely that we were going to live in Colombia for a long term. It was a country that was strange to us in many ways but the people we met were charming and intelligent. Real estate (finca raiz) in Bogotá was amazingly cheap by US standards so we began to shop for a house.

Friends introduced us to a real estate agent who spoke English quite well and had a lot of experience in the US real estate market before returning to Colombia. He showed us quite a few houses that were quite elaborate and expensive. They all had maid's quarters, which included a bathroom. Notably, the maid's toilet had no wooden or plastic seat. The rim of the toilet bowl was rounded to avoid discomfort, but it was apparent that the maid was not supposed to spend much time there.

After visiting and inspecting a number of such residences, we finally settled on a lovely house in the north of Bogotá, which is a more elegant part of the city. The area in which the house was located was named Chico Norte. The south of Bogotá was the poor area and the area between the North and South was the commercial part of the city.

The house had four bedrooms, three bathrooms, an enormous kitchen, maids' quarters (which included her bathroom), and an enormous tiled room that appeared to be a large laundry room. That room has a large ground-level metal cover over what appeared to be a tank, which was empty. The main bedroom had an attached bathroom that included a bidet. The house was built in four sections that formed a square around a large garden with an impressive fountain ('pila' - pronounced PEE-lah) in the center. The two-car garage was paved with a mosaic tile that extended up the walls as well, making it an elegant feature. I assumed that the elegance of the garage was because it was used to serve guests when the hosts threw a party.

The owner had built a new house about a mile away and he was asking a cash price of about $50,000. While I felt it to be quite a bargain, I offered him the equivalent of $46,000. He responded by taking the house off the market. I was shocked. I believed that he was insulted by this low offer. The real estate agent assured me otherwise by telling me that I may have actually offered too much. He said such a large offer told the landlord that he had better raise his price when he put it back on the market.

With our hopes dashed, we looked at other properties for the next few months without making an offer. To our surprise, the house of our dreams came back on the market with a price of $52,000. We negotiated through the real estate agent and the owner accepted a price of $48,000. First, he made several exceptions to the sale. They were fairly unusual and not of much value. One exception was the grating in front of the fireplace. It was fairly artistic and an unusual shape which made it doubtful that it would fit his new fireplace. I negotiated a price for the grating that was low enough to dissuade me from having to buy another one. The other exclusion was utter nonsense. He reserved the right to have his chauffer climb up onto the roof of the house to disconnect and remove the television antenna. I accepted that removal but I told him that he would have to pay for any of the clay tiles that cover the roof if they were broken by someone walking around up there. He decided that it was not worth taking that chance so he removed that restriction.

A somewhat unusual custom in Colombia was that the prior owner of a house was allowed to take away everything that was movable. This included the light bulbs, toilet paper, and even padlocks which, in the Bogotá environment, was a particularly dangerous practice.

Earlier, the steel container with the rest of our possessions had made its way from Long Island by ship. It had arrived in Barranquilla, Colombia, and then passed overland to Bogotá. The container had picked up a large gouge on its exterior, but it had not penetrated into the interior. It may have been accidental or intentional but we could never find out. When delivered to our rented home, the customs people visited us to ascertain whether the contents were new, which meant taxable, or used, which meant they were exempt. Now we had everything from our old home.

When they had arrived at the rental home, most of our items like the refrigerator were clearly used. One exception was the portable washing machine that we had bought just before we moved out of the US. It was slightly used and we had to debate that one with the customs people. My exercise bicycle got a lot of attention from the customs people. They wound up trying it out. They were having a lot of fun and I didn't mind that at all.

When we got the new house fixed up with all the furniture and equipment, it was comfortable. One problem developed when we connected up the portable washing machine in the 'laundry room.' I placed the drain into the top opening of the underground tank which I assumed drained off into the sewer system. It turned out that it was a storage tank for drinking water, to carry the household during times of water cut-off. When I noticed it filling up, I had to have it drained. Labor was fortunately cheap and the cost was insignificant.

Setting up my Ham rig was another story. In my Santa Ana home rental, the large antenna was mounted against the chimney of this two-story house. In my new home, there was only one story and I had to use a pole to raise the antenna above the adjoining houses in order to get better reception and a more powerful transmission. Some of the adjoining buildings were four stories in height. I was helped by an electrical contractor that I had met at my Long Island home years before when he visited his daughter who lived in Queens. She was a young lady that had been cleaning our home in the US once a week for a long time.

The contractor, Ernest Beltran, had several employees that he used to help put up my antenna. While I watched, they attached guy wires, consisting of steel tension cables, to the top of the tower just under the antenna. They were designed to add stability to the structure of tower and antenna. As each employee tugged on his guy wire with varying force, the steel tower rose from horizontal towards vertical. With the interplay of guy wires being pulled unevenly, the antenna began to lean over and was in danger of breaking off. I shouted to Señor Beltran to have them pull hardest on the guy wire that would move the tower to full vertical position. He shouted back that he is taking full responsibility for this job and to leave it to him. I had my way. The tower and antenna wound up vertical and the guy wires were tied to stakes in the ground.

The system worked well, depending on atmospheric conditions. We were able to communicate nicely with people in the US. Etta, as the second operator, was able to communicate with her family and friends back home. This made her feel much more comfortable. The Ham rig was particularly helpful since the telephone communication between Colombia and the US was poor in those days.

Etta learned enough Castellano to manage the household affairs and even visited friends using Bogotá's microbus system. She never did learn to drive in Colombia since it would have meant learning how to use a stick shift. Extending her religious background, she enjoyed the singing in the choir and the fact that kosher food was available. She never seemed to miss the good old US of America, although we did travel back home during vacations from school at which time I shopped for the latest medical books.

When I got back to school, I was able to embellish my answers to test questions with expressions from my newly purchased medical books, imploring contemporary research. My professors were impressed and it added to my stature in the class.

As the owners of an impressive home, we had to learn how to handle the day-to-day needs of the household. Our maid, Margarita, had the responsibility of buying the tanks of propane for cooking purposes when the trucks came around. On the other hand, firewood was available from a vendor on foot. He was always accompanied by a burro loaded with firewood that he had cut from the mountains surrounding Bogotá. The sluggish burro was named, inappropriately, Relampago, which translates into Lightning Bolt. Someone was being funny in naming the fellow.

Another addition to our household was a German shepherd dog that I received as a gift. One morning while walking the dog, I noticed a strange sight outside of my house. A small chubby man was pulling a wagon along the sidewalk. It consisted of a wooden box with an open top nailed to a long plank which extended a few feet ahead of the wooden box. A short plank mounted at right angles to the front end of the long plank could swivel back-and-forth for steering purposes, and was guided by a length of rope that was u-shaped. I was familiar with that construction from childhood when I had built the same kind of wagon starting with an empty orange box.

A small child was seated in the wagon coming my way. Under the child, there was a bunch of metal objects. The chubby man stopped the wagon on the sidewalk next to my home. He opened the small concrete lid to the water meter below. That water meter could not have been read for months since it was filled with water between the meter face and the glass cover. He explained that he was there to exchange my water meter. I was intrigued as I watched him shut off any water flow by turning the lever attached to the water meter to the off position. He removed the old water meter and took out the new one from under the child. As he put it in place, and screwed on the fitting at one end, I pointed out that the new meter was too short. He told me in Spanish not to worry. He reached into the wagon and took out a big metal ring loaded with washers, which are simply flat round metal discs with a round hole in the center. He placed an extension to the fitting leading to the meter and loaded it with enough washers so they could adapt the fitting to the new water meter. He then waved cheerfully at me and took off for the next repair job.

One day, when I was home, the doorbell rang. At the door three men stood wearing uniforms of the water company. Since they had identification cards as bona fide employees, I opened the door. They explained that my water usage had suddenly quadrupled and that usually indicated a leak in the system. One of the men had a stethoscope which had a block of brass at the end instead of the usual diaphragm. In the kitchen, he pressed the brass block against the floor in various spots. Close to the refrigerator he signaled that he could hear the water flow through the concrete floor. They drilled a hole in the floor about an inch in diameter with a long drill bit. The concrete floor was about a foot thick. When they checked again near the new hole, they realized it was the wrong spot. They put all their tools together and got ready to leave. They told me I would have to get a plumber to find out where the trouble was.

I complied and looking through the classified ads. I made a few appointments with plumbers. Those that did show up simply shrugged and said it was not up to them but up to me to tell them where the leak was. Finally, I was more successful with a plumber that had immigrated to Colombia from Italy. His name was Giuseppe and he was accompanied by a fourteen-year-old helper. He inspected the floor. He pointed to a small area where the uniform layer of the small hexagonal floor tiles became quite scattered, as though someone had run out of tiles.

Giuseppe said that area was where the problem was. We agreed upon a price which sounded reasonable to me, and he set his teenage assistant to pound away with a hammer and chisel at the concrete floor. After several hours, he had produced a hole in the floor that was about eight inches across at its top and about two inches across at the bottom. From that opening, the roar of escaping water was clearly evident. We filled pot, pans and even the bathtub with water and then closed the water feed to the house, overnight. In the morning, Giuseppe returned with two young assistants who began taking turns to enlarge the opening in the floor. As the opening enlarged, it was obvious that a T connection had rusted through and failed. There were two pipes. One on each side of the top of a T connector that fed water into the two sides of the house. The main feed pipe coming from the street had been threaded into the center of the T connection and that had rusted it through. Finally, the hole they were chopping was large enough for the young assistants to make their way through. I had to leave to go to my classes but, when I returned, I found that the problem had not been solved. The assistants had removed the rusted end and added a short threaded section to the end of the main water feed, held in place by an inside threaded collar. What they hadn't foreseen was that there was no way of tightening both ends of the short threaded section. If they tightened one end sufficiently so that it would not leak, the other end leaked instead and vice a versa. After seeing them struggling for a while, I suggested to Giuseppe that he purchase a flexible T connection which permits adjustments at both ends. He agreed.

Early the next morning, the crew returned with a flexible T connector but another problem presented itself. Some of the supplies to the hardware stores in Bogotá came from the US and, not surprisingly, were not always quality. The flexible joint leaked no matter how tightly they could clamp down on it. I had to get to classes so I left with them struggling. When I returned late that afternoon, they were preparing to close the opening in the floor. I looked down at the T-connection and, lo and behold, it was perfectly dry even with the water supply turned on.

I refrained from asking Giuseppe how he achieved that miracle but I soon noticed something odd. One of the teenage assistants was limping and I finally noticed the reason. The heel was missing from one of his shoes. I concluded that the heel of his shoe was now part of the T connection and that, from here on, our water supply would be passing through that heel.

I thought it was one of those foreign scenarios that usually makes for interesting dinner conversation should we ever return to the US. Should anyone ask the proverbial question, "How was the water?" I could then answer it was good, especially since it passed through the heel from the shoe of an Italian plumber's helper.

Second Semester – One of the 55 Students

When our schooling advanced to the second semester, only the 55 best students progressed, as predicted. The teaching became intense. My classmates had adopted me as one of them and the top scores still rested with me, Jennifer Lewis de Uribe, and Gloria Fernandez. The last two were the young mothers that aspired to become physicians.

On the first day, I ran into trouble. The problem was with the professor who taught bacteria and viruses. His pronunciation of Castellano was so bad that I had to use his blackboard scribbling to follow the material. It consisted of bacteria and viruses that caused diseases. That written material was just as bad since it consisted of tables with a heading and a body of the items relating to that heading. The tables were so disoriented that there was practically no relationship between headings and body. The table that I constructed below is just to give the reader an idea of what the trouble was. It is not an actual example.

Streptococcus Pneumoniae
Infection
Pneumonia
Illness
Surgery
Dr. Rojas
Cough
Hospital San Marcos
Skin
Bacteria
Lungs
Hospitalization
Staphylococcus Aureus
High fever

As we filed out of the first class, I complained to my Colombian classmates that I was going to have trouble with the class because I didn't understand the professor. They responded that they didn't understand him either. Somehow, we all struggled through the bacteria and virus class.

Another class that I had trouble with was surgery, but this was a different kind of trouble. There were two sections to the surgery class – the academic and the practical. The academic section consisted of lectures on surgical techniques and the use of surgical instruments. The problem was with the surgical patients: neighborhood stray dogs.

Fortunately, that class lasted only a few days. For a few weeks prior, the custodians of the school scoured the neighborhood for stray dogs. These were penned up and cleaned prior to the surgery. We were divided into groups of several students who operated on one dog per group. My group was assigned to do a cholecystectomy (removal of the gall bladder) on our dog. We had to anesthetize our dog and perform the surgery with minimal blood loss. The poor creature had to survive the surgery, which he did. That was better than the fate of the dogs in some of the other groups. We were graded on the survival and continuing health of our patients.

During our second semester, we had difficult exams with the same pattern of direct interrogation by one or more professors. After one particularly difficult exam, in a class taught by Dr. Piñeros, in which most of the students got miserable grades, the entire class gathered outside of the school building. There was lots of grumbling about how unfair the exam had been. Some of the questions had had no basis in material that had been taught in class. Several of the more rebellious students proposed that the group should select a committee to appeal to Dr. Piñeros as to how unfair the exam had been. The class was unanimous about accepting the idea.

Almost all of them looked unanimously at Jennifer Lewis and me. We could see each other's apprehension. The idea of the two of us confronting Dr. Piñeros was scary but we didn't want to let the rest of the class down. We accepted. Then one of the students started yelling that the Gringos are taking over everything in the school. He was shouted down by the rest of the class, telling him to shut up as we were the best choice to help the rest of them.

Dr. Piñeros was still in the exam room as Jennifer and I tiptoed in. He turned toward us and asked why we were there. We told him that the class was complaining that the exam was unfair. He calmly told us to bring them in and he would settle the issue. We went outside and told the class that he would address them. They filed silently into the room. Dr. Piñeros started asking a myriad of questions about the material. He worked over the bulk of the class with brief but important questions. Students started responding with a lot of stuttering and stammering. Jennifer and I were terrified that we might be caught up in the interrogation - or more appropriately 'inquisition.' Fortunately, the good doctor avoided asking us any of the questions.

The class slinked out with everyone feeling chastised but resolving to study much harder in the future.

Media Coverage: *Somos*

As we left the classroom after a lecture, I noticed Dr. Piñeros standing just outside the exit door. There was a man standing with him who was unknown to me. To my surprise, Dr. Piñeros pointed to me and motioned me over to them. He introduced the gentleman to me as the senior editor of the prominent monthly magazine, *Somos*.

Dr. Piñeros explained that the editorial staff of *Somos* magazine was interested in doing an article about the Escuela de Medicina Juan N. Corpas emphasizing its general appeal to the Colombian public. The concept of graduating family doctors, rather than using the medical training to create highly paid specialists, was a novelty in Colombia and in the US. They were particularly interested in my background and why I sold my business to move to Colombia.

The editor made an appointment for me to meet with one of his reporters and a photographer at my home in Chico Norte. They questioned me at length and took numerous photographs. Later, more photographs were taken at the school grounds and during classes.

A few months later, the issue of *Somos* containing the article appeared. What surprised me was that the article was more dedicated to the story of my life than the noble purpose of the Juan N. Corpas medical school. In fact, the article opens with a very exact description of my interview with Dr. Piñeros which led to my immediate acceptance.

Gendler ha ideado una red de comunicaciones a través de la radio, que enlazará a las más apartadas regiones de Colombia donde se presta servicio médico, con Bogotá y en caso de urgencia con la Escuela Albert Einstein de Nueva York.

Somos article

The Production Line

Alicia, Libardo's mother, introduced us to other foreigners or expatriots (extranjeros) that were interested in meeting us. One elderly Jewish business man went to the same synagogue where Etta sang in their choir. His daughter, Heidi, had married a young American named Jerry Harris, who had immigrated to Colombia. His father was a toy distributor in Brooklyn, and as Jerry had set up a toy manufacturing business in Bogotá, his father scouted the US for toys that had fallen out of popularity. His dad would buy up the plastic molds to produce those toys in Bogotá.

When we met the family, Jerry expressed interest in working out an arrangement with me to help him finance his Christmas shipments to toy dealers all over Colombia. I was receptive since I had a fixed income from the sale of Seg Electronics in the US and my expenses were modest. The way that Jerry handled the sale of the toys was that the customer would write a post-dated check for the full price of the shipment. The check was dated around Christmas and, by Colombian law, that became the legal due date. If the check couldn't be cashed then, the creditor could engage a lawyer to have the debtor imprisoned. The release, from prison, can occur only when the debt is paid off. During the imprisonment, the family has to arrange for meals to feed the debtor. If there is no family, or the family is too poor to pay for the food, the debtor has to survive on bread and water.

Jerry invited me to visit his factory to show me the production line for his new line of toys. His factory building was huge. He proudly stated he had about six hundred employees. I visited his plant one morning and Jerry walked me to the production floor. A toy was being assembled that had several large gears and a tiny electric motor inside of a metal frame.

We walked down the production line, stopping at each station. Part of the way along the line, Jerry turned to me and asked what I thought of his operation. I told him that I had never seen anything so bad. He was shocked and asked me why I had said that. I told him that the operation lacked the rigid limits to what each assembler could do. As an example, I pointed to an assembler connecting the wires that ran to the tiny electric motor. There was no predetermined exact route for the wires. As a result, the wires ran closer in some toys to the gears than in others. There was the potential for the wires getting caught in the gears.

At the next station, a metal surface had glue being painted on with a broad brush. There was no control over the amount of glue or the path that the brush would be allowed to take. I explained there had to be jigs and fixtures controlling both. Jerry shouted out to his production manager to bring a pad and pencil to take notes as we worked our way along.

At the end of the line, he asked me to give up the idea of medical school and join him there. He promised we could make a million dollars. I smiled and said that I would be glad to help him out, now and then, but I was not interested in a manufacturing career.

School Is Out At Last

Finally, the first year came to a close. It had seemed to take forever. I had the highest grades with Jennifer and Gloria close behind. The medical school was getting better known throughout Bogotá but government approval seemed far away.

As vacation time was the month of December, I decided to return to the US to visit our family and old friends. I had made some contacts through Ham radio and it seemed worthwhile to visit. From my earlier visit to Richmond Hill, Canada, I had met and been in contact with a famous physician, Dr. Barnett Berris, at the University of Toronto. I even had a brief visit with him. By Ham radio, I contacted him and we scheduled a visit during my vacation time. He had the reputation of being the top diagnostician of Canada and seemed quite friendly. From thereon, we communicated frequently.

Etta and I traveled from Bogotá to the New York area to visit family, mainly our two sons and our daughter. Our oldest son, Jeff, had lived in our home in Long Island and finally arranged to sell it. Etta remained in the New York area visiting her large family. I traveled to Canada to visit the University of Toronto, Princess Margaret Hospital, and the Hospital for Crippled Children.

I was impressed with the Canadian medical facilities, mainly for their cleanliness and the cheerfulness of the staff. The patients, after treatment, left the hospitals feeling very upbeat. On my way to visit Dr. Barnett Berris in Toronto, I had the great pleasure of visiting the

Shouldice Hospital in Richmond Hill where I had the innovative hernia surgery. I was welcomed there and noticed that it seemed as popular as ever. They invited me to stay overnight and assist in the hernia surgeries the next morning. I was delighted to agree and it turned out to be a wonderful opportunity. I went on rounds with the staff internist who impressed me with his practical, short physical exams and concise questions.

The next day at the University of Toronto, I enjoyed a full day's visit with Dr. Barnett Berris, the internal medicine genius. That night I was a guest at his home. I addressed the grand rounds at his hospital, delivering my favorite talk, which combined medical physiology with electronic feedback theory. The talk was very well received. Dr. Berris expressed a lot of interest in Colombian medicine. I promised him that I would attempt to find an eminent medical group that would invite him to lecture on his favorite topic, hepatitis. We parted but it was mutual on both sides to continue our friendship, for life. Afterward, I remained in contact with him through my Ham Radio.

I returned to Long Island and rejoined Etta. We were guests at the home of Bernie and Roz who lived close to our home in Long Island. This enabled us to resume our friendships with our neighbors and friends that we sorely missed. They had missed us as well and we spent much time answering their questions about life in Colombia. Several of the families told us they would come and visit us. One or two families did so.

December flew by rapidly and we prepared to fly back to Bogotá for my second year of medical school.

The Second Year & Dr. Fernandez

The second year of medical school opened with my feeling much more a part of the medical scene. The modern and clean hospitals that I had visited during vacation made me desirous of returning to the US eventually. I found myself becoming more anxious about my school's lack of government approval. No one seemed very concerned, as if it was a routine matter. I resolved to see if I could improve that situation in the future.

Our studies began with the internal medicine under Dr. Manuel Fernandez Arenas, an eminent cardiologist. He worked his way steadily through the course lecturing about approximately six hundred diseases. Many of the diseases had similar symptoms. I felt that I had most of them. Most had fever, cough, rash, malaise, rapid heartbeat, headache, etc.

One particular symptom that I was presented with troubled me greatly. That symptom began many years back when I would watch boxing matches on television. The matches were often very exciting and I would feel my heart beating irregularly. In Colombia, watching television or movies was boring because of the language barrier and the lack of up-to-date films. As I was a particular fan of Mohammed Ali, a.k.a. Cassius Clay, I made sure that I watched those movies. Whenever I did so, I would find myself getting very much into the scene - bobbing and weaving along with the prizefighters. This made my heart beat fast and it always frightened me.

I described this to Dr. Fernandez. He reassured me that the reaction was a perfectly normal one. With that reassurance, my symptoms vanished. Nothing like a quick remedy.

Dr. Fernandez's residence was only a few blocks from my house and, at his invitation, Etta and I would visit him and his wife, Garty. She was born in Germany, where Dr. Fernandez had lived for quite a while, and she spoke Spanish and English.

During one of those visits, Dr. Fernandez described an unusual situation in his house. When certain appliances like his refrigerator would start to run, lights in the other room with go dim. He had burned out several appliances and many light bulbs. He asked me the favor of trying to fix the problem. I agreed and went to his home carrying a small voltmeter.

Measuring the voltages from the power box where the cables entered his home, I found the problem. The power that was delivered to his home was through a three-phase cable, which required three thick wires, with a fourth wire as the neutral or ground wire. The three cables delivered their power to three areas of the house but all with respect to the neutral or ground wires. This would produce 120V between the first cable and the neutral wire, the second cable and the neutral wire, and the third cable and the neutral wire.

To prevent having a short circuit damaging any of the three circuits, fuses were connected between each of the three cables where they entered the house. Under those conditions the 120 volts was available and steady for each of the three circuits. The electricians who wired Dr. Fernandez's house however, had made the mistake of placing a fuse in the neutral or ground line. The power line coming in from the street had a high overall voltage which then was split into three circuits.

That fuse in the neutral or ground line had blown out and as a result, rather than having three circuits of 120V each, the three circuits split up the high-voltage depending on the nature of the equipment or lights attached.

Take this example of what could occur without the neutral or ground cable intact:

The refrigerator circuit would share the 230V input with, say, a bedroom circuit, and would not split the voltage to 120V each but, whenever the refrigerator motor turned on its voltage, would drop to say 50V which could damage the motor. Meanwhile the bedroom circuit would rise to possibly190V, blowing out the bulbs.

I checked the system by placing a piece of metal tubing into the neutral line fuse holder. All of these three circuits then were locked into delivering 120V each, which was the desired result. Dr. Fernandez was delighted but apprehensive. The idea of wiring around a fuse looked like a loss of protection. I had to persuade him that the absolute protection came from a solid neutral or ground connection that could not be blown out. The real danger exists if there is no fixed neutral or ground wire. He gave in to my orders and I exchanged the neutral or ground fuse for a solid thick wire soldered in place. The voltages stabilized at 120V per circuit.

We remained friends for the rest of my time in school and communicated even after I returned to the US. A few years after my return, Dr. Fernandez and his family moved to North Carolina where they lived until he passed away. His two daughters had studied medicine in Colombia. When the family moved to the US, his daughters transferred to US residency programs. Today they are practicing physicians.

Lights, Action, Camera

The foreign community of Bogotá was small but active in keeping the members aware of the latest news and opportunities for cultural opportunities in English. The US Embassy helped with occasional meetings and even a movie, now and then.

One interesting project sponsored by a Colombian film director who had done much of his directing in the US was a rerun of The Desperate Hours, a 1955 movie that was based on the Broadway play of the same title years earlier. The film starred Humphrey Bogart as the villain who invaded the household of the husband and father of the family, played by Frederick March. The villain, who had another desperado as his sidekick, had sought refuge while escaping from the police and keeping the family hostage (There was a revival in the 1990s of the same play).

The director sought volunteers for the roles. I applied and was accepted for the role of Jess Bard, the deputy Sheriff who eventually killed the villain. We rehearsed several times a week for several months. Finally, the opening night was approaching and the tension was growing. Our organization rented a large theater for the rehearsals and the seven evening performances. All proceeds in excess of expenses went to charity.

On opening night, the play was well received. Any minor glitches were covered up with no one in the audience the wiser. When I shot the villain, everyone in the audience enthusiastically applauded. That was not the high point for me. Earlier, I had a segment where I was on center stage, illuminated by one overhead spotlight, with the rest of the stage pitch dark. In my monologue, I described an incident in which a tough bad guy was goading me by telling me that he had served a jail term for some vile crime and how law officers like me couldn't touch him. I described him sneering at me whereupon I swung my fist in a mock punch that knocked him down.

Many of my professors went to the performance and loved it. Dr. Piñeros told a group of students that while the student body was studying for exams I was busy performing on stage. This was done in an admiring manner rather than critical.

After the seventh and final performance, there was a sudden vacuum, a word that always seemed to follow me throughout life. It was a big letdown from the intense activity. Imagine; the gratifying applause, and then…nothing. The next day at a department store, a man saw me with Etta and congratulated me on my performance. Nice to be recognized, but it was a rather weak sequel.

Military Field Hospitals

Our second year studies were interrupted for several weeks due to an unusual opportunity that presented itself.

During the worst of the Cold War, the US constructed about sixty field hospitals to handle the casualties of a nuclear war with the Soviet Union. As rational thinking took over on both sides, the threat of a nuclear war faded. That is, until the Cuban missile crisis occurred in the early1960s. By that time the field hospitals had become more or less obsolete. The US donated these hospitals to various nations that could make good use of them. One major problem with the hospitals was the fact that the expiration dates on the medications and sterilized components were expiring or had expired.

Colombia was the recipient of one of those field hospitals. It was received by the Colombian army and they didn't know quite what to do with it. Since Bogotá had a large and poor population, largely in the south of Bogota and underserved by the health system, the Colombian army officers decided to set up the hospital there on vacant land. The Escuela de Medicina Juan N. Corpas was selected to supply the medical staff to treat the impoverished patients over a two-week period. I had the suspicion that the well-established medical schools had their curriculum quite full and could not supply their own staff.

Dr. Piñeros addressed our second year class and told us that we were going to staff the field hospital for two weeks. He emphasized that the first-year students were not sufficiently experienced and the third and fourth year students were too busy.

The Colombian army notified us when the field hospital was ready to receive patients. We had prepared for the event by organizing our group into subgroups. Several tents were to be set aside for internal medicine and one tent was to be equipped with beds to handle the patients that required hospitalization. I was singled out to be the Ophthalmologist since I had the only ophthalmoscope of the group.

Unfortunately, the opening day coincided with the beginning of the rainy season in Bogotá. The long lines of patients waiting to be served at each tent had to contend with a drenching rain. The heavy rain ran down the mountainside where the tents were erected. The water flowed under the tents and down to the long lines of patients. We students had tried to prepare by soliciting medications as a donation. The updated medications had to be sorted out as to their function and expiration dates.

The first day opened in turmoil. The Colombian military had promised us two supervising physicians but they never appeared. We managed as well as our limited training permitted. There were no disasters, for which we were grateful, but we came close at times. I did all the eye exams which gave me a lot of practice. One of my colleagues treated a young woman for anxiety and bereavement as her father had suddenly passed away. She was given a few days worth of tranquilizers. Unfortunately, she was brought in the next day after taking them all in a suicide attempt. Fortunately, she wasn't given enough tranquilizers to do much harm, other than put her into a sound sleep in our hospital tent, rain and all.

The long lines of patients continued unabated all through the two weeks. The rain never let up either. We arrived home wet and exhausted every night. We were learning the hard way. If we weren't too tired on arriving home, we could look up the difficult cases. Since we had already studied how to conduct the physical examination, this helped us do a fairly professional job.

I had one more nagging problem as the two weeks drew to a close. Before we had learned about the field hospitals, I had contacted the medical school of the Javeriana, (Pontifical Xavier University), which was one of the oldest medical schools in Colombia. I had offered Dr. Barnett Berris' hepatitis presentation as I had promised. They had accepted the offer and Dr. Berris was due to arrive just before the hospital was dissembled.

At about that time, my daughter, Leslie, was visiting us. She drove to the hospital just as the tents were being dissembled by the army and the hospitalized patients sent off to area hospitals. She had picked up Dr. Berris at the El Dorado airport and he wanted to see our field hospital operation. As they arrived, I was examining a lady whose abdomen was distended and she was complaining of labor pains. Her pregnancy test, however, was negative. As Dr. Berris arrived at my tent, I asked him about the case. He looked at her standing up as the beds were being taken apart and the tents taken down. He said that he didn't have the faintest idea as to what her problem was. I told him that I suspected pseudo-cyesis (fake pregnancy). Dr. Berris shrugged and didn't respond. Not surprisingly, he looked sort of dazed through it all.

We all squeezed into my little Renault 6 and headed to our home in the North. As we passed through the main street through the center of Bogotá, one of my tires went flat. Two men hurried over and offered to repair the flat. This was a well-known trick where the bad guys scatter nails to cause the flat tire and then offer to help the victim in the hope of some tip.

In Colombia, tubeless tires were quite rare as the many deep potholes damaged the rims of the wheels so tubeless tires lost air promptly. There was an entire industry in Bogota dedicated to straightening out the wheel rims (rectificador de rines).

Our situation was complicated because a police officer came over and was demanding that we drive away, on the flat tire, to clear the busy lane that we were blocking. As I debated with the officer, the 'helpers' quickly repaired the tire. I tried to start the car, which was another problem. I gave the officer a few pesos as a tip so he was directing traffic around us. Meanwhile, I opened the hood and quickly took off the air filter over the carburetor. I propped up the air intake control, at the top of the carburetor, with a piece of cardboard. The car started and we were on our way home in the North of Bogotá - Transversal 23 101-01. It had taken fifteen minutes to clear the mess. Poor Dr. Berris. He didn't deliver his sigh of relief until we reached home. He had never encountered anything like this in Canada.

The next day we went to the Javeriana and Dr. Berris delivered his Hepatitis lecture. He was well received. He was invited to look at some difficult medical cases in the hospital of the Javeriana. I tagged along with him as we went from bed to bed. At one bed, there was a fifteen-year-old boy lying with his upper body propped up partially by a large pillow. Dr. Berris looked at him for a few seconds. He told the Javeriana professors that this was a case in which the pulmonary heart valve had failed. This caused the strong pulsation appearing in the neck veins and his shortness of breath (dyspnea). The Javeriana Professors nodded in admiration. Dr. Berris said that he doesn't know what was causing a rash on the patient's chest. He and I touched the rash. The Javeriana Professor said it was Hansen's disease. We looked at our fingers. We looked for where we could scrub them. Hansen's disease was another name for Leprosy.

Leslie & The Javeriana

During my daughter's visit to us that second year, she expressed interest in my medical career. Her Spanish language studies at Syracuse University had been augmented by her frequent visits to our old family friend, Libardo and his family, during summer vacations.

She offered to join me for a day at the Juan N. Corpas. One day, she accompanied me and sat in on the classes. The high point of the day was when I took her to the Amphitheater with its long rows of cadavers. It had been prepared for the first year students who would start working there shortly. I was concerned that Leslie might be horrified by what she was seeing but she surprised me by saying it wasn't half bad. She decided to change her career direction, as she had just completed her third year of Syracuse University in her major of Spanish Literature.

I offered to try to help her get into my school but she explained that she wouldn't like to compete with her father or be compared to him. The Javeriana would be her first choice. It was one of the most recognized medical schools in Colombia. Other foreign students, mainly US citizens, were enrolled in the Javeriana, but were in a tiny minority.

The next day, I arranged some appointments with the two deans of the Javeriana; the academic Doctor Calderón, and the ethical (religious) dean. All of their medical staff knew of the older engineer that had left his multi-million dollar industry designing NASA's moonwalks to enroll in the upstart, unapproved medical school, Juan N. Corpas, where he donated over a million dollars of high tech medical equipment. Talk about poor communications. No wonder I had received several hints that the Javeriana might be interested in a transfer by me to their 'real' medical school. I suspect that they might have had an interest in tapping into that giant bonanza that the Juan N. Corpas was enjoying.

We arrived at the Javeriana at the appointed time to speak with the padre (Father) that was the religious dean and whom I had never met. He asked me how I liked Colombia and I responded by telling him that I was excited by the country's prospects. He wished us luck and we left to visit Doctor Calderón. On our way there, Leslie gently admonished me. She said that in my conversation with the padre, I had used the wrong word, 'excitado,' which means sexually excited, and not 'animado,' which means 'animated.'

The academic dean knew of me. He greeted us in a friendly manner. He told us that it would be his pleasure to allow Leslie to take the SAT exam in competition with the Colombian pre-med students. The next SAT exam was scheduled about six months from our meeting. She would also have to take the basic pre-med courses, as a prerequisite for admission.

Leslie was delighted as we left the dean's office. She was confident that she could pass the SAT exam. She was leaving for the US in two days after our meeting with the Javeriana Deans. As we headed home, we stopped at my favorite bakery for a delicious loaf of bread. When we got home, Leslie realized that she had lost her wallet with her credit cards, airplane tickets, and a small amount of cash. The most likely place that she might have lost it was after making her purchase at the bakery. Naturally, we rushed back there but no one admitted to seeing the wallet.

That evening, we received a telephone call from a young Colombian woman who said that she had found the wallet. She came to our house with it the next day. The contents were intact except for the cash, which was gone, but even the credit cards and the airline tickets were safe. The mystery was how the woman got the Colombian home address and telephone number. There were many such mysteries like that in my life, and especially in Colombia.

Leslie changed her final year's curriculum at Syracuse University to satisfy the Javeriana requirements. Upon graduation, she enrolled in Kingston University, also in New York State, for an additional year to complete the Javeriana requirements.

Six months later, Leslie returned and took the SAT exam. About three months after that, she returned to see how she had fared on the tests. The grades were posted in a small room that had one exit to the campus. It took Leslie and me about an hour to get through the milling crowd of students trying to force their way in to get their scores. Sadly, Leslie's name was nowhere to be seen. We left quite dispirited.

The next day, Leslie was leaving for the US but, hoping against hope, I called the academic dean at the Javeriana and he was willing to see us, according to his secretary. When we met him in his office, I told him that we couldn't find Leslie's name where the grades were posted. He said that this was a 'different situation.' He pulled out a large ruled pad with names and grades, and found what he was looking for. Leslie had a high passing grade. She therefore was accepted as a first-year medical student for the next semester. Etta and I were ecstatic about her acceptance and the fact that she was going to live with us again.

Leslie moved into our home after her last year of pre-med ended and was well received by all the Colombians that were part of our life. She loved the house we had bought and its frequent visitor which was a beautiful female parrot that belonged to our next door neighbor. Her name was Rebecca and every day she climbed out of her cage and up to the ridge at the peak of the roof. From there, she climbed up onto our roof to visit us. She kept calling out her name, Rebecca, in a falsetto voice, trilling the R's, of course.

We were also given a parrot only a few months old, as a gift from one of the Libardo's brothers. We named him Arturo. When Rebecca was visiting, the bedlam was deafening. Unfortunately, someone stole sweet Rebecca but our beloved Arturo lived with us for more than thirty-five years.

Our house was all on one story. Leslie's bedroom had a tiny balcony facing the street. On her birthday, I knocked on her bedroom door. When she let me in, I opened the door leading to the balcony and there was a band of mariachis with their guitars singing any song that she or I requested. She enjoyed the quaint birthday surprise. It was just a small step in the new direction in her life. She was thrilled at this tremendous change in her life with the goal of becoming a medical doctor suddenly within reach.

What she also wanted within reach was her own telephone. One day she requested it. When we purchased our house, it had a telephone line and number. This was a rarity then as there was a two-year waiting period. Granting her wish, I took her to an area of Bogotá called San Andrecito, named after San Andres, a beautiful Colombian island that was a smuggler's haven as well as a vacation jewel.

We entered a large factory where there were many stalls with different classes of merchandise. One stall had new telephones that were cheap and I agreed to buy one. I asked how we could be sure that it would work at our house. The vendor took us over to a pay telephone mounted on a wall of the building. The two wires of the payphone came out of the top and ran up to the ceiling. A foot or so above the payphone someone had scraped the insulation off exposing the two bare wires. He clipped the new phone wires to the bare wires and told us to call our home. The connection was great but I was uneasy about not paying a peso for the connection.

My family and I took some delightful trips, mostly locally. We made sure that visiting friends and family saw the nicest parts of the beautiful country. A favorite of everyone was Lake Guatavita, which is a spectacular lake surrounded by quaint small cottages constructed by the government in the style of ancient Spain. It carries the legends of the Muisca Indian Chief who arrived regularly, covered by gold dust, on a boat filled with golden treasures which he threw overboard as a tribute to their gods. The Spanish Conquistadores plundered the golden treasures, sending many ships loaded with the precious metal to the King of Spain.

Not everything was fun and games. On a short trip outside of Bogotá, we drove to a cheese factory which was a favorite attraction of the Bogotanos. While Leslie and Etta were inside buying some cheeses, I headed outside to my Renault to get a book on cheeses that I had left in the car. As I approached the car, I saw a Gipsy woman with a young girl about ten years old near the Renault. The woman addressed me asked if I liked the girl, in Spanish. I looked at the woman in horror. I ran back into the cheese factory. That episode has remained graven in my memory to this day.

The Six - Shooter

There were several robberies in neighbors' homes, which took place while the families were away. Sometimes the house maid was the accomplice, or her friends chatting with her by telephone learned the neighbor's routine. There were usually strict prohibitions against opening the street door to strangers. The robbers used clever techniques, like one or two men would knock on the door with one man carrying a large bouquet of flowers. The maid would come to the door and she was told through the closed door that this was for a delivery of flowers. She would tell them to leave it outside and go away. They would refuse, stating that they had to get a signature. If the maid still declined to open the door, they would turn to leave and tell the maid that the Señora will be upset at missing such a gift. Imagine the torment of the poor girl faced with such a no-win situation.

Most of the crime was petty. There were numerous cases of a watch being snatched off the wrist of a driver waiting for a traffic light to change to green, while resting his hand on the frame of his open window. Leslie had an episode similar to that when she boarded one of the microbuses to school. There were no empty seats as she got on the microbus so she held onto the post in the middle of the little bus. A boy got onto the bus with her, carrying a stack of the main Bogotá newspaper, *El Tiempo*. He worked his way from the front entrance to the middle of bus and, as the bus made its next stop, he prepared to leave at the center exit. As he started his exit, he grabbed Leslie's Timex wrist watch and tugged hard. Amazingly, the strap didn't break or come loose, and Leslie pulled back hard still holding onto the post. He jumped off but without the Timex. Imagine what a great ad that would be for Timex.

Later, we got word of some serious nighttime break-ins with the family held at gun point in our upscale neighborhood. This really concerned me and I began to think about getting a gun, which I understood are ubiquitous in Bogota. Since we had several friends and VIPs visiting us, occasionally to be connected by Ham radio to their family in the US, I waited for the opportunity to find out how one goes about the process of acquiring a weapon.

My break came when a retired Colombian Colonel (Coronel) made an appointment to get connected with his son studying in the US. After he finished chatting with his son, he thanked me and, as usual for him, asked me if there was any way for him to repay the favor. That was the opportunity that I sought. His response was that it would be his pleasure to help me and that I should meet him on my next free day at the Ministry of Defense. He met me early in the morning and we headed for the office of his friend, an active Colonel. There was a line (*cola* or queue) of about a hundred men waiting to see the Coronel for the same purpose. My Coronel strode rapidly with me at his side down the entire length of the line to the active Coronel's office. Every man waiting on line glared daggers at me but I kept my eyes averted. We waited about 10 minutes for the Coronel to complete his meeting with someone inside, and then we entered. The two Coronels greeted each other by embracing.

In about 20 minutes, I had an official document to go to the defense ministry's warehouse and choose my gun, as well as a booklet on safe conduct (salvoconducto) with the appropriate signatures and stamps. I had to leave with my Coronel along that same line with the same baleful looks. He met me the next day. I bought a Smith & Wesson six-shooter revolver and a shoulder holster. It felt reassuring. I hoped I would never have to use it other than to practice, although I came close a few times.

One of those times was an evening when I was on my way from one of the clinics at which I had been working. As I was driving from the South to the North of Bogota. I suddenly remembered that I had to make an urgent telephone call. In the relatively poor area through which I was passing, I spotted a neighborhood grocery store with customers coming and going. Since they usually had a coin telephone, I parked my Renault 6 at the curb, placed my brief case of books and notes on the floor behind the front seats, got out, and locked the car. As I made my call using the pay telephone, a woman entered the store and went up to me. She told me someone had gotten into my car and taken what was there. I hung up and rushed out. The car was still locked but the briefcase was gone. I looked around but the people standing around paid no attention to me, although they must have seen someone unlocking the car and removing my briefcase. Even though I had my loaded revolver in its shoulder holster, my common sense told me that I had better not question the people nearby. Guns were everywhere in the population. I never could figure out how they got in and out of the car in such a short time. The briefcase was old and the few books in it were not expensive so I just drove away, but a little wiser.

Another such event took place in the commercial center of Bogota. I was walking through a busy street approaching a one-way cross street with two lanes. The far lane was filled with parked cars and the near lane was packed with traffic that was creeping at a snail's pace. There was a bus in the traffic that was hardly moving. A man behind me started running to catch the bus. In the crowded pedestrian walkway he bumped me lightly as he raced for the bus. As he boarded the bus, I checked my wallet, watch, and pockets. Everything was there. That is, until I reached the breast pocket of my jacket. My glasses were missing. I started walking toward the bus which was now stationary. I reasoned that I might board the bus and make my way to him. I would hold out my hand and ask for the 'gafas' (vernacular for glasses) with my jacket slightly held open to expose my weapon, only to him. As I got close to the bus, I was still weighing the pluses and minuses of the predicament. Fortunately, traffic started moving briskly and the bus took off – my gafas still on board.

One night, a more dangerous event occurred after Etta and I were returning home from the center of Bogotá after visiting some friends. We were driving along the main avenue, Avenida Cien (Avenue 100) and, as we were in the north and close to home, an old, large car drove alongside our Renault. In it were four burly men who looked our way. They continued driving alongside our car. I reasoned that I had better not make the left turn off the Avenida Cien toward our house as we would be isolated. My gun against the four of them, very likely armed, would be foolhardy. I chose to continue along the Avenida Cien about one extra mile to where it ended. There was an army base there with a single entrance guarded by a soldier with an automatic weapon. I figured that we would be challenged by the soldier and we would be able to explain the problem. Still, I hoped that he wasn't trigger-happy.

Fortunately, a police car with several police officers approached us and the other car took off. That was a close call. I'm convinced that we were in grave danger.

Less scary was an event while driving to school with several classmates as passengers. The day before, a Colombian General had been shot to death in his car while waiting for a traffic light to change. There were lots of police and soldier activity as we drove towards Suba, a suburb of Bogotá where the school had constructed its own buildings. About halfway there, all cars were being stopped and the drivers questioned. An army officer did the questioning with several soldiers standing by. When they approached my Renault, I slowly got out of the car. I opened my jacket and said to the officer, "Tengo arma" ("I have a weapon"), pointing to my other axilla (arm-pit). I then added, "Tengo Salvo Conducto" ("I have a Safe Conduct booklet"), which I showed him. I was obviously a gringo from the clothes and haircut that I sported.

All of this was done slowly and carefully. He nodded with a bored expression and that was the end of it. Boy, if my little Renault 6 could talk. Oh the tales it could tell.

La Calera Farm

My son, Howard, had sold the farm that he owned with several partners in West Virginia. I believed that I might be able to interest him in moving to Colombia if I bought a farm as a business investment. He could live on the farm and manage it. If successful, I could make him a partner. Farmland was cheap, I was told. I had no income, other than the monthly payoff from the sale of Seg Electronics, but it was a viable idea.

An opportunity appeared in the classified section of *El Tiempo*, offering a large farm (finca) in the suburbs, called La Calera, about 10km north of Bogotá. It was about 135 acres. In Spanish, this was equivalent to about 60 fanegadas. There was a nice house on the property, as well as a barn and several other structures. I met with the owner who turned to be Jewish. This was reassuring based on the special trust that I received from Señor Gurevich on exchanging money. He pointed to the freely flowing stream coming down from the high point at one end of the property. He explained that there was a spring up there, to which the owner of the farm had the prime rights to all of the water. He said the said owner would have to divert a small part of the stream in order to feed two very small farms higher on the hill. I felt that this was a bargain at the asking price of twenty-eight-thousand dollars and I bought the property.

One problem for me when I got to Bogotá was the 8,600 ft of altitude, which made itself felt when I walked up a flight of stairs and found myself quite short of breath. The farm was about 1,000 ft higher. It sloped from the road upward which made the effort even more difficult. After a few months, the body gets accustomed to the lower oxygen level and the symptoms disappear.

I took title to the farm, which had the form of a thick stack of paper with the cover emblazoned with the colorful government stamps and official signatures. There was a similar stack granting me the prime rights to the water spring (nacidero) close to the top of the hill behind the farm. The water rights document was written in a strange tense of Spanish that I had never seen before. It apparently was an old form of legal language with unusual word endings and whose English version would come through something like 'May it be understood.' I found that I could make sense of it after plowing through it. The day that I took possession was very similar to the same event with my home in Bogotá. When I arrived at the house, there were no padlocks on the doors of the house and barn, and no toilet tissue in the bathrooms. The missing padlocks were particularly worrisome. I could have found the interior stripped of everything that could be sold.

I still marveled at the bargain that I got until a few weeks later, which is when the rainy season ended. The stream of water coming from the spring decreased tremendously. The reduced flow sank into the ground on the way down so that nothing reached my farm. So much for one Jew treating another Jew with complete honesty and graciousness.

To rectify the situation, I hired a foreman (mayordomo) named Ruben. He had good references from a local church as being religious and honest. We had already bought a few dairy cows and two horses. A new student at the Juan N. Corpas, who had been a veterinarian in Canada, agreed to live in the house and keep the eventual herd healthy. I didn't charge him any rent but, on the other hand, there was no electric power or telephone. Neither was there any water anymore.

The other animals on the farm consisted of three dogs and one goat. 'Red Dog' was my favorite and he headed the pack whenever they raced to the road because someone was passing by. The barking was tumultuous and it was added to by the goat's bleating as she charged with the dogs. I guess she thought she was a bona fide member of the pack.

Our first order of business was to try to get water. We had found a flow of water on the property between two rocks. A small amount came down, at times, through the original stream bed which now was a ditch. I climbed up the hill to the nacidero's opening and noted that there was a reasonably flow but that the water sank into the sandy bottom of the long ditch. There was only enough flow to supply one neighbor's tiny farmhouse on the way down.

I reasoned that the correct approach was to stop the loss of water in the ditch. I went to a cement vendor in Bogota and ordered enough bags of cement and sand in the right proportions to line the ditch and easily stop the water loss. I explained this to Ruben who understood perfectly. He took on a few workers at a few dollars a day for each one. They used horses to carry the cement and sand up the hill. Once there, they would add water from the nacidero and using my tools they would apply the mixed cement and sand to the surface of the ditch.

During the week, I was busy with school and didn't get back to La Calera until the next weekend. Ruben proudly showed me the completed job. He had saved the extra cement in order to make a floor in the barn. The new floor appeared somewhat brown however, instead of the standard gray color of cement. I climbed the hill with Ruben and the same brown color was there all along the ditch. I scraped the brown cement with my fingernail and it scooped up with only slight resistance. The water flowed much better, feeding my neighbor's small farm and reaching my own. Unfortunately, the flow of water ended as the ditch lost its so-called cement in a few days. In retrospect, I was not prepared for the complete lack of education and experience.

As the water flow receded, I tried another approach. I used additional helpers to dig in the area around where the water was flowing weakly between two rocks right on my property. That approach seemed to show some promise. The ground turned muddy as they dug down. The mud was becoming watery as the digging went deeper. The men were having an increasing amount of trouble digging in the mud so I found a service that would rent us a tractor with a driver for about twenty-five dollars a day. The tractor started with great promise but got stuck. I reached the owner of the tractor service by telephone and he sent another tractor. The second tractor tugged the first one out of the muddy pond but then they both took off, heading home. It was quite a funny sight, but I didn't feel much like laughing at this point.

I bought enough lengths of sewer pipe to line the ditch as well as enough cement and sand to seal the joints. Ruben got strict instructions about sticking to the correct proportions of cement and sand, not trying to save me money by skimping. I also instructed him to dig a hole of a certain size next to the neighbor's farmhouse. He was to line it with the same proportions of cement and sand to form a storage tank thereby supplying the neighbor's water needs.

Our herd of Red Poll cows had increased and we were selling milk to a company that packaged it in one liter bags. However, our resident soon suffered the fate of those in the lower half of students admitted into the Juan N. Corpas School of Medicine. He went back to Canada but had helped us choose healthy cows while he was still living on the farm.

In order to improve communication between home and the farm, I had purchased a pair of Citizen Band radio transmitter/receivers on one of my trips to the US. The connection was uncertain and the quality was poor but it was still able to keep me connected.

Ruben was no longer with us. I had found out that he had been quietly selling much of the milk cheaply, for cash, to a different packager. This was during the big water shortage. In a round-about form of logic he blamed the reduced quantity of milk on the water shortage. He reasoned this shortage, in turn, resulted in less grass for the cows to graze.

My new mayordomo was Armando who seemed quite honest although this was far from certain. He lived in the farmhouse with his family and directed the employees. To his credit, the sale of milk rose to normal.

Our next enterprise was growing and selling potatoes. We had a small garden at first, where we grew potatoes for seed. The workers who seemed to know the ropes cut up the potatoes so that each piece they planted had an eye, which they called the small bud. I was troubled by one extra step they had added, which seemed to be standard for the area. When they harvested the crop, they threw the small and deformed potatoes into a pile and cut up the runts up for seeds. I still believe that this perpetuates the deformation but it wasn't obvious in the results, which surprised me. We planted our major crop early to catch a better price. It was threatened when a frost appeared, out of season, and slowly climbed up from lower altitudes to the opposite side of the road from my farm. Fortunately it never crossed the road. However, the frost did destroy the potato crops of several of my neighbors at lower altitudes.

Lipizzaner Horses I

To my relief, Howard contacted me. I hadn't heard from him for a long time. He was coming to visit with his girlfriend, Lynda, whom I had never met. They had been in Colombia for the past several months. He had sold the West Virginia farm before making the move. They had stayed with some North American friends in La Florida (pronounced floa-REE-dah) after arriving in Colombia. Lynda was pregnant and in her early months. They planned to live on the La Calera farm, which still had no electric power yet promised within a year or two. I had set up living quarters for Armando and his family in one of the farm's vacant buildings.

Around that time, La Calera still had no telephone service but that was on the way. We were able to communicate with the same limited connectivity of the Citizen's Band Transceivers, which I brought from the US.

Howard was eager to make the farm profitable. We gave it a lot of thought. We came up with the idea of producing cottage cheese, which the big Colombian cheese company was not producing at all. We named the cheese 'Wisconsin Queso de Cabana,' which more correctly translates into 'Wisconsin Cabin Cheese.' I shopped around and found a big bath tub. We sanitized it generously. We imported the right bacterial cultures from the US to add to the milk. We stirred the mixture well and covered the tub with a cloth that we had sterilized with steam and waited out the recommended time. The cheese looked and tasted great. I sold the product to several large supermarkets. A week later, we started receiving complaints from the stores that the containers of cheese were developing green mold. We accepted and credited the returns after which we closed up shop. It was obvious that we could not keep the operation sterile enough, or we would have to add preservatives. I had to chalk that up as one of my failures. I credited the loss to a learning cycle, for which I had lots of credits exceeding the lifetime of losses, comfortably.

Howard introduced me to a friend of his that he had met in La Florida, Colombia. The friend, Thomas McClendon, was nicknamed Jesse. He was visiting Bogotá frequently as part of his normal routine of visiting Colombia. He carried an attaché bag whose contents he displayed to Howard and me. The bag was filled with pictures of Lipizzaner horses that were his pride and joy. He told us that he had sent some of these horses from his home, in Florida, to Colombia. He explained that he used these horses for stud purposes. The overall objective would be to improve the characteristics of the Colombian horse population.

I had heard of the Lipizzaner horses, which were an elegant breed closely related to the Spanish Riding School of Vienna, Austria. They were trained for exhibitions during which they displayed their ability to dance and prance for audiences that might include royalty. They were extremely expensive and needed expensive care. Jesse explained that he had four Lipizzaner horses that had been shipped to Colombia, two horses sent to Bogotá, and the other two to Medellin. The horses sent to Bogotá were at a stable in the center of the city. He was certain that they were being used for stud services for which he was not being paid. That sounded about the way things worked in Colombia.

Jesse asked me if I would be willing to keep the Lipizzaner horses on my farm and he would refer the breeders to my farm for the stud services to the mares. He would set up the stalls for his horses in a vacant building on my land, which he would also equip with enough feed to last a few months. Leaving for the coast of Colombia, Jesse vowed he would call us from time to time until he got back.

The financial arrangements would be simple. A fifty-fifty split between us for the stud services. Howard and I agreed to the arrangement. Jesse set up the stalls and had feed delivered. We agreed to allow the horses to graze on our grass whenever possible. This would be limited by the fact that our grass was in short supply and our cows depended on it.

Over the months that followed, we received two mares for stud services for which we billed 50,000 pesos (about $100). Well we received half of it. With Jesse away, it became obvious that the pickings were going to be slim.

Over the next few months, water remained limited. The growing of grass and crops were barely adequate. The weather remained chilly and Linda's pregnancy was advancing. Electric power and telephone services were still promised but not delivered.

Howard and Lynda decided that it would be best if she went back to the US for more comfortable living conditions and adequate medical care. Howard would follow shortly. Lynda left for Oregon, where she would stay with friends. Howard left a few weeks later using his truck to pick up items that they had left in La Florida, after which he would sell the truck and fly to Oregon to join Lynda.

I next heard from Howard several months later. I had become concerned about lack of communication. As it turned out, I had good reason to. It was years later that I learned something of his adventures on his return to the US. As he described it, he intended to return to the US via Venezuela and was stopped at a reten. Retens are military or police checkpoints abound in Colombia.

The soldier that stopped his truck ordered him into the small building to be questioned by the officer-in-charge, who also examined his papers. Everything appeared to be in order until the soldier came into the building after searching the truck out front. The soldier was carrying a hand gun that he had found under the driver's seat. Howard told the officer that it was unloaded. The officer exclaimed, "Oh, unloaded, is it?" He pointed it at the soldier's abdomen and pulled the trigger. Only a click was heard. The gun was handed back to Howard and he was free to continue on his way.

What if it had bullets in the chamber? Would Howard have received the next bullet? What if the solider had been shot? Would Howard have been accused of killing the soldier? It is a king-size puzzlement. We will never know the answer to that one.

I am happy to say that Howard, always the adventurer, has changed enormously in his later years. He now owns a farm in Central California that occupies a quarter of a square mile. He also has crews installing the major appliances in newly constructed high-rise buildings in San Francisco, each with hundreds of condos.

Over the Cliff

Howard and Lynda had named their baby boy, Clifford, after he was born in the US. While Clifford was young, Howard and Lynda began to have their differences and their marriage ended in divorce. Each of them eventually remarried and they wound up living far apart with their respective spouses. It was arranged that Cliff divide his time more or less equally between the two parents. The situation was complicated by friction between Howard and Lynda. Raising Cliff became more complicated because Lynda's new mate showed a strong dislike to the boy, which he did not try to hide. After Etta and I had moved back to the US, we noticed that Cliff was having problems with the shuttling back and forth. We elected to raise him. Strangely, Lynda broke off all contact with her son, which continues to this day.

We raised Cliff at our home in Southern California. He did well in elementary and high school. At his graduation from high school, he surprised us when he showed up on the podium to address the crowd as the student representative. In CSU, Fullerton, he excelled in wrestling while he continued with extra-curricular work in the Reserve Officer Training Corps (ROTC). On graduation, he chose the Air Force program, which he entered as a Lieutenant. He wound up flying KC- 135s, the giant tanker planes that refuel the fighter planes. He saw service in the Iraq and Afghanistan theaters and carries the rank of Major. At present he serves as a Major in the Air Force Reserve. He is mostly employed training the Air Force pilots on a Flight Simulator with less frequent deployments around the globe. He decided to limit his military deployments and join one of the Airlines. Cliff has two children who, of course, are my great grandchildren. I love them very much.

Cliff was also recently hired by United Airlines to train for the Captain's position.

Lipizzaner Horses, II

A rather strange episode took place several months later. I was studying one evening after school, when I received a phone call in Spanish from someone who would not give me his name. He told me my mayordomo in La Calera and his brother were riding along the road on my horses whilst drunk. I was upset since the two horses were the expensive Lipizzaner horses for which I had full responsibility. I had never met Armando's brother but I had heard that he was just getting out of prison. I didn't realize that he was headed for my farm.

I headed for my car immediately with my revolver in its holster. It was pitch dark when I arrived at the farm. I headed towards the house making as little noise as possible. My efforts at arriving secretly were shaken up when Armando tapped me on the shoulder from behind. So much for my efforts. There was no sign of the brother and the two horses were in their stable. I never did learn who had called or even the purpose of the call but it did seem to be malicious.

With water still limited the Lipizzaner horses were competing with my cows for the sparse grass. As the horses were not particularly productive economically, I was anxious to hear from Jesse, wherever he was, and ask him to take the horses away. Finally, I received a call from him. He told me that he was at the coast of Colombia and expected to be back in two weeks. He told me that I should supply the horses with supplementary feed for which he would repay me when he got back.

That call relieved me substantially. A month later there was still with no sign of Jesse. I became anxious but I should not have been surprised. A month later I went to the consulate of the US to ask for the whereabouts of one Thomas McClendon. A member of the consulate staff that I was speaking to stepped out of the room, and returned with a large picture of Thomas McClendon. I was elated and asked how I can get touch with him but I was told that they could not give me the answer to that question. They denied me any further information.

The shroud of mystery continued. Since Jesse had been traveling through Colombia with his attaché bag that contained pictures of the horse and nothing else, I guessed that the attaché bag usually contained good old American greenbacks. He was probably trading for popular items, like drugs, and we all know what avenues of danger that can lead a person. With the lack of security and the nature of the drug trade, who knows what could have happened. He may have had to pay with his life for one of his deals.

About that time, I had visitors on my farm in La Calera. A young couple arrived and they identified themselves as friends of the missing Jesse. They said they had spent time with Jesse and the horses on a farm in La Florida, Colombia. The young lady said her name was Kathy Ergle and that the young man was her boyfriend, born in Ecuador. She said they loved the horses and asked if I would mind giving them permission to visit the horses from time to time. I agreed. They visited my farm several times over the next few weeks. On one of the visits, they brought a large sack of carrots which the horses ate. They did bring some other food from time to time. Once, the boyfriend turned his back on the younger Lipizzaner horse which promptly tried to bite him on the shoulder. He was unharmed but his shirt was torn.

One day, Kathy Ergle and her boyfriend arrived at my home. She showed some papers from the Colombian Customs office which stated that the horses had originally been shipped from Thomas McClendon, in Florida, to Kathy Ergle, in Bogotá. She explained that, since the horses were considered perishable and had to be fed, they were released to the shipper Thomas McClendon, for a nominal sum of something like twenty-five dollars, before they were appraised by Customs for their true value. Now the customs people had located her as the intended receiver and wanted a settlement based on the true value of the coveted horses.

While I was not unhappy with the idea that the horses would be taken off my hands, I felt there had to be some repayment for the feed and services that I had provided. In addition, I understood that I had the responsibility to care for the horses until the rightful owner showed up. I needed assurance that I was doing the correct thing. I asked her to meet me at the office of my lawyer, David Rosental Rosental, the following day.

The plot thickens. The next day, they met me at my attorney's office. He looked over the paperwork. He commented that the horses had been left with me by their original owner, Thomas McClendon, and so, under

Colombian law, I had a grave responsibility not to release them without the rightful owner's explicit permission. Given the present situation with the custom papers in hand, he could prepare an agreement for both of us to sign. It would assure that I would get reimbursed for their care up to the date that the horses were turned over to her.

In addition, if and when Thomas McClendon reappears, she must turn them over to him unless she can prove ownership. She agreed. David Rosental Rosental started a handwritten agreement. He noted the spelling of her name and asked for her cédula number. This is issued to all legal residents of Colombia. She said that she doesn't have a cédula, and is in Colombia on a US passport with a tourist visa which she showed to him.

Complications continued when, upon checking out the visa, he noted it had expired. He stated that, in Colombia, it is strictly prohibited to enter into a contract with an illegal alien. He told her to return to the office when she gets her papers straightened out. She became furious with that edict but agreed to return with the correct papers. As she and the boyfriend stormed out, she turned to him and said something to the effect that they should have engaged their own attorney right away as had been recommended.

I didn't hear from her for many months after that. I never heard from Thomas McClendon ever again. I assumed that he had met his end by foul play. Recently, my son, Howard, told me that Jesse was alive and lived in Florida.

P Waves, Q Waves, T Waves & More

Prior to the end of the second year, I had met the Israeli Ambassador to Colombia at a party in his residence. I asked him about opportunities to spend a month at the famous Hadassah Hospital in Jerusalem. He recommended that I visit the Israeli Consulate in the center of Bogotá. I went there at my first opportunity and found that the Consulate was located on an upper floor in a tall office building. The heavily fortified entrance was on the floor below the consulate and the communication was by intercom. There was a lockbox which was opened up remotely for me to store my gun, and to be picked up later when I left.

All of these precautions were necessitated by a major attack on the Israeli embassy in London in 1972. There had been many similar attacks or threats over the years.

On entering, I applied for permission to work with Israeli doctors at the Hadassah Hospital. It was granted soon thereafter. I prepared for the trip, which I would make alone as Etta had commitments at the synagogue. She was also kept busy with my Ham radio setup as the auxiliary radio operator.

The Hadassah Hospital was in a suburb of Jerusalem called Ein Kerem and I was assigned to an internal medicine ward called, pneemy dalid in Hebrew. That ward was selected for me as I knew only a few words or expressions in Hebrew. English was spoken on that ward more often than on the others. I was placed under the direction of the medical residents attached to that ward. They were proud of their knowledge in the medical field and I was impressed by the elaborate progress reports that they wrote in Hebrew from right to left. When they entered a word in English like penicillin, however, they did most of the sentence in Hebrew. When they reached the English word they still approached it from the right, skipped over an adequate space, and entered penicillin from left to right. They then skipped over the English word and resumed the right to left script in Hebrew.

I was assigned to a small dormitory room for sleeping quarters. It was used by medical students of the Hebrew University. The Hebrew University Medical School was located in a building next to the Hadassah Hospital. It was unusual to have vacancies in the dormitory but the empty rooms had been assigned to the Muslim students. They had gone out on strike. When their demands were not recognized, they went home.

I found the small room comfortable and clean. After the hours of working at the Hadassah Hospital, it felt great to relax and study my own medical texts. I also tried to learn some Hebrew so that I could interface with the patients better. That turned out to be useless since the patients spoke all different kinds of languages. The predominant languages were English, Hebrew, Arabic, and Yiddish. Of course, I spoke English and a little Yiddish, which my parents had used when I was young. My parents had used Yiddish between themselves so that we would not understand something personal that they did not want to share with us.

One Friday, which was a day that our work ended early, I had supper at the hospital cafeteria and went to my room to study. There was a knock on the door and when I opened it there was a young man standing there. He queried if I was going to be there during the weekend. I said I would be there all weekend. He asked me if I would mind doing guard duty as he had some pressing engagement in a different part of Israel. It sounded interesting so I agreed. He said he would bring his gun. I told him he would have to teach me how to use it. He looked quite disappointed saying he couldn't teach me and that I needed to have prior training. That ended that. There would be no guard duty. I went back to my studying.

Every day I would have a big breakfast in the hospital cafeteria. I would arrive on the ward just as the medical residents were starting their rounds, visiting their patients for bedside discussions. I was assigned to the scut work, which I started as the staff began their rounds. This consisted of checking the urine specimens for those patients that were ordered to fill a specimen jar. It involved dipping a plastic strip into urine specimen, with various bands of colors to be matched against color bands on the outside of the metal case of the urine strips. I also had to draw blood for testing which I inspected under the microscope.

The drawing of the blood at the Hadassah Hospital was different from the same process in US hospitals. In the Hadassah Hospital, ordinary sterilized hypodermic syringes and needles were used instead of the vacutainers in the US. I had to go to the patient's room with the hypodermic syringe and needle, clean the site with an alcohol pad, wrap a rubber tourniquet band tightly around the upper arm, find the best vein, and draw the blood. Often, we ran out of smaller syringes.

We had to use 60 ml syringes which are awfully big. I would have to approach the patient with my hand holding the syringe behind my back. They would try to look behind me but I would turn my body to make that difficult. If they saw the great big syringe, they would turn pale. It worried me they might faint. It never happened.

After my blood and urine work were done, I scurried after the residents on their rounds. They obliged me by speaking English wherever possible. It was rare that I could offer much to the conversation as I had only finished my second year, which was half of the academic curriculum of the Juan N. Corpas. Once a week, we met with our attending physicians to discuss our cases. As I was assigned some simple cases, I would be caught up in the attending physician's interrogation. At one such interrogation, the chief attending physician asked me, in English, why my patient was in so much pain. I answered that I believed that he suffered from osteoarthritis. He asked me on what did I base that diagnosis. My reply was that his fingers were deformed with Heberden's and Bouchard's nodes. He turned to the chief resident in my group and asked in Hebrew, "Mah nee shmah Bouchard's?" I understood those few words which stood for, "What does Bouchard's mean?" The chief resident explained that Bouchard's nodes were a different form of Heberden's nodes. The chief attending physician nodded in satisfaction. He learned something - and from a medical student no less.

Another discussion that the residents engaged in about a particular patient was in reading his EKG (Electrocardiogram). The electrical pulsations of the patient's heart begin with a tiny upward blip on the baseline. That is the trigger and is called the 'p' wave. It starts in the upper regions of the heart. That 'p' wave starts an electrical shock wave that travels to the big chambers of the heart below. It starts a powerful contraction that pushes the blood into the circulation. The EKG displays the powerful pulsation first as a tiny upside down blip, or the 'q' wave, a short distance to the right of the p wave.

This is followed immediately by the big 'r' wave which is all above the baseline. As the 'r' wave dies out, there is a tiny upside down 's' wave. The last three waves form the 'qrs' complex. When the heart resets itself a while later, there is a rounded upright wave called the 't' wave. Then the heart waits for the next 'p' wave trigger.

Two examples of the diagnostic value of the EKG follow:

1. If the 'p' wave is absent, the qrs wave pulses irregularly – this is called fibrillation.
2. If the 'q' wave is deep and wide, this often indicates a heart attack or myocardial infarction.

In the EKG of the particular patient above, the 'p' wave drifted along the baseline sometimes close to and sometimes far away from the 'qrs' complex. The residents called that dissociation, meaning that the 'p' wave trigger was appearing every beat of the heart, but it was not setting off the big 'qrs' pulse, which was beating slowly on its own. I told the residents that it was not dissociation but that there was a weak coupling between the 'p' and 'qrs' waves and, consequently, the 'p' wave was hunting for its target, the 'qrs.' That opinion came from my experience as an electrical engineer.

They laughed at the opinion of a second-year medical student, until we took several questionable EKGs to the EKG specialist. He looked at my patient's EKG and announced that there was retrograde coupling, around the back of the heart. The residents look at me with surprise. I just smiled at them.

My assistant chief attending physician was also the 'Chief Flight Surgeon of Israel.' We got along well together as we were about the same age. One day, he asked me to do him a favor. As the chief flight surgeon, he had duties which took him away from the hospital. That day, he had to fly to an important military meeting. He would not be able to return in time for him to stay at the hospital overnight since he was scheduled to be on call for the entire night. He told me that I had a mature judgment. Would I be willing to be on call for my wing of the hospital all that night? I agreed and it worked out well. In retrospect, I was on call overnight with full responsibility for a large chunk of the world-famous Hadassah Hospital with two years of medical school under my belt.

My assistant chief attending physician took me along a few times when he visited some distant clinics of Israel's socialized medicine. One time, we had a call from a clinic on the West Bank which was run by a female doctor who had emigrated from the Soviet Union. When we arrived, there was a Rabbi waiting to be examined by a visiting male doctor. His religious principles forbade him to be touched by a woman. As my assistant chief prepared to examine him, the female doctor rushed in and asked him to see a case that needed immediate care. I was left with the Rabbi and I conferred with him in Yiddish, which I learned from my parents. He was short and heavy and had a history of poorly controlled diabetes. He told me that he was not worried at all about his health and that he was in God's hands. Whenever God wanted him, he was ready to go to him. He said that his family coerced him go to the clinic. That is why he was there. His health was not important to him anyway. I was examining his throat and then his ears during his monologue. As I finished these two areas, he turned to me and asked if I found anything wrong. I told him that I hadn't, at least not yet. This was repeated after I checked his heart and lungs. Around then my Chief returned and I passed the buck to him.

As my month's stay was running down, I had discussed amateur radio with my assistant chief who was a Ham as well. He invited me to come to his home that Saturday morning since he would not be on duty. I showed up early and anxious. He showed me how to use his Ham equipment and I got busy listening for and trying to establish a contact by calling, CQ, CQ repeatedly, but without success.

I calculated the time of day in Bogotá and it turned out to be early evening which was the time when Etta used to have a scheduled appointment to call a friend in Long Island. At the correct time, I heard Etta calling, "W2XYZ, here is W2KEE Portable HK3 calling." I blurted out after pressing the microphone switch, "Break, Break – Here is your husband." She was pleasantly surprised and we three Hams got busy talking.

The next Monday I told the medical residents that this would be my last week with them. They shouted, "What do you mean? Who is going to do the work?" They invited me to come back whenever I liked. I wished them all good luck in their careers. We parted sadly and with deep respect for each other.

Third Year of Medical School & WHO Approval

As we entered the third year of medical school, I became concerned with the fact that we were not an approved school yet. I had been learning that it was getting more difficult for the foreign graduates to be accepted into medical programs for their residency in the US. Since my third year began in February, and the American schools went on vacation in July, I decided to see if I couldn't transfer to an American medical school. I hired a typist that could handle English and we put together a package. It showed me to be at the top of my medical class for the last two years and my 'Magna Cum Laude' diploma from the Polytechnic Institute of Brooklyn. We sent these packages out to many of the medical schools and there was one positive response. Penn State University, Hershey, said that they would be delighted to admit me into their third year medical school program. They admit only if there was at least one vacationing student who did not show up after their vacation ended in August. However, it turned out that all of their students returned from vacation. This was unusual. I would not be transferring to the University of Pennsylvania. I was disappointed but, on the other hand, I would have been set back by one whole semester. I looked much harder into the situation with my own school.

We all had expected that by now the Juan N. Corpas would have been approved by the government. Our school was not even listed by the World Health Organization (WHO) yet. I decided to see if I couldn't help out in that matter. I did some checking and learned that the World Health Organization had an office in Bogotá. At the first opportunity, I headed over to that office and got some startling news. The last WHO sealed Courier dispatch, which could get to the Secretariat before it convened in May, would have to reach their offices in Bogotá within the next two days. I was supplied by the Bogotá office with the necessary application and schedule of the basic requirements. I rushed back to the school and the Rector assigned several helpers from the administration to help me in the huge task. We had to count all of the books in the library and record its resources, including a full history of the school, to the World Health Organization.

We were finished by the afternoon of the second day. I rushed over to the offices of the Minister of Education whom I had met earlier. I explained what I had to do. He had agreed to cooperate by applying his signature to the document. He was not there when I got to his office however, and time was short. I waited in his busy office and he arrived within the hour. I begged for an immediate audience with him and the kindly secretary helped by ushering me in. He seemed annoyed but signed the documents. I left him with one copy and rushed the original signed application, with the Minister's governmental seal, to the Bogotá offices of the WHO. It made the last Courier dispatch. It got to the Geneva secretariat of the WHO in sufficient time to be approved and listed in that year's published record of the world's medical schools where it has appeared ever since.

The WHO listing was the last requirement that the Colombian government Ministry of Education needed to grant approval to the Escuela de Medicina Juan N. Corpas to grant degrees of Doctor of Medicine to its graduates. The approval came through quietly but was warmly welcomed.

Success at the IUPS Conference

My school received a brochure from the Javeriana describing an interesting meeting sponsored by the International Union of Physiological Sciences (IUPS). Physiology is the science of how the body's circuits work - the science behind the functioning of human systems. This includes how the components of the human body do their job and how they interact.

This proved interesting to me as I was trained in electronic circuitry, which had its parallels in the organic systems of the human body. In electronic system design, there is a powerful use of negative feedback circuitry, which makes the system more dependable and stable. In my medical studies, I noticed the body using negative feedback extensively. The reason it is called negative feedback is that a small amount of the output of a system is connected back to the input of the system in such a way as to subtract from the input. Done that way, an amplifier of sound using negative feedback reduces any distortion by the amplifier itself.

A crude example of negative feedback is the steering system of a car. The driver thinks that he feels the effort of turning the wheels as he turns the steering wheel but he doesn't realize that a powerful hydraulic pump is doing the pushing with a feedback system giving him the feeling of resistance as he turns the steering wheel. It is calibrated to give him precise control. Imagine if all the driver had was a switch that he snapped to the right or left.

In the human system, the thyroid gland is the thermostat of the body. It maintains the body temperature at the normal level that we are used to unless the person is ill. The thyroid gland produces thyroid enzymes which stimulate the energy production of the body depending on the amount of enzymes released from little packages in the gland. The brain picks up signals from all over the body and uses those signals to control the release of a thyroid stimulating hormone, TSH. TSH is a sensitive liberator of the thyroid enzymes. Specifically, this is an example of a control system.

I made a few telephone calls to the Javeriana to find out who was in charge of the conference. When I connected with the professor, I arranged an appointment and met the professor. He looked at my paper work and my resume. He asked what I was looking for. I explained that I wanted to give a talk on Feedback Systems in Human Physiology. He told me that this was an international conference with famous speakers from all over the world and not a third year medical student's hobby.

I explained that the material was novel and new, that I had founded a successful company that used those principles, and that company was still in existence in the US with national and international customers.

With some reluctance, he granted my request to deliver a paper at the conference. My slot was at the end of one day, after dark. I assumed that the reason for the poor time slot was that I was a third year medical student at an upstart medical school no less. Oh well. I was somewhat disappointed but my reward came. My talk was very well attended and very well received. The applause was strong.

XII Congreso Latinoamericano de Ciencias Fisiológicas
Reunión Regional de la
INTERNATIONAL UNION OF PHYSIOLOGICAL SCIENCES
X *Congreso de la Asociación Colombiana de Ciencias Biológicas*
9 - 15 Noviembre/75

During this third year, Leslie needed to have her educational visa renewed. According to Colombian law, every second year the foreigner has to leave the country. Upon reentry, the renewal is stamped into the foreigner's passport. Since I left Columbia during my vacations and flew back in, my renewal was automatic. Thank goodness for small favors. One less thing to worry about.

In Leslie's case, she left the country traveling by air to Cúcuta, which is at the border of Colombia and connected by a small bridge to Venezuela. Upon crossing the bridge, and then walking back across the bridge, she had her passport stamped by Venezuelan and Colombian immigration. That was the typical route taken by the majority of foreigners and it satisfied the Colombian law for renewal of visas.

I knew that Leslie was leaving that morning but I did not expect the phone call she made to me late that afternoon. She called me at home in Chico Norte, crying. She explained that she had a pleasant trip to Cúcuta and then crossed the bridge to Venezuela. After she crossed back to Cúcuta and had her passport stamped, she headed for the airport. To her dismay, there was a notice that the plane to Bogotá was delayed. To make matters worse, it was heavily overbooked. She was calling from the pay telephone at the airport waiting room and described a big mob of people circling around and taking turns at using the pay telephone. The airport manager was a big gorilla type and he showed no compassion for the plight of his passengers. She pleaded with me to help her in any way I could. I told her I'll see what I could do.

I recalled that Libardo had been a junior executive at Avianca Airlines, the national carrier. By telephone, I reached the Avianca offices in Bogotá and explained to a nice lady the predicament that my daughter was in. She actually agreed to help me for which I thanked her profusely. An hour later, I got a call from Leslie at the airport in Cúcuta. She said that when she was in the mob that was circling, the gorilla type manager came out of his office munching on a banana, scanned the mob until he found her, and told her to come with him to the gate, and that she was leaving on the next plane trip that was due in right away. Her relief brought tears to my eyes.

There was a similar episode that Leslie handled by herself on the same kind of trip out of the country for renewal of her student visa. She had arranged a trip to Panama and made a hotel reservation overnight in Panama City. Her problem presented itself when she made an international phone call via the hotel operator to her friend in Bogotá. She kept it brief and hung up after a few minutes. When she checked out in the morning, she was staggered to find telephone charges of over a thousand dollars. It turned out that she was supposed to have the hotel operator close the call when the conversation was over. As usual, she just hung up. The charges had continued all through the night. Leslie finally had the bright idea of reversing charges to her phone number in Colombia. Once home, she was able to straighten out the matter with her local telephone company. Whew.

Profesor De La Javeriana

In my third year of the Juan N Corpas, I reviewed where I stood in my life goals. I was generally satisfied but there was one promise that I had made that I had not moved on at all.

When I decided to move out of electrical engineering into medicine, I had the vague idea that my engineering training would somehow help my medical career. Years later, I was slowly forgetting my engineering and mathematics. The insights that I had developed which led to the modest successes in design and development of my products were all a satisfying part of my life.

One of my concepts, in my move to Colombia, was that I would teach the Colombians what I knew in the engineering field with the goal of advancing their knowledge base. That profession had created a decent living for me and my family, as well as for my employees. I went to the engineering department of the Javeriana University where my daughter, Leslie, was studying medicine. I met with the engineering department chief and offered to teach on a part-time basis. He was delighted and added that I would be given the title of professor (profesor) of electrical engineering. My class would meet twice a week in the evening, and so would not interfere with my medical studies. I was even given a salary of 10,000 pesos a month (about $200).

At my first few classes, I had to learn the translation of basic words such as volts and amperes into Spanish. I also had to explore the students' knowledge of the concepts of differential equations, as well as pole/zero diagrams. All of this seemed to go well until I gave my first exam.

I arrived in class with the exam papers and noticed something strange. The students had seated themselves toward the back of the room. I guessed that the purpose was to make it easy to copy answers from each other. I went to the last row of seats in the classroom and sat down. Marking the papers at home was quite disappointing as I expected. One week later, I handed out the papers and sat down in the teacher's seat at the front of the room. With practiced ease, the students all jumped up into single file to appeal their poor grades. It was obvious that they were not going to gain a lot of knowledge from my efforts as they were poor at the basics. Somehow, no student dropped the course nor fell asleep in class, even though it ended at 10 p.m.

During the semester, I was invited for an afternoon meeting of the engineering professors (un coctel). Snacks and alcoholic beverages were plentiful. I learned that the purpose of the coctel was to select a representative from our department to send to a retreat of the Javeriana faculty in the Hot Country. The mood was jovial – even giddy, as the first vote took place and ended in a draw. There was lots of laughter as a new slate of nominees was set up on the blackboard. I wasn't paying a lot of attention but all of a sudden there was a burst of applause for the winner – me.

We were driven to the 'Hot Country' ('Tierra Caliente') by autobus over a weekend. We were addressed by the dignitaries of the Javeriana, with some invocation of religious beliefs by the Padres (Fathers) and various suggestions by the professorate. I don't recall if I contributed much but I was treated courteously - like one of the boys.

After about six months of teaching at the Javeriana, I received a demand notice from DAS (Departmento Administrativo de Seguridad), a much feared agency of the police, to report to a Colonel of DAS. DAS had been informed that I was working and receiving pay despite the fact that I was a resident of Colombia with only a student visa.

I met with the Colonel at his office at the El Dorado International Airport. He informed me that I was working illegally and would have to surrender my earnings to that date. I pointed out that my purpose in teaching was to advance the knowledge of the Colombian students and that I was passing on valuable information. He responded that he would allow me to keep half of my earnings and advised me, not too harshly, that I was getting a good deal. It was true. The full punishment could be zero pay and a prison sentence.

With that kind of threatening situation hanging over my head, I did not continue teaching at that Javeriana after the semester ended. I did write up a booklet, with the framework of my original talk at the Javeriana, called 'Feedback in Physiological Systems,' for use in their engineering department.

Fourth Year of Medical School & 'A difference of Opinion'

As the third year of my medical studies ended, I went back to the US during our year-end vacation. During the third year, I had attended an orthopedic conference at the Javeriana with an orthopedic professor of the Vanderbilt University, Tennessee, as the guest speaker. After his excellent talk, I struck up a conversation with him. As usual, I offered him communication with the US via my Ham radio at home. In those days, telephone communication between the US and Colombia was poor.

He gladly accepted. When he arrived at my house, I was successful in making a very good connection with a Nashville Ham who connected the professor to his family. After the connection, I chatted with him. He asked about the possibility of a brief externship during my vacation at year end. He said that he would be pleased to have me visit. I took him up on that offer. I travelled to Nashville when my third year classes ended.

The University's facilities were magnificent and the orthopedic department was a treasure. I was made to feel very welcome. The Professor took me under his wing and I had excellent exposure. At one point, he showed me an x-ray study of a young woman with Scoliosis, which is characterized by a curvature of the spine. This is usually measured by drawing two lines, one along the upper part of the curvature and the other along the lower part. Where the two lines cross, the angle that is formed is measured and compared to the same angle on prior, as well as later studies. The professor was amazed when I estimated the angle very accurately due to my engineering background. He recommended that I see him after I finished my fourth year of medical school in Colombia. I was grateful but I preferred family medicine to orthopedics.

On returning to Colombia, Jeffrey came to visit us in Bogotá. Despite the fact that he enjoyed his visits with us, he did not want to pursue a medical career as Leslie was doing. I was still undecided about whether I would stay in Colombia or go back to the US.

The Last Year at the Juan n. Corpas

The fourth year of medical school began with most of our work being done at the Police Clinic. This was a hospital for the police. DAS had its own hospital. We went back to the faculty from time to time for special classes, including Cardiology and ENT (Otorinolaringología). Aside from accepting responsibility for managing several individual patients for each student, we had to stay once or twice a week overnight which was considered being on-call. Those of us on-call were responsible for all of the patients in hospital. Our attending physicians, who were our teachers, only spent a few hours a day at the Police Clinic and the rest of the time at their own private practice or some government agency. The reason for so much activity was that the pay was limited. The quality of the attending doctors was quite variable. While most were well trained and enjoyed teaching the medical students, others were a disappointment.

As an example, we were given a quarterly exam by two professors. They sat at the front of the room behind a large desk while the examinees sat facing them. The professor that was the head of the department of gastroenterology was questioning me and he asked me about the blood circulation of the colon. I was confident that I answered correctly but he denied that my answer was correct. While we debated the answer, the other professor, who was silent, stood up and walked behind me to the back of the room. I noticed that my questioner looked over my shoulder to where his colleague must have been standing. He dropped his denial and announced that there was a difference of opinion among experts to the correct answer. We were both correct. To me it was obvious that the professor behind me had motioned to my questioner that I was correct. I thought his handling of my case was petty. As a surgeon, he should have known the right answer.

Later on, I was assisting in orthopedic surgery. The orthopedic surgeon asked me how the Escuela de Medicina was doing. I said it was doing well and had finally gotten its governmental stamp of approval.

He said that he had wanted his niece to apply, and he was encouraged by the fact that a generous donor had given the school a four-million-dollar gift. I said that was news to me. I asked for details about the donor. The orthopedic surgeon said that he didn't know the details except that the donor was an engineer. He was talking about me. In regards to the four-million-dollar gift, things have of a way of getting exaggerated quickly in Colombia.

In another example, as part of the final exam, a different professor went into a short discourse about a disease affecting the colon named after an American surgeon. I didn't remember that this disease was called Crohn's disease. He started to drill me intensively and punitively. The other two professors at the exam asked him to stop the punishment as he was asking for something beyond the scope of a medical student. He backed away. Later, I heard a rumor that that the professor had a special relationship with one of the female students in my class. Since I was at the top of the class, he was trying to even up our relative standings. In his defense, I should have known the right answer.

During one of my nights on-call, I went to the emergency room to see if I could help out. The evening staff of the emergency room had gone off duty but the next shift had not arrived yet. I was the only one caring for the patients. For a while, everything was peaceful and quiet. Suddenly there were sirens and roaring motors outside. Wounded people were being helped inside by their colleagues, some gravely injured.

I checked a few cases while calling for the staff to get the surgeons, STAT (immediately). The next patient I looked at had a bullet wound in his ear. Miraculously, the bullet had exited behind the ear. Fortunately, the senior staff and surgeons arrived around that time. The story unfolded that someone had called the police and DAS separately, that there would be a drug delivery at a certain location and a certain time. Forces from both sides arrived at the same time, and since they were not in uniform, there was no recognition that they were on the same side of the law. There was a big shootout at close range. The most severely wounded was a female operative of DAS who was hit in the back by a bullet that entered her abdomen. Since she was from DAS and we were from the police clinic, the solution was to send her to the DAS hospital by ambulance.

In general, we were seeing lots of serious cases and learning where the rubber meets the road. As an example of how we learned, another student and I were working with a pediatrician who was a favorite of ours for being knowledgeable and also patient with us. We came to the crib of a newborn baby and the pediatrician asked us to check over the baby and report to him. We checked heart, lungs, and limbs, and then reported that the baby was fine. His reply was, "Mal Hecho!" ("Badly done!") He turned the baby over. At the center of the baby's lower back, there was a mass of nerve tissue projecting from the spinal column. Later, I looked up the condition of spina bifida in the books. In rare cases the spinal column of the fetus does not completely close up all the way down. That leaves an opening from which the spinal cord could bulge out. The spinal cord, instead of continuing into the pelvis and lower extremities, formed that big bulging mass which has to be cut away. After, there is no control over the lower extremities, genitalia, and urination.

As a break from the routine, our school was preparing a party at our faculty for professors, students, administrators, and the directors of competing schools. We received word at the police clinic that the administrators of our school would like to invite the police officials to the party. We formed a committee of the few students at the police clinic to visit the police headquarters and invite the officers and directors to our party. I was invited to join my fellow students for the visit to the police headquarters.

One afternoon, we visited the heads of the various departments of the police. I was interested in noting that each office had its titles incorporated into a series of initials which were abbreviations of their official functions. We received a mixture of acceptances and refusals but we felt that it was going well. That is until we passed one doorway at which point I began to laugh since the initials were RAPED. It was probably abbreviated for something like Rama Administrativa Policial Emergencia Division. The English equivalent is easy to figure out if it is understood that "rama" means "department."

My classmates were surprised by my laughing but I made light of it. I told them that RAPED reminded me of something in English.

Lipizzaner Horses, III

Our schedule for the on-call nights began in the morning. Since we were not able to catch much sleep that night, we were allowed to go home after morning rounds. Arriving home in the morning saved me from quite a disaster.

After being on-call one Wednesday night, I arrived home late in the morning and found a telegram waiting for me on my foyer table. It had been sent from downtown Bogotá on the prior Monday. In just a few lines, it changed my life. It stated that I was to appear by 3 p.m. that same day at the offices of a judge in downtown Bogotá or an order for my arrest would follow. An address was given with no telephone number and there was no mention of the nature of the complaint. I placed a telephone call to my attorney, David Rosental Rosental. He told me that he could not represent me at the Judge's offices since this was a criminal matter and he was not practicing criminal law. He recommended another attorney, however, one who we will call Valdavieso.

My panic picked up steam as I realized that we were almost at the siesta time when all work stops and a large lunch is followed by a nap. I called Valdvieso and was fortunate to find him in. By now it was after 1 p.m. and I told him about the matter and asked him to meet me at the judge's office. Not knowing the ropes of such proceedings, I also mentioned that I don't see how I could make it by 3 p.m. He told me that there was an Hora Judicial (an hour of grace) and I just had to get there before 4 p.m.

I got into my Renault 6 to head downtown. It was the worst traffic I had ever seen. The time zoomed by but I was traveling at a snail's pace. At one point in my trip, I considered leaving my car in traffic and running the rest of the way. I got there about 3:45 p.m. The judge's offices were on the second floor so I didn't take the elevator but climbed the stairs. I had to stay to the left on the stairs. The right side was occupied by a long line of young men. They were all handcuffed together in a long line, reaching from the street level to the second floor, with a few guards watching over them.

Once in the judge's office, I passed an industrial steel rack containing numerous packages of paper wrapped with string. Many of them had a piece of paper pasted to the outside with a hand written statement, "Hay preso," which translates to, "There is a prisoner." My lawyer appeared shortly thereafter. I got the feeling that this had to do with the horses on my farm in La Calera. I reviewed what had transpired after the horses were delivered to the farm by Jesse (Thomas McClendon). About a year had passed since the meeting with Kathy Ergle and her boyfriend in the attorney's office. She had never shown up with her correct papers. I had accidently run across the boyfriend outside of a bakery a few months prior. I asked him what happened to Kathy and her papers. He replied that she had her papers and they would get in touch with me shortly.

I was told to sit down in a chair next to a secretary seated in front of a typewriter. The judge whispered questions in her ear and she repeated them to me while typing the questions and my answers. After questions involving my name and cédula number, I was asked if I had the two Lipizzaner horses on my farm to which I answered in the affirmative. I was asked how much money I had received for their services. I replied that I had billed 50,000 pesos (about $100) and collected 25,000 pesos (about $50). In my fright, I had an uncontrollable urge to urinate so I asked for permission to go to a bathroom. I was given permission to go to the bathroom which was down the same set of stairs with the same long chain gang of prisoners. I considered running out of the building. Dutifully, I went back upstairs.

There wasn't much more questioning and I waited for the next step which was to determine which prison I would go to. At that point, Valdavieso bargained with the judge. He made the deal that I would not have to go to El Modelo prison, about which I heard horror stories, but I would have to sign the judge's registry each weekday. This was not very difficult as I spent my weekdays at the Police Clinic which was not far away.

So I visited the judge's office every weekday, chatted with him, to which he responded in a kindly manner. When he showed me some of his family pictures, I commented on the poor quality of the processing. I offered to send them to the US for processing. He accepted and I sent his films out several times. I realized that if the case went against me, our newly-formed friendship would not count for many brownie points. The weekday signing of the judge's registry was soon eased to every other weekday. Finally, it was lifted entirely.

This balmy situation was ended when I received a telephone call from the attorney for Kathy Ergle. He wanted to meet with me at my home the next day. I agreed and the next morning he showed up with Kathy Ergle. I had called my attorney, Valdevieso, the night before and asked him to join the meeting. He showed up just before the others arrived. The other Attorney stated that the court had granted him custody of the two Lipizzaner horses and he planned to pick them up today. I looked at Valdevieso. He theatrically turned to face the wall, extended both hands to lean against it, and announced I would not be surrendering the horses.

I stared at him. He repeated the same decision. The other attorney threatened my imprisonment by the afternoon. He stamped out of the room with Kathy Ergle in tow.

I looked at Valdevieso and asked him if he wanted me to drop him off downtown as he had no car. He agreed and I hustled him downtown. After I dropped him off, I drove immediately to the judge's office. I sat down alongside of him at his desk. I asked him if I had to give up the horses and he nodded. I said I would give up the horses since he said that I had to. Like something out of a Hollywood movie, the door to the Judge's office swung open and Kathy Ergle, with her Attorney, burst into the room. They stopped dead in their tracks as they saw me with the judge. I half smiled and told them the judge had told me to give up the horses, and asked what time they would be picking up the horses. The Attorney stammered that he would try to pick them up that afternoon. I'm sure that he didn't have transportation for them or a place to keep them. He arranged to pick up one of them two weeks later and the other horse about a month after that.

I shook the Judge's hand as I left and thanked him. I was glad to be rid of the horses even though they were worth many thousands of dollars each. I had no intention of getting deeper into that mess. I realized that I had a particularly close shave. If I had actually been arrested, I would never have been allowed to leave Colombia until the full case was resolved. What did become obvious to me was that I had better get out of Colombia as soon as possible. Which would be, by the end of the fourth year, now six months away.

I found out that the people that were trying to put me in prison so as to acquire the expensive horses, without having to pay me a feed bill, never wound up with the horses. The older horse died, so they said, and the people that were caring for the horse conveniently forgot where he was buried. The younger horse went to the Colombian Ambassador to Jamaica to be cared for and his children were enjoying the horse very much. He probably wound up with the title to the horse too.

Many years after I left Colombia, I learned that the case against me had continued and even reached the Colombian equivalent of the Supreme Court, the Tribunal (tree-BOON- al). My professors and Dr. Piñeros had to testify. The final decision exonerated me and included an order for the arrest of Kathy Ergle for trying to use the Colombian judicial system to obtain possession of the horses illegally.

Preparing To Leave

Although I had moved to Colombia to study medicine and I was now finishing the last semester of the academic part of my studies, the trauma of the Lipizzaner horses had pulled the rug from under me. I reviewed my life up to this date.

Years ago, when I considered moving to Colombia to study medicine, I believed that I had enough of a scientific background to benefit my new country. I was awakened to find that I could make very little impact. The people were warm and wonderful but I had to stay on the alert for petty and not so petty crime. In my four years in Colombia, I had lost a pair of eye glasses, a spare tire, some books, and notes - as well as several windshield wipers. A lawyer that had collected about $150, that I had loaned someone, soon took off with the money. I was never repaid. Etta had a tug of war with some gamines (roaming, homeless young boys) over a fine gold chain she was wearing. It turned out to be a tie between them - the chain broke but she held onto both sides. Leslie won her tug of war with a newspaper vendor who couldn't break the watch band of the Timex watch that she was wearing.

I carried my Smith and Wesson revolver even while driving to school and came close to needing its protection several times. Having had to use it would have changed my life for the worse.

The police and judicial system were the most frightening of all. During my residence in Colombia, I had heard many stories of incursions by the different agencies of the police or DAS. These incursions had sometimes resulting in the death of the person held. There was a law that, in the case of an accident or a crime, all people, including witnesses, are arrested and held until the case is sorted out.

I studied and read up on the possibilities that might be available to me if we moved back to the US. I had no diploma as yet. I was completing my fourth year of medical school. The Escuela de Medicina Juan N. Corpas required completion of four years of academia followed by two additional years of internship.

I had been following the course of the Fifth Pathway Program in the US. This required an additional year of medical training in a US school that honors the program, following completion of the usual four years training in a foreign country. If a medical student followed his or her four years of medical school abroad with an internship, that action would render the student ineligible for the Fifth Pathway Program.

That fitted perfectly. I wrote to all of the medical schools in the US that ran the Fifth Pathway Program. I enclosed a copy of the brochure of the Escuela de Medicina Juan N. Corpas showing that my program met their requirements. I also enclosed my CV which listed my licenses, work experience, and age. Two programs answered me showing interest in interviewing me.

One program was in Brooklyn, the very hospital in which Etta, and our daughter, were born. The other was at the University of California, Irvine Medical Center. Etta and I searched for a map that would give us the location of Irvine, California. All we had an atlas which showed the entire US on one page. According to that reference material, the state of California appeared one inch long on the map with the names of three of its cities printed over the Pacific Ocean close to its border – Los Angeles at the bottom, San Francisco at the top, and Irvine in the middle and further out over the ocean. We tried to judge whether Irvine was closer to Los Angeles or San Francisco, or dead center. It took a Ham radio phone call to the University Of California, Irvine, to tell us that Irvine was about 45 miles south of Los Angeles, which was great.

At my next break, I flew to the US and went to the Brooklyn program first. They were only mildly interested. I would have to wait out the results of a national examination that I would have to take next year. That was not very attractive. I had reached fifty-five years of age and worried that I would not have many years to practice.

I flew from JFK International Airport to LAX shortly after the interview and I rented a car. The rental was for one week. The only car they had for me was an older Ford Pinto. This was the mid-seventies and soon the Pinto would make headlines as being one of the most dangerous cars on the road. Its fuel tank was in the rear of the car, a combustible position for a fuel tank to be in. It was not much better than my Renault 6 in Colombia. I drove from LA to my hotel in Irvine, which had been reserved for me by the Secretary of the Fifth Pathway Program dean at the University of California.

Driving the Freeway south to Irvine, I was surprised that my speedometer showed that I was driving 80 mph. Most cars were passing me. I reasoned that the US roads were so much smoother than those in Colombia that it seemed to be a slower speed. I found out what the problem really was when I entered the driveway to the Irvine hotel. According to the speedometer reading I was going 70 mph. My Renault 6 didn't seem quite as junky after that discovery.

At my next interview, Jane King, the Secretary of Dr. Combs, the Dean of the Fifth Pathway Program of the University of California, Irvine, interviewed me. She introduced me to Dr. Combs, a kindly gentleman. I had communicated with Jane and she had been friendly and enthusiastic. I felt that I was among friends. I was told that I had one more hurdle to leap over, which was that I was to be interviewed by Dr. Thomas Nelson, the Assistant Dean of the Fifth Pathway Program and the Chairman of the Pediatric department.

I headed out of my hotel early the next morning and went to his office at the campus of the university. Both the campus and the medical center were magnificent. At the office of Dr. Thomas Nelson, I was put at ease as Dr. Nelson was about my age. He told me that he was born in Cartagena, Colombia, the son of missionaries. He was also a Ham radio operator. We had so much in common that it seemed like a sign from above. He told me that he had been fascinated by my career and had rooted for me with Dr. Combs.

I had to wait for their decision and it was positive. I was accepted for admission in January of next year, 1977, since the Escuela de Medicina Juan N. Corpas school year ended at year end, instead of July, for the American students. Since I was out of phase with the American medical school cycle, I would do my first six months in Pediatrics, before continuing to rotate through the different disciplines. The extended pediatric rotation was courtesy of Dr. Nelson.

As I was finishing up with the Police Clinic, and getting my affairs in order for the big move, I still touched base periodically with Dr. Combs and Jane King. At one of the Ham radio contacts, Dr. Combs asked me a serious question:

"Sam, the State of California is giving us $15,000 for your education in the Fifth Pathway Program. Do you intend to transfer back to the New York area upon completion? It would be very embarrassing to us."

It took me about three seconds to reply that I had always dreamed of moving to California and I had no intention of moving back East. Unlike the thousands upon thousands of immigrants a century or so before me, I was finally going West. (Go West young man.)

I was left with one difficult task that I had to face. I needed a diploma from the Escuela de Medicina Juan N. Corpas, or some document that would satisfy the state of California and the University of California, Irvine. This took a lot of thought. I came up with the idea of a document, in English, that acknowledged my completion of the four academic years of the Escuela de Medicina Juan N. Corpas program of medicine, but not the two years of internship required for their diploma. This would match the Fifth Pathway Program Preamble requirements. Any prior internship training makes the applicant ineligible for the program.

I typed it all up and presented it to Dr. Piñeros while telling him that circumstances have forced me to return to the US. He understood English well and signed it without hesitation. He recommended that I take it to the Notary Public in Bogotá, where his signature is on file, for applying his seal and verifying his signature to make it a legal document. I did so and sent a copy to Dr. Combs. It was accepted immediately by the University of California, Irvine, and the State of California. I realized that students from the South American and Mexican medical schools are required to complete a certain number of academic years, typically four to six years. They then enter a rural year (año rural) before receiving their diplomas. Those students, who wanted to avoid the año rural, since it is often served in the jungle, would need some version of a document like mine to enter the Fifth Pathway Program. That signifies that my document, bypassing the years after the academic part of the curriculum, is a fairly common requirement for those medical students planning to enroll in the program.

ESCUELA DE MEDICINA - JUAN N. CORPAS
(EN FUNDACION)
SUBA, D. E. Avenida a Flores de los Andes
Teléfono 54 56 12

TO WHOM IT MAY CONCERN

With this letter, I hereby certify that Samuel E. Gendler, bearer of Cédula No. 151963 of Bogotá has completed the 4 year sequence of the program of medical studies of the Escuela de Medicina Juan N. Corpas with excellent grades. This sequence completes the formal academic or didactic requirements of the curriculum up to the internship.

In accordance with Colombian law and the charter of our faculty, a diploma of "Doctor of Medicina and Surgery" is granted only upon satisfactory completion of the next 2 years of internship.

ESCUELA DE MEDICINA JUAN N. CORPAS

Dr. JORGE PIÑEROS CORPAS
Decano

DILIGENCIA DE AUTENTICACION

Bogotá, D. E. Diciembre 16, 1.976

16 DIC. 1976

(Copy of Document of Completion of 4 Academic Years of Escuela de Medicina Juan N. Corpas)

My son, Howard, had returned to Bogotá after his wife and new-born son had settled in Eugene, Oregon. In a family conference, we decided that I would travel back to Orange County, California, alone at year end. Etta and Howard would remain in Bogotá until the house and farm were sold. Meanwhile, we would start packing and shipping our household goods to be stored at the home of our friends, Bernie and Roslyn Gold who stilled lived on Long Island.

Part III

Back Home To Roost

It was December, 1976. I had flown from Bogotá to Miami, and then on to Los Angeles. I had left behind four years of medical school, my wife, daughter, son, house, and farm, as well as our parrot, Arturo, and our cat, Smoky, or Esmoki as she was sometimes called. (In Spanish, Smoky was called Esmoki as all words that would normally begin with 'S' need an 'E' at the beginning to adapt to the Spanish pronunciation.)

Upon my arrival in Los Angeles, I rented a small apartment in Garden Grove, California, about one mile from the University of California Medical Center. After that, I got busy with setting up my life in my home country.

Buying and erecting my Ham antenna was a bit of a problem. It was important since the long distance telephone circuitry between the US and Colombia was still primitive. I wanted to be able to help Etta make decisions about the sale of the house, farm, and furniture, as well as the things she had to do to exit Colombia. Howard was there to help her pack and do any necessary heavy work, as well as getting the paperwork. These included exit visas, shipping papers for personal items, and even permission for Arturo the parrot to leave Colombia.

The manager of my apartment complex was friendly. I asked him to permit me to mount the antenna support that I would need for my Ham radio in a spot where a tree had been dug out. He was uneasy about it but agreed that it was okay, just as long as I didn't put up an elaborate massive antenna on a tall pole. I was careful to limit the size and use little power for the transmitter, which otherwise might interfere with neighboring TV sets. It worked well. When the area supervisor of the property came by he was upset with its presence on the property. The manager told him that he had given me his permission and that was that.

While I was taking care of the home fires here in the US, it took Etta and Howard about two months to close out our affairs in Colombia. The house, which had cost us about $49,000, was sold for about $10,000 more than that sum. If we had waited several years to sell, houses and real estate became a far more attractive investment, like drug money. The estimated sale price then would have been about $300,000. The value of the house was its location. Perhaps it was the sign of the times, but it was later torn down. A high rise was built in its place and each floor rented or sold like condominiums. In Colombia, that kind of structure bears the name "propiedad horizontal" (horizontal property).

As for the farm, I had paid $28,000 for it. It sold for about $60,000. Years later, the real estate boom would have driven the price up into the million-dollar range due to its large, 85 fanegada size (about 134 acres), and its proximity to Bogotá. Like the house, it too would have been reinvented and split up into numerous lots.

Leaving our properties in Colombia, while we all lived in the US, was not a good option. Renters were entitled to seek title to the property after a number of years of absentee ownership by their landlords.

Our pets were not to be reinvented however, just relocated. About two months after I left for the US, Etta arrived with Smoky and Arturo in hand. Arturo had to be quarantined for sixty days at the LA airport, otherwise known as LAX. This quarantine is mandatory to prevent an epidemic of Exotic Newcastle Disease, which can infect poultry and other birds. We worried about him surviving but he did. He looked cared for. His feathers looked shiny. He was happy to see us and we were delighted to see him. Etta thought that the apartment was comfortable and clean. It would be satisfactory until we bought a house.

During the day we placed Arturo in his cage out on our tiny patio and surrounded by a concrete block wall. When he got accustomed to his surroundings he became noisy at times, screaming out his limited vocabulary. Nobody complained to us directly. What we didn't realize was that a nearby neighbor slept during the day since he had a night job. He let us know that he was annoyed by recording Arturo's squawking and playing it back to us from his patio at night. He made his point. We kept Arturo indoors as much as we could.

Soon after I arrived in California I noticed an interesting phenomenon as, unlike Arturo who had to stay indoors as much as possible, there were a lot more people outside on the street than I had ever encountered when I was living on Long Island. People all over were jogging outdoors for exercise. It inspired me to do the same.

I noticed that they all had special running shoes. While I had a pair of shoes that I had purchased in Bogotá that came close, the heels were thinner than the soles. Oh well. I began to jog anyway using those special shoes. What I did not realize was that my Achilles tendon was being stretched abnormally. Whenever I finished my brief jog, there was a slight ache along the tendon. It was mild enough but it worsened until it could not be ignored. I took some over-the-counter ibuprofen. It seemed to help temporarily. Wearing shoes with a thicker heel helped even more. The combination of medicine and better shoes allowed the tendon to heal. It took a long time. Later on in my studies, I learned that I had developed Achilles tendinitis.

University of California Medical Center, Sleepless in the City of Orange

With or without Achilles tendinitis, on Monday morning, January 3, 1977, I had to report in to start the Fifth Pathway Program. I had an early morning appointment with one of the professors at the University Of California Medical Center in the city of Orange. I got lost when I tried to find parking at the large, empty expanse opposite the medical center. That parking area had been cleared to make way for a shopping mall scheduled for completion a few years later. The parking markings were nonexistent. I did the best I could as no other cars were parked there at that early hour.

I rushed into the medical center and found the right office. At the outer office, the secretary was there but she told me that the professor was not in yet. She invited me to wait for him inside. I sat down in his office and looked around. The pictures adorning the walls attracted my attention. One in particular looked strange and I got up to get a closer look. It consisted of a single sheet of unframed white plastic with about six raised circles ranging from large to small. Their diameters were listed below each circle in centimeters. I realized the significance of the setup. The circles represented the diameters of dilation of a cervix during labor. While delivering babies in Colombia, I had to estimate the dilations by the spacing between my second and third fingers of my right hand touching across the dilating cervix. I took the opportunity to test my accuracy by checking the circles in stepped sizes on the wall placard. As I was busy with that procedure, I heard a gentle cough behind me. I turned to face the secretary who must have thought that I was some kind of weirdo. I stammered something of an explanation. She appeared disinterested as she informed me that the professor was on the way. The professor finally showed and handed me over to a second year pediatric resident to show me around the magnificent facility.

I was shown around and my pediatrics program was laid out for me. Early each morning, my colleagues and I would meet with our attending physician and perform our rounds of the pediatric patients. My colleagues would consist of interns, residents, or Fifth Pathway trainees. Each child or baby would be assigned to one of us. All of us would approach the respective bed or crib during these rounds. The one who was assigned to that patient had to inform the rest of us as to that patient's illness, condition, degree of improvement or deterioration, and the plan for further treatment, if any. They also had to answer any questions presented by the group.

It was exciting. I could hardly wait to get into the pattern. The opportunity to follow that routine was what I had been fighting for over the last four years. Since I had just finished my fourth year in Colombia, the routine laid out for me and my group, today, seemed similar to what I had been handling for the last year. In the back of my mind there was the apprehension that I would be competing with the vaunted American medical students, arguably the world's best.

Later that day, I found my way out and went to the giant parking area. By now, it was densely packed. There were no posted numbers of pavement markings. It took quite a while to find my car which was straddled across three parking spaces. Since the parking area was under construction there was no police inspection. I considered myself lucky not to have gotten a traffic ticket.

I began the day to day routine. The early mornings were laid out in the pattern that I described. The rest of each day was filled with a blur of activity. The time would be spent attending to our assigned patients, receiving and working up new patients from direct admissions or the emergency room, attending scheduled conferences or study and classroom periods, researching any areas needed for patient care, and meeting with department heads if scheduled. The days were full of learning and studying. I loved it.

The on call days were the same but, as the day ended, we had to report to exam rooms. We would go alone or with one or two colleagues to await patients that parents were bringing to the medical center. The nurses processed the new arrivals. They also checked vital signs and wrote up that information. Today with EHR (Electronic Health Records), it is much easier with all the information entered into a computer. Back then, it was not the case. The patients were passed to us with the written or recorded materials. We examined the children and questioned them, and/or their parents. It was exciting. I told myself that I was finally among US students with their world-famous medical training. They didn't seem super bright to me at the time. Time would tell.

It took a week or so to get used to the routine. I learned just how busy our routine was. It was gratifying to me that the physical demands and the long hours were handled by my mid-life body without complaints.

The routine was more complicated than what was laid out for us on that first day. After the early morning rounds, we would all rush upstairs to a classroom. We each had to tell our supervising physician about our patients with the latest lab reports available and answer questions. This interrogation was mostly concentrated on the patients that we had admitted, during the night, while on call. Certain days of the week I would be on call, which means an all-nighter. After a sleepless night, the lab results and vital signs were often a confused jumble. We tried to have a few scribbled notes to help us but most were illegible. Needing them was frowned upon.

One night, the workload was fairly light so I decided to put humor into the next post-rounds meeting with our supervising physician. I memorized the lab results on the few patients seen that night. After morning rounds, we rushed upstairs and the interrogation started as usual. When the supervising physician questioned me, I described my case and started quoting the lab tests but out to four-decimal places. I heard the group begin to snicker. I turned away from facing front to facing the rest of the group and said, "You guys just can't handle a stellar performance, can you?" They all broke into loud laughter. Even our supervising physician covered his face behind some papers to hide his smile.

There were wide ranging illnesses in the children that I attended which required a lot of learning and observation. After checking in a new child, the nurse whispered to me that I should be alert to a possible child abuse case as she had noted bruising on the child's legs. I first checked the child's head and face. I didn't want it to appear obvious that I was checking for possible abuse. The child had been brought in by his grandmother as his parents were working. He was neatly dressed with a clean blouse and new-looking jeans. He appeared quite comfortable with me and his Grandmother rather than frightened and guarded. I had the boy remove his pants and I noticed the blue discolorations on his thighs and legs. The grandma was calm. She didn't seem worried. Since the bruises weren't tender, I took a cotton pad and wet it with alcohol and rubbed it over the bruise. The bruise disappeared and the cotton pad now had a blue stain. It was obvious that the blue jeans were not color fast and any sweating dissolved the dye onto his skin.

I was moved by another case, which was attended to by one of my fellow students but quickly passed on to the Chief Pediatric Resident. The patient was an adorable female baby just several months old that had been brought in with a mild viral illness. She was admitted as an in-patient but her condition deteriorated rapidly. Despite transfer to the Pediatric ICU (Intensive Care Unit) where she was treated with various heroic measures, including intubation, she passed away. The final diagnosis was Reye's disease, a mysterious and deadly illness that doctors learned was caused by parents treating babies' fevers with aspirin. The discovery was made too late for that precious baby. Since that discovery, the use of aspirin to bring down body temperature in the young has been prohibited. The disease is fortunately limited to children that have a fatty acid oxidation disorder, which is inherited but usually is unknown until triggered by aspirin given for a viral illness or infection.

At the medical center, very ill children or babies were transferred to the hospital beds or cribs for a full in-patient admission. In severe cases they were transferred to the ICU, or the Intensive Care Unit. If the babies were very young and extremely ill, they were transferred to the NICU, the Neonatal Intensive Care Unit, where they were cared for by the specially-trained neonatologists.

In those days, we prescribed lots of antibiotics to our patients. That practice has been severely curtailed in the last few years as experience grew, as it caused increased resistance to antibiotics. For instance, amoxicillin used to be 98 percent effective against a streptococcus bacterial infection when it first appeared on the market. Now it has dropped below a 40 percent effectiveness rating. This is due to all of the prescribing and administering of amoxicillin over the years for viral infections where it is useless. Meanwhile, the bacteria built up a strong resistance to the streptococcus.

Since Fifth Pathway students and interns are new graduates, they are mostly managed and guided by residents, who are second-year and above post-graduates. The residents are mostly licensed to practice medicine having met the state's educational requirements and passed the qualifying examinations. As an example of their training functions, new graduates are taught how to clean the cerumen (wax) out of a child's ears so that we could then use an otoscope to visualize the tympanic membrane (TM-Ear Drum).

Bulging or red TMs are usually due to a bacterial infection of the middle ear, which is right behind the TM. It requires the use of antibiotics. It is quite an ordeal to hold a child's head motionless while cleaning the ear canal with a speculum which is a long stiff wire with a handle at one end and a tiny ring with sharp edges at the other end.

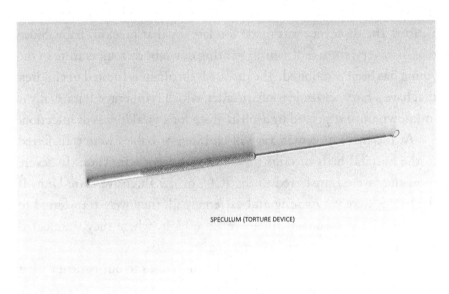

SPECULUM (TORTURE DEVICE)

Ear Speculum- Illustration

The resident showed us how to handle the child and the procedure and then checked the TM after we had done so. There must be a clear view of the TM with its landmarks and color. Any blood showing is a no-no although it happens frequently. I found that particular procedure as unpleasant as operating on dogs, which we had to do at the Escuela de Medicina Juan N. Corpas.

To make matters worse, some of the residents take likes or dislikes to their trainees. The dislike shows itself particularly in TM visualization where it can result in strong verbal abuse.

I was the victim of one particular dislike. It started early one morning in rounds when we all reached the crib of a baby that had been there for the past four days. During the presentation by the intern, we stood around the crib encapsulating it in a circle. I had been on call the prior night. The intern droned on with the same material that I had heard for the past four days. I sort of dozed with eyes wide open but unfocused.

As the talk was ending, I began to focus. I sharpened my focus which wound up looking at the other side of the circle. That point was occupied by Sharon, a third-year resident. She was shifting side-to-side and glaring daggers at me. I surmised that was because she thought I was staring at her pubic area. I was too ashamed to go over to her and explain that I was innocent of any such aggression on my part. I was convinced that she was too angry to accept my apology anyway. That tense situation lasted all year long. Whenever she supervised me at ear cleaning time she was loudly critical. I persevered and mustered through.

I had to leave the medical center and drive to the Irvine campus once a week to spend an hour with my mentor, Dr. Thomas Nelson. He seemed pleased to meet with me and was comfortable that I was fitting into the program. That did not stop him from asking me some tough questions. He asked, "If it is necessary to perforate an eardrum (Tympanic Membrane) in order to drain the pus from an infected middle ear, which part of the tympanic membrane is the preferred area to be perforated?" The correct answer, which is not what I gave him, was posterior/inferior. Thinking about the answer later I realized it was logical. However, in general I did well in the questioning.

The six months of pediatrics were intensely interesting and there wasn't a single day in which I didn't learn something new. We spent several days in the neonatal intensive care unit (NICU). I was assigned to work next to a nurse attending these newborns. She started to show me the routines in managing the newborn but was speaking rapidly. I had to ask her to repeat herself several times. She stopped, turned away from the incubator, and stated firmly, "I will show you one more time and that's it." The only thing lacking in that curt statement was being called Sonny. I watched the procedure she was showing me carefully as there would be no more chances for doing so. I felt humbled, but grateful however, for the state-of-the-art information that I was learning.

In general, I felt that I was part of a highly advanced team of hard-working dedicated individuals. They accepted me as part of their group even though they were young enough to be my children. My learning level matched the level of the team and I did not look for any favors or special consideration based on my age.

There Is No Place Like Home

Etta and I spent the small amount of spare time away from my medical training looking for a permanent home. The California weather was excellent. As spring approached, we tried to touch base with family and friends in the Northeast. We also made contact with Dorothy and Joe Gould in Los Angeles whom we met through their son, Mark, when we were living in Bogotá. At the time, Mark was serving in the Peace Corps. I had sometimes connected him to his parents via my Ham radio whenever he came to Bogotá from the countryside. They were grateful and the friendship quickly formed. Little could I foresee how valuable this friendship would turn out to be.

The Goulds living in Los Angeles invited us to visit them, which we did from time to time. Joe Gould was president of a small chain of California banks that stretched from Los Angeles into Orange County. Etta and I had two other goals in mind. The first was to find a house in a decent neighborhood that was not far from the medical center. In our search we gradually learned our way around the area. We had to be fairly selective as our budget was rather limited. My income from the sale of Seg Electronics was diminishing and would end in about a year.

We found a nice home in Tustin, California, with a large backyard and within 10 miles of the medical center. The negotiated price that we paid was $110,000, which was much more expensive than real estate in Colombia. I sold it about eighteen years later for three times that amount after spending $150,000 for a new Master Bedroom. A few years beyond that it was offered for sale at over $1,000,000. That gives one an indication of the run up in real estate prices in Southern California. The house was spacious enough to allow me a study, which doubled as a communications center for my Ham equipment.

With that, we were settling in. The first six months of pediatrics drew rapidly to a close and then it was on to Ob-Gyn for a month.

Obstetrics & Gynecology, Babies Born At Night

Obstetrical and gynecological studies began at Irvine with a gynecology clinic staffed by one or two of the staff and Fifth Pathway, intern, or resident students. It was our routine to handle vaginal bleeding, possible or active pregnancies, genital infections, or any combination thereof.

In the Juan N. Corpas Escuela de Medicina, I had gotten a lot of experience with gynecology problems, as well as handling pregnancies. I didn't feel like a novice. Still, I knew I had a lot to learn.

The threat of a malpractice lawsuit was almost non-existent in Colombia. Here in the US, it would be a large obstacle for a trainee to join his or her first medical practice with a history of a lawsuit settlement, or an award to a plaintiff. These histories would weigh heavily against the new physician.

The month passed quickly but was exhausting. It seemed like all the babies were born at night. The UCI Medical Center handled lots of patients without insurance. They were mostly illegal aliens who were afraid of being arrested and transported back to their native country, usually Mexico. The county government reimbursed the University of California, Irvine, for the costs since there was a substantial risk that the patient, who was not supervised during pregnancy, had a greater risk of a complicated delivery, which was usually very costly.

The gynecology clinic was relatively easy with lots of urinary tract infections, vaginal infections, and suspected pregnancies. There were frequent cases of UTIs that had been neglected by the patient because he or she consumed a lot of cranberry juice as a self-prescribed treatment, which was of doubtful benefit. The main danger there was that the infection would spread up into the kidneys causing a Pyelonephritis with the risk of severe kidney damage.

There were also some odd problems caused by sex toys, like vibrators, that had come apart during sexual intercourse. Sometimes the pieces had to be fished out. There were even cases where the vibrator motor had become imbedded in the wall between the vagina and bladder. This was due to the fact that this foreign object was left trapped inside and ignored for a long time period. If the patient had to be hospitalized, we were usually responsible for following the case.

If there was a case that was too difficult for us at the gynecological clinic, there were always the senior residents with whom we could confer. These third-year and fourth-year residents were extremely capable and experienced. Sometimes, the patient could be whisked off to surgery or intensive care as things could get serious quickly.

There was one extremely interesting case that the senior residents urged us to examine as a learning experience. The in-patient was a fifteen-year-old girl that had been born at UCLA with no connection between the bottom end of the uterus and the upper end of a short vagina. A few years later, the brilliant surgeons at UCLA built in a connection by transplanting skin from her axilla (arm pit) to extend the vagina and reach the bottom of the uterus. Since her family lived in Orange County, she wound up at Irvine when a severe UTI threatened the transplant. As she was recuperating, we trainees learned about this unusual case. We tried to find the opportunity to examine the patient. She became annoyed at the intrusions and refused the extra examinations. During the physical examination, there was a change of texture of the mucus membranes at the lower vagina to the rougher texture of the axillary skin of the upper vagina.

Obstetrics gave us lots of experience as the medical center handled a tremendous number of deliveries. On the nights that we were on call, we rotated through numerous pregnancies. After delivering a baby and tying off the umbilical cord, we would hand the baby to the nurse for clean up. We would head for a room full of bunk beds and collapse onto the first empty one we saw. We were lucky to get a full hour of sleep before the nurse tugged our sleeve to get up for the next delivery.

I still remember my fifth delivery at the Escuela de Medicina Juan N. Corpas in Colombia. The delivery went well. As the baby was handed to the nurse, I was confronted by the sight of a powerful hemorrhage jetting from the woman's vagina. I struggled to stop the powerful loss of blood. Fortunately, I was successful. Otherwise, she would have gone into shock from the loss of blood. The next day I checked on the patient. She was awake and feeling fine. I asked her about the hemorrhage. Her blood levels were only mildly affected. She said that it had happened at each prior delivery. I asked her why she didn't warn me. Her response was that she had been too embarrassed. In Spanish, a pregnant woman is said to be, "embarasada."

I was glad when the month of chronic fatigue ended. My skills and confidence had been boosted. I was dazzled by the miracle of being involved with the birthing process.

One month of psychiatry was the next stop.

Psychiatry & The Demons Within

When I was studying medicine in Colombia, psychiatry was one area that was underplayed at my school. That was unfortunate. I would come upon many emotional problems treating patients there. I realized they were somewhat unique to the Hispanic female population, although the rest of the world was not immune to that type of problem either.

In Colombia, the population was dedicated to Catholicism with only minor exceptions. Female youngsters were taught by their parents, that if they lost their virginity before marriage they would face eternal damnation. In religious families, a girl could not be alone with a boy without a chaperone accompanying them. In families where these strict rules were practiced, many young females grew up with a dread of male contact. When they did marry, the family told the daughter to keep him sexually satisfied and have lots of children. That was sometimes too radical of a change. Not every bride could make that transition. As a result, a young woman would wind up with many problems like chronic headaches, insomnia, and even obesity. Today, television, the internet, and co-education, have created enlightenment. That kind of problem has become much more infrequent.

In advance of the class, I read as much as I could about psychiatry and its treatment with medication and counseling. UCI Medical Center had a separate small building for its mental health section. Each floor had beds for fifteen mental health patients. I was assigned to the second floor to share it with a psychiatric, second-year resident. Since I was at the intern level, or below, I was assigned to treat seven patients and the second-year resident cared for the other half of the floor. That arrangement lasted only half a day when the resident physician came to me. He told me that his most recent patient was pregnant and spoke only Spanish. Since he didn't speak Spanish, he asked if I would accept her. I agreed. Now I was caring for eight patients and the resident only seven.

The second day, our nurse told me that my new patient had a slightly bloody vaginal discharge. My first reaction was to order her transferred to the gynecological clinic. I reconsidered since I had been one of the two trainees that were running the gynecological clinic up to a few days before. I checked her. By then, the bloody discharge had stopped, although she had a slight UTI that I treated with antibiotics that were safe for the pregnancy.

I also learned to do both individual and group therapy sessions with my patients. One evening when I got home, I happened to look at the classified ads in the local newspaper. One of the ads was under the name of one of my patients who was seeking followers because he was God and would promise them a long or infinite life. I asked him about the ad the next day. He admitted that he had put it in the paper but he retracted the concept that he was God.

The most interesting psychiatric patient that month wasn't God but a knight. This knight manifested himself as a big, pleasant man that was brought in by the Anaheim police on a rainy night. He was found to be completely naked, under a raincoat, and carrying a long toy sword with which he was trying to knight any passersby. He said that his Mazda truck had a little meter on the dashboard that, at times, indicated a high reading. When the needle trembled, it meant that God was trying to contact him. Later in the month, he was much more rational and able to be released.

Exposed to almost every type of psychiatric condition that existed within the Southern California population, I also learned how to handle schizophrenic and bipolar patients, as well as plain, old depression. It was sad to see how small changes in brain circuitry could cause such erratic thought processes to occur. It makes one wonder what demons lurk inside all of us.

Medication in many cases would help them. But whenever they felt and behaved normally, they would believe that they no longer needed the medication. Upon stopping their medications they often relapsed. I was impressed by the ability to convert an irrational, non-functional human being into a normal person, at least by our standards, just by prescribing a few pills and providing a little counseling.

Group therapy was disappointing to me. There was a poor response from my group of about ten patients. I found that there was a struggle to get a patient response after I started the discussion. I had to invent solutions and direct my drive toward the more alert patients.

Next stop was Urology for a month.

Urology, Erectile Dysfunction & the Suicidal Patient

The next month was spent at the Long Beach Veterans Administration Hospital in the urology department. The patient census was essentially male since the patients were exclusively military veterans, which was in sharp contrast to my earlier rotation in obstetrics and gynecology.

The only known exceptions to admissions of military veterans took place when a certain patient arrived in the emergency room. This was a story that circulated throughout the staff and supposed to be true. It was related to the case of a man who was treated at the emergency room on a Sunday. He did not have the necessary veterans' discharge documents with him but he insisted that he was a war veteran and had seen active duty during World War II. He promised to prove his military status in a few days after admission.

It turned out that he was indeed a World War II veteran, but as a German soldier. The only other exception that I heard about during that month was that of a female student of the neighboring Long Beach State University. She had been pregnant and suddenly went into labor while attending classes. With the labor advancing rapidly, she went to the nearest emergency room which was in the VA Hospital adjacent to her school.

During my stint in the urology rotation, I encountered the older male's difficulty with urination frequently. This was almost always due to an enlarged prostate gland that squeezes the urethra, which is the tube that carries the urine from the bladder to the penis. This enlargement can block the urine flow. In such an emergency, quick relief while in the hospital is obtained by passing a catheter, which is a plastic tube, through the penis, urethra, and prostate. The patient has to bear that tube in place until a more permanent method of relief can be implemented, such as surgery. Until the blockage can be removed or the situation stabilized, the patient has to allow the urine to flow into a plastic bag that is taped to his leg.

Another large segment of the patient census at the hospital that afflicted the aging male was erectile dysfunction. Diseases like diabetes, that affect the circulation of the blood, cause problems with erections. That is also true of advanced age. During my rotation, so many years ago, there were not many successful treatments. Some of the treatments that were fairly popular consisted of injections into the penis, vacuum pumps, or actual surgical replacement of the two penile (cavernous) glands that store the blood under pressure during sexual excitement. The replacement glands were made of a special plastic composition.

I was involved with one case whereby the patient had both penile glands replaced but an infection set in. The patient was hospitalized for the infection. With antibiotic therapy it finally cleared it up. He was told that the replacement glands had to be removed surgically and could not be replaced. The news depressed the poor fellow. When I tried to lift his depression by offering him treatment with antidepressants, his reply was simply, "Don't bother. When I am discharged from here, I plan to go home and kill myself."

At that point I brought in the hospital psychiatrists. I never learned the final results as I was assigned to treat other patients.

The discovery of Viagra, followed by Levitta, and then Cialis, caused a revolution in the field of Erectile Dysfunction.

Search For Internship

As that poor fellow considered his fate, I moved on to meet mine. I approached the end of my year of Fifth Pathway rotations. I faced the same problem that I had before that year began. Since my medical education in Colombia began at the beginning of the year, and ended just short of the end of the year, I was six months out of phase with the American system. I ran into difficulty finding an internship, which would begin in January, rather than July. The only internships that seemed flexible enough to accept me for January admission were those in psychiatry.

I reasoned that if I had to accept a six-month delay to be admitted into one of the other disciplines, such as family medicine, I had better apply for an internship at one of the excellent programs in family practice. I spent quite a bit of time in the last month of my Fifth Pathway rotations contacting and interviewing for an internship in that discipline, within the state of California. The procedure for doing this was to register with the Match program.

The Match program is set up for applicants, and the heads of programs in the different disciplines, to register toward the end of the year for selection of suitable candidates for July admission of the following year. The applicants pursue obtaining interviews at their most desired programs. After all of the interviews are completed, the programs rank the applicants in the order of their desirability. The applicants rank the programs the same way. On a fixed day in the following March, a computer program matches those rankings and publishes the order of acceptance for each applicant in each program.

It seemed fair enough to me. I carefully considered my choices. My interviews seemed to go well but the interviewers did not seem very enthusiastic about setting a preference for a 56-year-old medical student who had trained abroad. They had to consider the fact that the intern they accepted would be expected to continue for at least two or three additional years in order to become board certified in the chosen specialty. Those two or three additional years would bring me close to 60 years of age. I had to weigh how many years I could expect to practice. The average male life expectancy was about 75 years. My work was cut out for me but I wasn't discouraged, especially when I remembered that 40-year-old medical student whose photo I had seen back on the Riviera. He had been my original inspiration to become a doctor. In other words, "If he can do it, so can I."

Before making my decision, I interviewed at several psychiatric programs in California. This included one at the Long Beach Veterans Administration Hospital. They were friendly and seemed willing to accept me six months early. That made it an attractive alternative, although the idea of a four-year program in psychiatry was not terribly exciting. One additional factor helped me make a decision. The California Medical Board required that interns, in psychiatry, had to devote three months of the one-year program to internal medicine. They would be eligible to apply for licensure at the end of that year. I compared those factors with the possibility that I may not be accepted under the Match program six months later. It made psychiatry more attractive.

I had to select which psychiatry program I preferred. The only other California psychiatry program that would accept me, out of turn, was at the Harbor, UCLA Medical Center. Their chief of the department was quite pleased with my qualifications but had to clear any offer of a contract with several other hospital officials. She seemed certain that there would be no problem. The situation grew more complicated when the program at the Long Beach VA Hospital accepted me subject to my acceptance of the offer within the following two weeks. My preference at that point was with Harbor, UCLA. I was waiting to hear from them for a firm contract.

Disconcerted about the whole affair, I went to the office of the chief of the psychiatry department at Harbor, UCLA but her secretary informed me that the chief was away at a conference. She was expected to call in shortly. I tried to explain that I was ready to enter into a contract with Harbor, UCLA, but I needed a firm acceptance within the next two weeks. My built-in radar antennas signaled me that the young secretary was not happy with that statement although the acceptance had been assured by the Chief, subject to certain signatures. I was skeptical of my message being conveyed properly and not taken as some kind of ultimatum.

Later, and lacking all but a few days, I grew anxious as I had not been able to reach the chief at Harbor, UCLA. I accepted and signed my contract with the Long Beach VA hospital. One week later, the Chief at Harbor, UCLA called me about the final acceptance of my offer. When I told her what had transpired, she admitted that the information forwarded by her secretary had not adequately described the situation. She was furious. I felt that I had made a wise choice since the travel time from my home in Orange County, California, to Long Beach was about thirty minutes compared to an hour, or ninety minutes to Harbor, UCLA. Perhaps it was another sign from above that I was making the right choice. The Long Beach VA hospital program was associated with UC- Irvine. My performance and experience there had been quite favorable.

Within a few weeks of my signing the contract, I entered the internship with some confidence as my one month of psychiatry under the Fifth Pathway program had gone well. In effect, I had been fully functioning as a psychiatrist, although for eight patients only. I had issued all of the necessary orders, and the resident had the job of countersigning my orders, which took him about ten minutes each day. I anticipated the pleasant fact that I would actually be earning a salary, at last. It would be a small one but something is better than nothing.

In March, 1978, I received a surprise letter from the family practice department of Kaiser-Permanente in Fontana, California, where I had interviewed. They asked me why I had not accepted the family practice internship that they made available to me under the Match program. As I had mentioned previously, I did not believe that my interviewers were particularly enthusiastic about a considerably older applicant, who had studied in a foreign country, applying for a spot in their program in competition with younger applicants that were American graduates. I had not considered my case to be particularly attractive, despite the fact that the University of Pennsylvania at Hershey had been willing to transfer me into their program if a space opened. It hadn't.

Psychiatry and the "5150"

Touring the VA hospital at which I was going to work for the next year, I was impressed with the wounded war veterans that were lying face down on mobile Gurneys that they propelled by spinning the wheels with their hands. They were hemiplegics, usually due to a spinal cord injury. I surmised that these unlucky guys must have been hit by shrapnel, bullets, or high explosives. I was told later that not all of them were injured in battle. Some were the victims of swimming pool or auto accidents. The end result was the same. I pitied them all. I was glad that the US government was dedicated to helping them. More recently, following our wars in Iraq and Afghanistan, the new flood of veterans had overwhelmed the Veteran's Administration system with dismal results.

Our day at the hospital typically began with a staff consisting of psychiatrists, residents and interns, as well as nurses, interviewing patients that had been seen in the emergency room at the hospital and admitted to the floor. Some patients were brought in by the police and these were usually locked in a special enclosure. The usually simple admission document was called the 5150. It allowed for forty eight hours of attended care in a secure facility. The criterion for issuing the 5150 was that the police consider that person to be a threat to him, her, or others. At the VA hospital, that facility was always crowded. As the time limit approaches, the police, or appropriate authorities, may release the person under the 5150, or obtain a court order for a lengthier stay.

These early morning interviews allowed the staff to become familiar with the new admissions and to participate in questioning them. With the rest of the staff listening to the interview by the psychiatrists, they become skilled at gleaning as much information as possible. Before the patient leaves the interview process, there is a session with the patient being retained outside the interviewing area while the treatment plan is worked out by staff.

At one of these early morning interviews, I arrived a little late. I had been busy admitting a patient. A senior psychiatrist was interviewing a patient that had been dropped off by the police during the night. The patient was friendly and cheerful and delivered an amazing story. He related that he lived in a rented house in Anaheim and had accumulated an assortment of toy tanks and planes as a hobby. One rainy night, he looked out of his windows and insisted that he saw an invasion of Japanese toys and planes attacking his house. He barricaded half of his house but this did not seem to deter the invasion. He put on a helmet and raincoat. He headed for the local police station to alert them about the imminent invasion. The police intercepted him halfway up the police station steps. They agreed that he was wearing a helmet and raincoat and nothing else.

This reminded me of a patient (that I described previously) from my Fifth Pathway days who was picked up on a rainy night by the police. This was the one who was trying to knight people in Anaheim with a toy sword. I was beginning to ask him a question when I realized that he was my former patient. He smiled and waved at me. He remembered me too. He was treated and released on medication that blocked his delusional responses.

I was sure that this was not the last time that he would become a guest of the VA hospital like so many mentally ill patients who were chronic residents. Many of them moved from one VA hospital to another. Major depression was a frequent diagnosis. Bipolar disorder was another. This disorder was one in which the patient alternates between major depression and high excitement called manic. These mood swings can vary from hours to months. Treatment is difficult since medication for depression can force the patient into the manic phase, and vice versa. The manic phase, in its full expression, can cause the patient to become irrational.

Another mental health illness which was prevalent was schizophrenia. In that disorder, the patient frequently hears a flow of voices in his head. The voices could be pleasant, unpleasant, or confrontational. In some patients they may be ignored. In others they could be unbearable.

Another symptom of Schizophrenia that I witnessed frequently is when the patient believes television characters are speaking to him. Sometimes, on passing people speaking on the street, the patient believes the speakers had been speaking about him or her. There are a number of medications that can suppress such delusions. Again, the problem arises when the voices disappear. The patient feels there is no need for taking his medication and so the symptoms recur.

An example of a bipolar patient in the manic phase, who was assigned to me, had been brought in under a 5150 by the police the night before. It was my duty to interview him and complete a history and physical exam, write orders for diet and medication, and visit him each day in the secured facility. On my first interview with him he was pleasant, alert, and cooperative. As I prepared to leave he told me that he was not prepared to stay in the locked facility long. He said he had a fleet of FBI cars circling the VA hospital awaiting his orders.

I assured him that it was not our intention to keep him any longer that we had to. The next day when I visited him, he was wearing an expensive watch that had belonged to an elderly patient in the same facility. My patient had swapped his ordinary watch for the expensive one. I ordered him to return it. To my surprise, he obeyed.

Another case, in which I had to improvise a treatment plan, my patient was a chronic inhabitant of the VA hospital system. According to his history, he suffered from severe migraine headaches that were so powerful he would pass out from the pain. He would be transported to the nearest VA hospital each time he was found unconscious. During each stay, he would be injected with pain killers to control the migraine headaches. I attempted an unusual treatment, which would usually be frowned upon. I ordered the staff at the nursing station to inject him with 1ml of normal saline solution every four hours. This is simply a sterile salt water solution at the same concentration of salt as the human body liquids. It is used extensively in treating dehydration as well as other conditions or emergencies. To my satisfaction and surprise, it worked wonders on his migraine headaches. The four hour schedule proved to be just right for the routine. He lined up at the nursing station with the other patients that were treated with shots.

A few months later, the migraine patient informed me that he was ready to leave the hospital and was planning to move to the East Coast. He confided that he probably would wind up at a VA hospital there, according to his past history. He asked if he could get the formula for his wonderful shots to use if he was admitted elsewhere. I told him that if he wound up in the VA system, they could call me. He asked me if it was sugar water they were using on him. I denied that firmly. It's normally considered improper to mislead a patient that way, but I felt that it was the best course for the patient.

On those occasions when patients arrived at the emergency room during the day, we interns took turns at doing the interview and admitting the patient, or declining to admit as the case might be. During the on-call nights, the interns would be called into the emergency room to question the patient if the problem was mental health. One such episode took place when I was on call and I recognized the patient as one who had been there quite a while before. Since the administration had started to clamp down on frequent E/R visitors, I questioned the patient as to whether he was still taking his medications. He said he was. I did a physical exam. Upon questioning, I did not believe that he should be admitted.

When I informed him he got upset and shouted at me. A large patient, with the same problem, joined him. They were getting increasingly agitated and started shaking their fists at me. I asked one of the nurses to call security to usher them out. I was surprised when security, a little lady, arrived. She grabbed one arm of each of the two patients who towered over her and took them away peacefully.

In the hospital, one intern per night was always on call. He or she was responsible for the mental health problems of the 400-bed VA facility. We could call on the senior residents to guide us if the problem was too difficult. The last time that I was ever on call for an entire hospital wing was as a second-year medical student at the Hadassah Hospital, near Jerusalem, Israel. This facility was dwarfed by the VA hospital for mental health problems.

Early in my year of internship, I was on call during my three-month requirement of internal medicine. Just before midnight, a nurse called and told me that an elderly man on another floor was in distress. I hurried to the bedside and noticed that he was in respiratory distress. His middle-aged son was standing next to his bed and was watching him. I started CPR and called for oxygen. His son grabbed my arm and said, "Let him go. He has ALS. He has suffered enough." ALS stands for Amyotrophic Lateral Sclerosis, also known as Lou Gehrig disease. Lou Gehrig was a champion baseball player who at the height of his career, in the Yankee Stadium, announced to the world that he had to retire from baseball due to the fact that he had ALS which was paralyzing him. He passed away a few years after that statement.

I paused in my CPR and looked at the nurse. She nodded in agreement. All of these hands-on experiences were so important for interns on the way to becoming medical doctors. None of these experiences were wasted on me.

I found that my three months of internal medicine were also interesting and should prove valuable in my future practice of medicine. The internal medicine rotation included several weeks of a 'Lumps and Bumps Clinic.' We were divided into pairs consisting of the surgeon and the assistant surgeon. We switched roles after each patient.

In one particular case, the surgeon was a resident who went on to become a well-known surgeon in one of the nearby cities in California. The patient in question had noticed a lump in the soft tissue in front of the right elbow. I was the assistant surgeon and cleaned the area with an antiseptic solution. I injected lidocaine to control the pain of the procedure. My partner cut through the skin over the lump which turned out to be fatty material. After he did so, there was a strip running through the lump. He slipped the blade of his scissors under the ribbon to cut through it.

I called out, "Isn't that the median nerve?"

He gulped and withdrew the scissors. He gingerly scraped away the fatty tissue over the nerve and closed the skin with sutures. I shudder when I think about the close call we had. The cut would have paralyzed the hand of the patient.

Several months later while on call in psychiatry, I was called by a nurse who informed me that the chief resident of another department was acting strangely. I went to her office feeling uncomfortable about it since a chief resident was so many levels above me. I felt it would be akin to asking me to examine the president of the US. I will call her Doctor Claire. She didn't appear nervous when I appeared. I told her that I heard that she was not feeling well. She agreed. She told me that she had been working hard and with long hours. Her stress level was high and made worse since someone had broken into a condo that she owned in San Juan Capistrano and had stolen valuable items. I sympathized with her.

A secretary walked into the office that we were using and set down a stapler that she was carrying. Doctor Claire and I were silent during the intrusion until the secretary left. I thought everything was okay. Dr. Claire looked at me and asked, to my surprise, "Are you part of the conspiracy?" I answered, "No, but tell me about it." She responded, "Did you notice that woman who put the stapler on the desk, pointed it at me, and the design on her sweater was also pointed at me?" I questioned her further and recommended some days off for her to rest. I believed that she was close to a nervous breakdown due to the real and perceived high pressure under which she was working. She agreed and I prescribed a mild tranquilizer as well. Nervous breakdown is an old expression. It means that the person has become so overwhelmed by depression and stress that he or she has become non-functional.

I learned that she had been taking a stimulant, Ritalin, to give her the energy to handle the long hours. My diagnoses were Stress Reaction and Ritalin Psychosis. I have been cautious ever since that episode about prescribing Ritalin. It is prescribed with high frequency to our children who have a diagnosis of ADHD (Attention Deficit Hyperactivity Disorder). These children or adults, who don't respond sufficiently to Ritalin in its various forms, are frequently advanced to other stimulants that are based on amphetamines or dextro-amphetamines.

While it was important to research various drugs and their uses, it was also important to research different subdivisions of psychiatry. During our internship, that's what we did. This meant attending conferences and classes in that subdivision. I found myself interested in hypnosis. I had memories of my childhood experience with my cousin, Sam Goldberg – the one who said he could hypnotize himself if we all left the room. One of the senior residents formed a group for us that received notices about various lectures and we attended several conferences on the subject.

- We were urged to prepare one or more lectures ourselves for delivery to the entire staff at Grand Rounds which were scheduled once a week.

I naturally chose hypnosis as the theme of my lecture. I felt nervous facing the entire psychiatric staff of the Long Beach VA hospital. My presentation began with a description of hypnosis and continued into proven efficacies, such as in alcoholism and tobacco dependence. My audience seemed attentive and I continued into trying to hypnotize the entire staff. My expectation was that about 25 percent of the staff would be hypnotized. I was surprised to note that about 75 percent of the staff seemed to be hypnotized - or just sound asleep. The applause at the end was gratifying. I vowed not to abandon hypnosis when I went to practice for myself.

Part of my routine consisted of group therapy sessions which I felt were not useful as the patients, most of whom were chronic, never contributed much. This required me to keep talking to stimulate an interchange of ideas. They were mostly my ideas and my group contributed little.

While my internship was interesting and rewarding, both in psychiatry and internal medicine, I began to doubt whether I should continue in psychiatry or seek opportunities in family medicine, which was my first intention. The chief of psychiatry pressed me to continue with the additional years needed to become a board-certified psychiatrist. I realized that the additional years of training would subtract from the time that I would have to practice medicine. On the other hand, in family medicine there was a need for board certification as many services required, or were going to require, board certification for their medical discipline. The projected length of time for the average longevity for a male in the US was about seventy-five years. That projected term could be lengthened by the fact that my father lived until his mid eighties, and my mother into her early nineties.

In the last few months of my internship, I studied hard for the Flex exams, as administered by the California Board of Medical Quality Assurance (BMQA), to meet my requirements for licensure. If I passed that exam I would be eligible for licensure on completion of my internship. I applied for permission to take the Flex exams. It was granted. Having completed the Fifth Pathway exam gave me an additional cushion.

During the three days of the examination, I was apprehensive about my performance. I remember just one incident on the first day that made me anxious. It occurred when I was leaving the examination. I overheard two candidates discussing how difficult the exam was. One of them asked the other, "On the chest x-ray question, did you notice a notch in one of the ribs, which means aortic stenosis?" I was shocked. I had not noticed any notch.

Waiting out the time needed for marking the exam was difficult but I finally learned that I had achieved a grade of 83, which was quite high. After all these years I was so close to achieving my full license, my dream. Before completion of my internship, I applied for licensure to take effect upon completion.

On one of my required trips to the UCI Medical Center, I came across Dr. Thomas Nelson. I had the pleasure of telling him that I had passed the Flex exam. He responded he knew that I would pass without any doubt.

First Medical Office, What A Moment

A vote of confidence like that can go a long way in one's career. As the end of 1978 approached, I was still considering whether to continue in psychiatry or open my own practice in family medicine. There was a front page article one morning in the local Orange County newspaper. It was about a young board-certified family physician with a practice in Huntington Beach, California, that had perished in a rented airplane crash. It was a sad story, which I'll explain later, but I recognized an opportunity.

I looked up the doctor's name, office address, and telephone number. I called and spoke to a member of the staff. She said that they were all confused and shocked about the terrible accident. They had no idea what was going to happen to the practice. I told her that I was interested.

I would head over there that afternoon. I requested permission to leave as I was trying to plan my next year's activity.

The practice was located in an attractive, brick building in a busy, upscale part of Huntington Beach. As I entered the lobby, I tried to find the suite of the deceased physician. A distinguished looking gentleman passed by me. I asked if he could help me find what I was looking for. He identified himself as Dr. Samuel Cohen, a surgeon with an office in the building, one who had known the deceased for several years. He pointed out the physician's office on the first floor.

The suite itself was attractive and well-equipped. It even had its own x-ray room. Concealing my excitement, I asked who I was to deal with. I was told that the deceased doctor's brother was a San Diego attorney and I was given his number. He told me that he was having the practice appraised. I checked over the furniture and equipment by myself, estimating the cost the best I could.

My rough estimate, at fire sale prices, was about $9,000. I conveyed this to the attorney and he promised to call me in a few days with his appraisal quotation. I anxiously awaited the results. Meanwhile, I accumulated further information such as knowledge about the neighbors in the building.

From this inquiry, and with the help of Dr. Samuel Cohen, I learned that there were no other bidders yet. Another family practice doctor in the building was trying to buy the charts for $1,000 to $2,000, while a team of pediatricians next door wanted to acquire the suite to expand their practice.

When the attorney called and told me that the appraisal came in at $19,000, I told him that I had hoped to pay no more than $13,000 but that I would accept that $19,000 price. That did it. I became the proud owner of the suite and its equipment, and the employer of two medical assistants with the stroke of a ballpoint pen on a check.

While negotiating, I heard rumors about the sad circumstances of young Dr. Kerchner's death. He was the physician who had passed away.

When Dr. Kerchner was in medical school, he participated in a class in physical examination. It involved dividing into pairs of students.

An ophthalmoscope was distributed to each pair and each student took turns in examining his partner's internal eye structure. After Dr. Kerchner examined his partner's eyes, he passed the ophthalmoscope to his partner to be examined by him. His partner looked into Dr. Kerchner's eye structure and was puzzled at what he saw. He called over the professor who reported a mass. Although the mass was surgically removed it apparently had recurred elsewhere in his body later. His continued treatment had been causing a lot of pain. He was reputed to have developed a strong opioid dependency because of it. It was said that the habit got so severe that he kept prescribing increasingly stronger doses for himself. When the authorities became alerted, they started an investigation which involved local pharmacists that had been coerced by the doctor for drugs.

As the situation became threatening, and the pain level probably became intolerable for the doctor, he needed more drugs. He rented a private plane to go to Canada or Mexico perhaps, which he had done before. This time he had crashed the plane into a non-populated area. There was no way of ascertaining whether the crash was due to mechanical failure or suicide.

This was all hearsay but it may explain the stack of about thirty hospital patient charts stacked against the back wall of his former office, all missing the required patient discharge summaries and physician signatures. I returned them to the hospital administration of the Pacifica Hospital for their review and processing.

It would take another few weeks until I became licensed. In the meanwhile, I received my diploma of completion of my internship at the Long Beach VA Hospital, as issued by the University of California-rvine. The medical board issued my license effective on January 2, 1979. I was busy learning my way through all of the equipment and paperwork. Suddenly, my medical assistant, Pauline Annan, came into my office and said, "Doctor, your first patient is here." What a moment.

I took a deep breath and remained seated for a few minutes to give my heart rate time to slow down. I walked slowly to the exam room, my very own patient waiting. I tried to control the pitch of my voice as I introduced myself to the female patient and reviewed her chief complaint as written into her chart by my medical assistant. Within a few minutes of my meeting with her, I was able to fall into the routine which I had practiced in my years of seeing patients in Colombia, the University of California-Irvine, and the Long Beach Veterans Administration Hospital. I took my time with this special event. The patient was both relaxed and seemed to enjoy the visit.

I saw several more patients that first day. I went home feeling content. That evening, Etta listened with pleasure to my description of each encounter. She was slightly dazed at the path that her husband had chosen and how he had been successful at clearing so many barriers.

Of course, without her full cooperation over the years, I could not have been successful. Without discussing it openly, we both realized that I was now fifty-eight years old. We did not know what the future would hold and how much time I would be allowed to practice before I got too old and feeble.

The Early Years

I had applied for family medicine privileges at the Pacifica Hospital which was across the parking lot from my building. After licensure, my application had been approved quickly and I was also accepted as an attending physician by the skilled nursing facility next door to the hospital. My patient census consisted of about 50 percent of MediCal patients, 40 percent of private insurance patients, and about 10 percent of Medicare patients. The MediCal program in California is named the Medicaid program in all the other states. Its pay scale was quite low but improved over the years. The Medicare program paid better at a fee-for-service rate and had become a great benefit to the senior patients particularly, those on limited income or living entirely on their Social Security income.

It was gratifying to learn that my training had been more than adequate. Since I had what amounted to two internships, when counting the Fifth Pathway Program, I rarely had to access my books to research the cases that I was dealing with. My forced choice of psychiatry, as one of my internships, turned out to be of great benefit. There always has been lots of anxiety and stress in our population, and the training of psychiatric counseling put me at an advantage. My new patients welcomed the substantial attention that I paid to them. This made my standard office visit longer than most other primary care doctors. It made days longer for me but my patient census grew. I lost very few patients in the changeover as the word spread that I spent lots of time with my patients. Among them were an American Airlines flight captain, a television news anchorwoman, and a drummer with the Rolling Stones.

The census grew but mainly in the MediCal section. It involved a lot of work for not much pay. While there were a few large practices in the Los Angeles area that prospered on MediCal rates, they employed foreign-born physicians that usually saw more than fifty patients per day at 5 to 10 minutes each. The way it was explained to me was that the physician walked into the room with his prescription pad open, listened to the patient for a minute or two, and started writing a prescription. I didn't operate that way.

My income was not great but kept increasing as the census grew. Since I spent more time with each patient, my hours were quite long. My outcomes were good and my reputation spread throughout the community. My patients reported that the word was out that I was a doctor that really listened and answered all the questions that the patients might have for physical and psychiatric problems. In addition, I administered to many skilled nursing facility patients and managed my own hospital patients.

One particular case stands out in my mind as helped greatly by my psychiatry training. I spent extra counselling time with a 23-year-old mother of three children whose marriage was in trouble. Her husband, in his early thirties, had developed the habit of heading to their garage, right after dinner, where he assembled models of ships and planes until late into the night. She found herself burdened by raising the three children herself with little support from her husband. Her retired parents would drive up to Huntington Beach to help her often. Suddenly, her husband took off and went to live with an 18-year-old girl. My patient went into a very deep depression. She felt that her life was shattered. I worked with her and suggested that she go back to school to develop a career since her parents seemed willing to help with raising the children. She perked up. She responded that she had completed one year of nursing school before she was married.

I lost track of her after she restarted nursing school. About ten years later, I ran into her again when I was looking for a certain piece of electronic equipment in a Huntington Beach store. She was there with a girl friend of hers. They were both Intensive Care Nurses at a major hospital. My ex-patient was dressed in outstanding clothes. I was very impressed by her elegant pastel leather coat. She was long since divorced from the husband that so neglected his family. She was then considering an offer of marriage by one of the hospital's top cardiologists. She was radiant. She was happy. I felt elated that I had been able to help make such a great change in her life.

For the older patient, my approach was somewhat unusual. One example was that of a 95-year-old lady resident of a nursing facility who was confined to a wheelchair. Her nurse took me aside and commented that they were having a problem with her. The problem was that she was masturbating whenever she had the chance. The nurse was shocked when I answered, "At her age, she has such limited possibilities for pleasure so I certainly would not force her to stop but rather encourage more privacy."

Of course, the older patient is usually less agile. At times, I have to examine the patient who was sitting in a chair rather than on the exam table, which makes the physical exam more limited. I am reminded of a quite elderly lady, named Mary, who I helped get into a sitting position at the exam table. I am usually reluctant to use a tongue depressor since it frequently causes the patient to retch or vomit, but I held one at the ready while I aimed a penlight at her lips. I said, "Mary, say ah." She responded with something barely audible, lips parted only about half an inch. I couldn't see past the tip of her tongue so I urged her to do a big "ah." With her lips still parted half an inch, she responded with a barely audible, "big ah." I thought that was one of the cutest responses that I had ever encountered.

It was sobering to see the effects of Alzheimer's Dementia in my medical practice, which I had not seen much in Colombia. As an unusual case, a delightful 75-year-old lady that lived alone had a grave complaint. Mexicans were breaking into her apartment and stealing odd items like a jewelry items or her checkbooks. There was no obvious way they got in as the door and windows were locked and not broken. She also admitted that they didn't remove the stolen items but left them elsewhere in her apartment in unexpected places like leaving the checkbook between the sheets in her linen closet. Otherwise she was quite rational but very fixed in her delusions.

In another case, I was helped by my electronics background where I had to diagnose a problem from scattered clues. There were twin brothers in their twenties who lived together. I treated one of the brothers for open sores over one of his kneecaps (the patella). A laboratory culture showed that the infection was due to a particularly nasty bacterium named Staphylococcus Aureus, which in those days was easily treated by Penicillin as well as other antibiotics. The infection cleared. About two weeks later his brother came to see me with the same problem, open sores over the same patella. The infection cleared with the use of the same antibiotics. I was fascinated and questioned both brothers carefully at their next respective office visits. Putting it all together, it turned out that the second brother had put on the same pants one morning that the first brother had worn while the knee was infected. The second brother had an incident that day where a dog charged at him in the street. To avoid getting bitten, he jumped up onto the hood of a car landing on his knees. That would have caused the infected cloth of the pants to press into the skin of his knee cap, causing the infection.

I also learned that there are occasional hazards in managing patients. In one instance, a strongly-built young man complained of a small growth on his Gluteal region (rear end) that was increasing in size. It appeared to me to be a small basal cell carcinoma, which is a cancer that grows slowly but metastasizes (spreads to other parts of the body) only rarely. I told him that I would numb the area with an injection, cut it out and send it to a pathologist for full diagnosis. He agreed. As I proceeded to apply an antiseptic solution with him lying on my exam table, he appeared calm and comfortable. After I injected around the small lesion, he suddenly passed out as I cut into the skin. I slapped on a gauze pad and my medical assistant opened an ammonia vial under his nostrils. I was leaning over him as he opened his eyes with a dazed expression. He started swinging his fists wildly. Fortunately, he didn't connect with me or my assistant. I calmed him down. Since the area of the lesion was quite numb, I was able to excise it in a minute or two. The pathology report agreed that it was a basal cell carcinoma but it had been excised completely. It never recurred.

Despite the increasing income from my young practice's growth, money was tight since the income from the sale of Seg Electronics many years earlier had stopped. A psychiatrist that I had worked with at the Long Beach Veterans' Administration Hospital during my internship stayed in touch with me. He offered me a part-time position at a mental health clinic that he managed in Orange County. The position involved reading electrocardiograms (EKGs), which were done on all of his clinic's patients. I was able to head over to his clinic after my office hours once a week. It helped my income and made me become proficient in reading EKGs. When the EKG reading ended about a year later, my practice growth had more than made up for the loss of income.

Etta Joins In & Mom Comes to Live With Us

Time passed. Etta entered into medical assistant training with the idea of helping me in my practice. She ran into unanticipated problems after she completed training. As a fair number of my female patients saw me for Pap testing, Etta found that distressing. She was able to assist me more in the financial and bookkeeping end of the practice however, and that was a real help to me.

In general, she was thrilled that her husband had become a physician. As I described earlier in this book, when we had suffered financial hardships, her parents told her that she should have married a doctor. During the occasional heated arguments, she reminded me that before we were married, her older sister in Buffalo, New York, had invited her to visit with her family one summer. The ulterior motive wasn't just a nice gesture. It was to have her meet a young man from a Buffalo family who was studying to be a dentist. Whenever that subject came up, I would point out that when that fellow did marry and have children. They had had some grave handicaps with the childrens' mental and physical health. When I pointed that out, it usually settled the argument.

In my new practice, I was invited to many physician dinners at excellent restaurants with the main purpose of having us listen to a lecture on the host company's products. Wives were often welcomed. At the first of those dinners where we both attended, Etta felt uneasy about being in a room with so many physicians and their wives. That uneasiness did not last past the second or third dinner to which we were both invited.

While I had my wife now working with me, we soon had my mother living with us. My parents had been residing in Miami, Florida, for several years when I started medical school. My father passed away from a stroke within a few months after I started my studies in the 1970s. They had been together for well over fifty years through thick and thin. My mother, Rebecca, gave up her home after my father died and she went to live in a residential facility. She welcomed the social life at first but soon tired of the facility. On moving to another residential facility, the pattern was the same. Then, she met a man that met her standards. They got married. The marriage lasted several years until her new husband passed away. Several years later, she married again and this marriage lasted longer.

On what was now her third husband's passing, I invited her to stay with us in California, which she accepted. I flew to Florida to pick her up as she was always afraid of flying. On the flight back, with me at her side, she actually enjoyed her first flight. When I tried to point out that the field of sparkling lights down below was a well-known city, she simply smiled. I assumed that since this was her first flight, the concept was just too much for her to bear.

She stayed with us for about a year. Then the restlessness appeared again since she had very little social life with us. I arranged her next stay at a residential facility close to my office in Huntington Beach. She delighted in visiting my office and remained seated in the waiting room for hours at a time, watching the ebb and flow of my patients. It is almost every Jewish mother's dream to have her son become a doctor, even if it happened so late in life. My brother, Paul, used to complain that our mother did not consider him to be a doctor despite the fact that he had earned a PhD in Education. A great part of my happiness in succeeding at being a doctor was that it brought so much pride and joy to my mother and wife.

Sometimes I jokingly asked a person a question, which I first qualify by stating that different cultures specify different times for when a fetus becomes viable. I start by saying that the Chinese choose the end of the first year of life as to when the fetus becomes viable. Other cultures choose the moment of conception or the moment of birth. I follow with a question, "At what stage does the fetus becomes viable in the Jewish religion?" If the correct answer is not given, and usually it is not, I state, "When it graduates from medical school."

My mother's social life at the new residential facility in Huntington Beach seemed satisfactory for quite a while. One weekend, I received a telephone call from my mother complaining about suffering from a severe case of diarrhea. I told that I would be there shortly. I bought a large bottle of apple juice on the way which I delivered to her. I instructed her to avoid eating regular meals for the next day or two, and to concentrate more on apple juice for a diet plus some carbohydrates like cereal cooked in water. She objected. She said that the apple juice would run right through her digestive system due to her diarrhea. I countered with, "Mom, I'm the doctor now. Please do as I say."

The next day, I called and asked her how she felt. She told me that she felt fine and added that she never realized that apple juice was binding. I explained that the body could handle its own cure, if not overburdened with food, and fluids were replaced by the apple juice which contained the lost minerals.

Things proved to be more serious in her case and I was on the alert. When she had first arrived in California I had taken the opportunity to examine her. I was distressed at encountering a rough heart murmur, which led me to believe that she had suffered from rheumatic fever as a child. In the early twentieth century, rheumatic fever was rampant and entire hospitals were filled with patients suffering from damaged hearts. She was in her late eighties when she was with us and gradually grew more dyspneic. That is, short of breath. Having her checked out further by a cardiologist, she was reported as having a third-degree heart block. That is extremely dangerous due to the fact that the heart could stop beating at any time and, if prolonged beyond a few minutes, would result in death. The obvious treatment is the implantation of a pacemaker. I proposed that to my mother but also had to consult with my family in the East at her request.

While she was reluctant, we persuaded her to go for the procedure. As she had never had any surgery, despite a gall bladder full of stones, we waited at the hospital for the procedure to be completed. To our dismay, the implantation was a failure, since as the surgeon cut through the skin, her blood pressure and heart rate soared. The mild tranquilizer that had been administered was insufficient to prevent her from panicking.

The procedure was postponed until it could be repeated under general anesthetic. By that time, I was contacted by my brother, Paul, who told me that our family felt that she should not be subjected to that panic again. I objected but was overruled. The problem was left to its inevitable result. She passed away in her sleep a few months later, and was cremated according to her own prior decision, as my father had been. All family decisions.

While life dishes out its sorrows, in almost equal measure, it also hands out joys. One of ours was our daughter, Leslie. She had just completed her medical school studies at the Pontifiicia Universidad Javeriana and received her diploma, although she still required completion of her rural year (año rural) to obtain licensure in Colombia. Toward the end of her curriculum, she had met and married a Colombian psychiatrist named Dr. Jorge Betancourt. Jorge was a graduate of the Universidad Nacional and, after completing his año rural, he had established a psychiatric practice in Bogotá.

As Leslie had planned to complete her medical training in the US, she did not intend to enter the año rural. She and her husband moved to the US and Leslie enrolled in an internship at Mercy Hospital in Pittsburgh, Pennsylvania. From there, she enrolled in an excellent ob-gyn residency program at the Aultman Hospital, located in Canton, Ohio. Their daughter was born in 1983 and they named her Isadora. Jorge prepared for his licensure in the US by studying for English and Flex exams, which he passed, and then did his fellowship training at the Jackson Memorial Hospital in Florida.

When I met him, I found his company enjoyable and we spent several hours together speaking both English and Castellano. He described an episode in his año rural, which fascinated me. He spent that year in the deep jungle of Colombia. Traveling between Bogotá and the jungle clinic was difficult. A complicated case which required higher level medical or surgical care necessitated the services of a surgeon or other specialist, flying in a small airplane and landing on an unpaved earthen field. In the case that he described to me, he needed the help of a surgeon whose services were normally ordered thirty days in advance.

A few days prior to the scheduled surgery, he read up on the surgical procedure requirements as he would be expected to assist in the surgery. On the morning of surgery, he prepared the patient and the instruments, and waited for the arrival of the surgeon who was also the pilot. The arrival was obviously delayed. Since the surgeon had not shown up on time and the patient was under anesthetic, Jorge began the surgery himself but intentionally slowly. As he was proceeding, he heard the roar of the plane's motor so he slowed down even more. The plane landed and there was a loud crash and then silence. A few minutes later the surgeon walked into the operating theater carrying the steering wheel of the plane. He was bruised and covered with dirt from the rough landing since he had come in between two trees which broke off both wings. The surgeon looked over Jorge's shoulder and commented that Jorge was doing fine and should continue while he cleaned up. He then disappeared. I don't believe that he was much help after that.

Leslie, after completing her residency training in Ohio, entered into ob-gyn practice with a large established group in Canton. The geographical separation between Leslie and Jorge turned into a complete separation and an eventual friendly divorce. Her medical group ran into some internal disruptions, which made her environment there quite uncomfortable. She contemplated making changes in her practice environment.

My practice in Huntington Beach continued to grow but as competition picked up, due to more physicians moving into the area, the available patients were mostly MediCal. In addition, the trip between my home in North Tustin and my office in Huntington Beach were quite far apart. Since I had a solo practice, I often had to make a middle-of-the-night trip to the Pacifica Hospital adjacent to my practice location, usually to assist in an emergency surgery.

The Patient is the Doctor

One day, I felt a mild pain just under my right front rib cage. The pain did not resolve during the day. When I tried to sleep that night, the pain had increased to the point that it was intolerable. From its location, I assumed that the pain was due to gall bladder calculi (gall stones), especially since my mother had been diagnosed in the past with that problem. The best solution would be to arrange direct admission at the Pacifica Hospital for surgery by Dr. Samuel Cohen the next day.

The only way that I could handle the pain until then was to get an injection of narcotics, such as Demerol, which we had at my office. Getting to the office involved bearing the pain during the trip, although the real hazard was driving home after the injection. I reasoned that traffic would be light late at night and I might be able to get home in time to catch some sleep before reporting to the hospital early the next morning. However, the pain had become so severe that I was not even thinking sensibly. I swallowed some ibuprofen that I had at home and took off. I got to my office, injected the Demerol, and ran to my car. As I started the car, the pain had already begun to subside but as I traveled towards the freeway, within a half-mile I began to feel strange. I pulled into the parking lot of a fast food store, leaned my head back and fell sound asleep. I was awakened about 30 minutes later by two policemen shining a flashlight on my face. I felt somewhat alert and the policeman told me that they had received a report of a man passed out in a car.

I told them that I was a medical doctor and gave myself a shot of pain killer for my gallbladder attack. They asked for proof that I was a medical doctor and I searched my wallet for the medical board's identification card. There were just a few cards. With a little difficulty I was able to hand them the right one. They examined the card and asked me if I was able to continue my trip. I said that I could continue. They advised me to be careful. The rest of my trip was uneventful, although I do recall that a big trailer tractor tooted its horn at me.

I had my surgery the next day at Pacifica Hospital. I had to remain hospitalized for about a week after that. A couple of days before I was discharged, I was visited by my medical assistant, Pauline Annan, with some news for me. She told me that another doctor had offered her the same job in his office, but with more pay. She was quitting without further notice. As an employer who paid his staff decent wages and was never harsh, I always tried to be a model employer. It was quite a shock but it only took a few days to replace her. I promised myself to be more alert to the fact that there were unethical doctors out there who could lure an employee to leave his or her job without notice to the present employer.

Next Step Forward?

As my first five years of medical practice were drawing to a close, and I was ready to negotiate another five-year lease with my landlord, I began to consider some other possibilities. I had been gaining knowledge of the surrounding areas, including Los Angeles and the Inland Empire, which were essentially Orange County's bedroom area. It began about 20 miles northeast of Orange County and extended beyond into Riverside and San Bernardino Counties. Its population was expanding. Construction was springing up all through the area. Corona was not far from my home in North Tustin and was thriving. A more important factor was that my daughter, Leslie, was considering giving up on her contentious medical group and moving to California. We even contemplated setting up a medical practice together.

Leslie had been separated from Jorge for years as they pursued their careers in different parts of the country and then divorced. I had recently received an attractive offer by a young Indian cardiologist who was looking for a family medical practice that could feed him cardiology patients and also make use of his internal medicine training. His offer was $150,000 to be paid as $50,000 cash and the $100,000 paid out over the next five years.

I looked for a practice for sale in the Corona area. I found a small one, which might be a good starting point. The asking price was $28,000, which was not much more than the cost of the equipment. It was located in a well-placed office. I saw it as good opportunity and went ahead with the sale and purchase.

The new practice started off as a disappointment however. The Los Angeles Summer Olympics of 1984 had just started and this jammed up the freeways, making my travel back and forth lengthy and uncomfortable due to the summer weather. Even worse, patients showed up for follow ups of small surgeries that had been botched by the physician that sold me the practice. To complicate matters, my daughter, Leslie, had accepted an excellent offer with a different ob-gyn practice in Canton, Ohio, although she was much happier there and I was happy for that. In addition, she was dating a young man who was an executive of his family's steel fabricating business.

All of these problems and situations showed me that I had a lot to learn. They proved what a great deal I had gotten in my first practice by pure chance.

Suddenly, the whole picture changed. I received an urgent call from my friend, Dr. Samuel Cohen. He told me of an opportunity in Garden Grove, California, where there was a busy, well-established practice whose owner had died of a heart attack. His widow was in charge of the practice and trying to sell it. Meanwhile, she needed family medicine doctors to staff the practice until it could be sold. I called Myra Rosswell, the widow, and we made an agreement for me to see patients there three days a week. The remaining two days a week, I would see my patients in the new practice that I had purchased.

I started seeing patients at the Garden Grove office the following week. This started a learning process that was extremely important. The practice was in an old building that had been owned by the Rosswell family for years. Many of the adult patients had been babies delivered by Dr. Morris Rosswell. Their children were patients as well.

Myra Rosswell supervised the front office and transactions were simplified. For the most part, patients paid in cash. If they were well known, checks were also accepted. There was no insurance billing but on request blank insurance papers would be provided. The total revenue received was high. The percentage that was the net income was about 60 percent of that figure, which is a very high ratio.

There was one hitch however, and it was a big one. A large number of the patients were on a medication schedule of a tranquilizer, Alprazolam, whose brand name is Xanax. This was prescribed at the full, three-times-a-day dosage. 100 pills was the quantity prescribed. The patient was advised early in the drug's administration to take the medication steadily at the three-times-a-day rate and it would make him or her feel great.

What apparently was not conveyed to the patients was that that medication, taken steadily, would cause the patient to become dependent on it. The patient would be told that he or she needed a regular monthly appointment. Using simple arithmetic, a thirty-day supply of this medication, three-times a day, equals 90 pills per month. If the patient did not appear for his or her next appointment at a month's end, the pills would run out in three days. Within that time the craving for the tranquilizer would begin.

During my time at the practice, I counseled the patients on the need to cut back on their use of the Alprazolam. Myra Rosswell would frequently complain to me that my cutting back was harming her deceased husband's reputation, but it was the ethical thing to do in my judgment.

During the few weeks that I worked there, several teams of doctors arrived to learn about the details of the sale. The initial asking price was about $800,000. The potential buyers, obtaining more information, walked away from the deal. I heard that local hospitals, reluctant to lose such a large practice to their competition, were willing to finance the purchase for potential buyers that were already active members of the hospital.

I drew the conclusion that, without the Alprazolam attraction, the income would drop substantially but still should be much above what I was earning in the past five years.

I approached Myra Rosswell as the prospective buyers became scarcer and she was getting more desperate since the medical licensing board was temporarily turning a blind eye to the fact that no medical practice can be owned by an unlicensed person. She knew she was within an imaginary grace period and one day the board would have to take action.

I offered a price, way above my means, of $200,000, which she rejected. We finally went to contract as I added a kicker. A formula was added that included a sliding scale above what I considered to be overly optimistic annual total revenue. Provided that I could obtain the financing, I estimated that I would not need to reach that optimistic total revenue in order to make a decent living, while I could still support the expenses and pay the staff decent wages.

I discussed the overall picture with Dr. Samuel Cohen. He offered to recommend that his bank, the Farmers' and Merchants' Bank, finance my purchase as he was a substantial depositor. He did meet with them on my behalf but was turned down. I had also asked my old friend, Joe Gould, if he could talk to his board of directors on my behalf. He was the chief executive officer of the First State Bank in Garden Grove, close to the office in which I was working. We had met them in Bogotá when they visited their son Mark, in the Peace Corps. They too lived in California and traveled to my office in Huntington Beach every three months for a routine checkup. They were great friends and it was always a pleasure to see them but each routine visit lasted much too long. Anyway, he did go before his Board of Directors on my behalf but, as he described, not without twisting some arms. They agreed and the $200,000 for the purchase was thereby available.

I worked long hours. The practice did not lose as many patients as I had predicted cutting back the liberal use of Alprazolam. Three years after I purchased the practice, the Garden Grove First Bank office that had loaned me the money produced their annual financial report. It featured me as their best customer. The front cover bore a picture of me and the bank manager side-by-side with wide smiles.

A female head of a department at the First State branch office had married a vice president of the Farmers and Merchants Bank. When I crossed paths with her, and after a brief discussion, she confided that she had once asked her husband why his bank turned down my loan. She said that he smiled sheepishly and told her that the Farmers and Merchants Bank was very conservative.

The practice regained its popularity. The patients welcomed the generous time I spent with them. They also welcomed my handling of their emotional well being, and that I could speak in either English or Spanish. Here in Southern California, I began to realize the tremendous advantage that I had achieved by becoming fluent in Castellaño, which is considered to be a somewhat more elegant form of Spanish.

On the downside, the building and equipment were old and obsolete. The parking was crowded and the waiting room small. The rental agreement that I had signed with Myra Rosswell stipulated a five-year term. If things went well, I decided I would make plans to find more modern quarters.

Always optimistic, I also made plans to commence work on a new project to be added to my medical practice. That new project was psychiatric counseling by telephone. The future goal would be the maturation of this service toward television and the internet. A small advertisement produced a tremendous response but landed only a few patients, as well as lots of irate psychiatrists who even complained to the Medical Licensing Board.

The board publicly commented that they trusted I didn't intend to prescribe medications without having examined the patients first. That was enough for me to close down the nascent operation. The timing wasn't right for this type of treatment. Recently, there has been much more interest in treating patients by way of television and the internet. Various startups have already sprung up and blossomed.

New Role as Professor

One day, I received a phone call from my mentor, Dr. Thomas Nelson, who had been elevated to Acting Dean of the University of California, Irvine. Tom and I had been having occasional lunches together. He was interested in my career. We usually picked a restaurant for our lunches that had a South American menu since he had been born and spent his early childhood in Colombia. I still felt a lot for the people and customs of Colombia.

One afternoon as I was seeing my patients at the office, I remembered that I had just missed my luncheon appointment with my friend Dr. Tom Nelson. I called him and he was gracious about the mishap. He said that he understood that I was busy and it just slipped my mind. Those were the days when there was no blackberry or smart phones. Later I carried a clumsy electronic storage device for my contacts and appointments. They've gotten progressively smaller since.

His surprise news was that he had nominated me as an Assistant Clinical Professor in Family Medicine at a meeting of Irvine's administrators. Like Joe Gould before him, he did some arm twisting and I was accepted. The appointment was prestigious. I was extremely proud and grateful. There was no salary involved as it was a volunteer position but I was expected to be teaching just a minimum number of hours per year to maintain my faculty appointment. Being able to add the Assistant Professorship to my business cards and letterhead was quite a feather in my cap.

Aside from delivering an occasional lecture on campus, I would receive a third year medical student at my practice several times a year, whom I would tutor. I would introduce him or her to my patients. The externship students in my office became useful. They first saw patients with me present. Gradually, they came to deal with patients without me. They were required to discuss the patient's case with me before making any important decisions.

Aside from the prestige, the program kept me on my toes. After they well indoctrinated, the students began helping with the patient load. There were some special privileges at the University of California, Irvine Medical Center, such as reserved parking slots and access to research facilities. After about five years with that faculty appointment, I was promoted to Associate Clinical Professor. My faculty appointments lasted twenty-three years until I retired. At one time, I was considered for a full professorship which never worked out but each year I received a certificate of appreciation from the Department of Family Medicine.

The Next Move

As my five-year contract with Myra Rosswell drew to a close, an accounting of the practice verified that I had exceeded the contract level for revenue that we had set by agreement. I was obligated to pay a percentage of the amount over that level. However, I had some offsets for failures on her part. We entered into some discussions, which turned bitter, and when she learned that I was planning to move the practice out to more modern quarters, she threatened to sue me. She went as far as serving legal papers on me. Finally, common sense prevailed. We settled the matter between us. I arranged to make the additional payments on a monthly basis, which made it less onerous.

Meanwhile I had been scouting for a better location and facility. A yoghurt shop at the corner of two major intersections in Garden Grove had been vacant for two years. The store had large windows opening on the two avenues. The available useful area was a little more than 1,000 ft square which was relatively small. Taking advantage of my training in engineering, I laid out the space for an ample-sized business office, waiting room, x-ray room, two bathrooms, and a private office. I had drawings prepared by an engineering office and I supervised the construction. It turned out to be an efficient medical office. I had my name on the signs facing both avenues. The arrangement of my new medical office fitted well into the upscale plaza while visibility of the signage on two major thoroughfares was a marketer's dream comes true.

With everything moving along smoothly, I applied for and received staff physician approval at three hospitals: Garden Grove Hospital, Fountain Valley Regional Hospital, and St. Joseph Hospital. I made friends with the physician community at the new hospitals. From them, I gathered that it was assumed I was a wealthy, older guy who was in medicine as some sort of a hobby. On the other side of the coin, it was rumored that I was some sort of a marketing genius to have wound up with such an efficient office in such an excellent location since I recognized that the vacant yoghurt shop was a hidden treasure.

I frequently attended hour-long medical conferences at the Garden Grove Hospital to satisfy the medical board's requirement for annual CME (Continuing Medical Education). These conferences were given once a week during lunch time.

At one of the conferences, the speaker was a well-known female Rheumatologist, Dr. Lalita Pandit. She was presenting her material backed up by an excellent slide presentation. At one point, the full screen showed an ugly hand with gnarled fingers outstretched. She questioned the audience as to what the picture represented. None of the physicians ventured an answer until I spoke up by calling it Tophi. She instantly responded, "Good." Tophi are the lumpy formations of uric acid crystals over the joints of the body in people suffering from gout. In severe cases the fingers become gnarled and twisted.

All of the physicians turned to look at me with broad smiles, particularly a urologist named Stanley Cohen (not to be confused with Dr. Samuel Cohen) to whom I had referred some of my patients. We became fast friends. After that episode, no one ever repeated that medicine was just a hobby for me.

I delivered one of the lectures at Garden Grove Hospital for the staff's CME. My material was on the effect and treatment of high lipids, which include the good and bad cholesterol as well as the triglycerides. The latter is the form in which fats travel through the blood. I was innovative in using high dose Niacin, a B vitamin, as a booster of the good cholesterol. At that meeting, I recall that I was asked a question about the dosing of Niacin by an internal medicine specialist who was a favorite of the hospital administration. He had been Chief of Staff for several years. His father had retired from his internal medicine practice at the Garden Grove Hospital and his son took over the practice. The administration and staff of the hospital were all in shock when he passed away at the age of thirty seven. He had stayed at his office late one night to catch up with some paper work but didn't return home. His family called hospital security who found him slumped over his desk. As an only child, his parents were inconsolable at his passing.

Opportunity Knocks – Surgeon General of the US

While reading an article in *The New York Times*, another opportunity presented itself to me. It was about the trials and tribulations of the female Surgeon General of the United States. She had raised a fury with her broadcast advice to our young people that masturbation was a better substitute for early sex. That storm resulted in her resignation.

On a daring impulse, I brought my Curriculum Vita up to date. I added it to a letter that I addressed to our then President Bill Clinton, c/o the White House, Washington DC. It was a long shot. A few weeks later, I received a letter from his assistant, William Nash, thanking me for offering to serve in the administration. He informed me that my letter would be forwarded to the appropriate authorities evaluating candidates for the Surgeon General position.

I was proud of that interchange because technically, I can say that I had been a candidate for the position of Surgeon General of the United States. Beneath is the letter.

THE WHITE HOUSE
WASHINGTON

July 12, 1995

Dr. Samuel E. Gendler
13010 Harbor Boulevard
Garden Grove, California 92643

Dear Dr. Gendler:

On behalf of President Clinton, I want to thank you for your interest in serving in the Administration.

I have forwarded your portfolio to the appropriate staff handling the Surgeon General appointment. You can be certain that you will be contacted should an opportunity arise where we can utilize your skills.

Your offer of service is welcomed, and I hope that we can count on your continued support.

Yours truly,

Bob J. Nash
Assistant to the President and
Director of Presidential Personnel

Illustration --Copy of Surgeon General Letter

Health Problems and Mr. Pritikin

Before going to the office each morning, I would jog for a half an hour in the area around my home in North Tustin. My jogging was mostly along level ground but included several inclines. Occasionally, I would feel a mild jabbing pain in the left side of my chest which lasted a few minutes at the most. I was never short of breath and I had no history of heart disease although I was aware that my bad Cholesterol (LDL-Cholesterol) was high and my good cholesterol (HDL-Cholesterol) was low. I had learned to be careful of those mild jabbing pains from my gall bladder episode.

Dr. Isaza, in Colombia, had tested my blood once and found that my total cholesterol was around 280, but in those days, the role of cholesterol in heart disease was not well known and the division between LDL and HDL cholesterol was totally unknown.

When I got back to the US in 1977, I heard about Nathan Pritikin who was an engineer that had researched world literature for the relationship between cholesterol, one of the lipids (fats) in the blood and heart disease. He did that study because he had been, in his own words, a "cardiac cripple."

He reported two bodies of evidence backing his theory that cholesterol was the major villain in heart disease. In one finding he pointed out that in WWII soldiers who had died in battle despite extensive surgery to try to save them had fatty streaks in their arteries as early as eighteen years of age. The fatty streaks contained substantial cholesterol.

In the other report, the white governors of South Africa, in building housing for the native population, would include a hospital for each housing unit with sufficient capacity. These capacities would be calculated by the illness records for the white population. Within each hospital, there was a cardiac division. The sizes of these divisions were based on the percentages of those same records and what could be expected from that statistic. To their amazement, the non-white, native population, whose diet mostly consisted of roots and little meat, had so little heart disease that those new cardiac wards were practically empty.

Nathan Pritikin followed his own theories with a carbohydrate diet consisting of lots of fruits, vegetables, and some carbohydrates like grains. The proteins and fats were kept low. His heart disease cleared almost completely and his angina pains disappeared. He described several cases with the same favorable results. Many years later, my brother, Dr. Paul Gendler, and his wife, Rochelle, went into a program that the Pritikin Organization was running. They both lost substantial amounts of weight and felt healthy and energetic from the prescribed diet.

Several years later, I attended a conference where Nathan Pritikin had a debate with Dr. Robert C. Atkins, who became a successful proponent of his low-carb diet. Nathan Pritikin spoke first and I was impressed with his logic, possibly because I am also an engineer. When Dr. Atkins arose to speak, he began loudly. He practically shouted, "Mr. Pritikin," and expounded on a diet filled with many more succulent goodies that are so beloved by our generation. He went on to become a smashing success. He passed away years later from injuries sustained from a fall on an icy sidewalk.

In my case, I contacted the cardiologist that had taken over my Huntington Beach practice, Dr. Harshad Shah. He scheduled an angiogram for me at the Fountain Valley Regional Hospital. It was read as having four major blockages of the coronary arteries and immediate open heart surgery was recommended. The surgeon, Dr. Trivedi, who was a colleague of Dr. Shah, came to my office to persuade me to proceed to surgery without delay. I politely cut him off as I was busy seeing my patients. This was not to be rude, as I knew his credentials were top notch. Neither had I any trepidation about the outcome but duty called. I had to finish with my patients first.

Monday, the CABG (Coronary Artery Bypass Graft) surgery went well and by Wednesday I felt well enough to go home. Dr. Trivedi insisted that I stay another day. I agreed reluctantly and went home on Thursday. Later on I learned that Etta had pressured Dr. Trivedi to keep me there the extra day. On Friday, I went back to work but limited myself to a shorter day at Dr. Trivedi's orders. When I got home that evening, Etta told me that Joe and Dorothy Gould (he was the CEO of the bank that loaned me all that money) had visited early that morning expecting me to be recuperating in bed.

Maybe I should have stayed in bed awhile as it took a few months for my blood supply to return to normal from my post-surgical hemoglobin level, of 10.5, to the normal level, which is over 13. When it did, my energy returned. Meanwhile, I got used to a clicking feeling in my chest whenever I moved to certain positions. The reason for this is the CABG is accomplished by cutting the sternum (breast bone) in half, lengthwise, to expose the heart. It is then closed by twisting wires to hold the two halves together. When I lay in bed, I would feel a thumping that was actually shaking the bed. This was due to the membrane that retains the liquid cushion surrounding the heart, slowly becoming leak proof. Things eventually got back to normal. I was ready to pursue my next project, whatever that would be.

American Breast Centers

It didn't take long. The next project came to me soon after I moved my practice to the new location. I was attracted to an article in a medical journal. It described an experiment by the American Cancer Society in Chicago. They had obtained the cooperation of radiology groups that had mammography practices. For the period of one month, the offices offered mammography studies for $50 each. Before that time, the mammography studies had been priced at about $200 each. They had been successful in attracting women for the studies. Prior to the special rate, mammograms had been unpopular by being unaffordable. Nothing like that was being done in Southern California so I decided to investigate.

The mammography machines were quite primitive compared to today. One version was made by Xerox but was very expensive. There were many competitors out there trying to produce the equipment at more affordable prices.

I settled for one that cost about $75,000 but I could lease it for about $1,000 a month. I hired a mammography technician and rented a store front. Etta was the front office person that signed the patients in. She would collect $50 payments from the patients as they left. A retired radiologist read the mammograms on a fixed price per reading. If we were successful we could save lives by detecting breast cancer early, hopefully before it spread. The radiologists in our area would compete by dropping their prices for routine mammograms. That should make mammography more popular and successful in saving lives and disfigurement.

Before we could open our doors, I experienced a setback. I had set a task for myself to prepare a computer questionnaire to be prepared on the computer keyboard for each patient. The intention was something like present-day Electronic Health Records (EHR). Word processing programs were flimsy then. I had shopped and bought an early version of a program that was helpful but crude. A few times I had to call its designer who was a brilliant gentleman from Alameda, California. His name is Martel Firing and we have been friends ever since.

The day before we were ready for our first patient, I worked feverishly setting up the questionnaire until late that night. It finally came out right and I went to bed. I didn't realize it but the intensity with which I was working must have raised my blood pressure dangerously. In the morning when I awoke, my right eye was bright red. The vision through it was tinged red as well. I went to an ophthalmologist colleague who said that my blood pressure must have been high, which ballooned an artery in the retina. That swelling blocked a retinal vein that burst.

He recommended that I reduce my blood pressure with medication to let the hemorrhage get absorbed and clear up. That happened as predicted. Several months later, when I woke up one morning, I rubbed my left eye and looking through the affected right one there was a black disk in the middle of my eye field. It was due to macular edema, since the deficient circulation caused leaky young blood vessels to crop up.

The treatment consisted of zapping the leaky blood vessels by laser to dry up the macula, which is the part of the retina in the back of the eye with the sharpest vision. If I close my left eye today, any straight lines that I look at with my right eye appear to have small wiggles in them.

All in all, we did open our American Breast Center on time. Overall, we enjoyed some modest success so that we could slowly open others. We opened six centers that soon gained in popularity but their future was cloudy. This was due to the new popularity of mammography which had attracted the watchful eyes of the legal profession as missing a lesion meant a juicy law suit.

Etta was the office manager of the first American Breast facility and enjoyed the opportunity to be part of a growing enterprise. My pleasure at seeing her taking pride in our success was dampened when she was found to have a mild case of CLL (Chronic Lymphocytic Leukemia). The prognosis is bad but the life expectancy averages about fifteen years from diagnosis. We could only hope for the best but she was determined not to use the only definitive treatment which helped prolong life further. That was IVIG and it consists of lengthy blood infusions done on a regular basis.

When I first started the American Breast Centers, my malpractice insurer charged me only $125 for the clerical work to add them to my existing malpractice insurance. After the first missed diagnosis, which was settled for about $30,000 by the insurance company, I was told that I had to find another insurance company. It was an unusual case as the patient was only twenty-six years old, which was a young age to develop breast cancer. In actuality, the mammography field was found to be profitable for malpractice attorneys and premiums soared.

I had tried to get consultations from experts in the field to recheck some of our films. I was able to get some help and they did help somewhat, but the equipment that was available at the time was poor. We did not have the capital necessary to continue upgrading our equipment. One of the experts I was able to attract was Dr. Lazlo Tabar. He was world famous having made mammography available to all through a large program he ran in Uppsala, Sweden. A large percentage of the female population there had already received mammograms.

I went to a conference by him as a visiting Professor to a Southern California University. I also arranged a consultation by him. After his lecture, he drove to my first American Breast Center and reviewed some of our films. I invited him to dinner with us at an upscale restaurant but we almost lost him as he zoomed out of his parking space at my breast center into dense high speed traffic.

As I could ill afford consultants of that caliber, I decided that I needed ongoing supervision of the quality of our work. I ran a classified advertisement in one of the local papers. The most interesting respondent was a young woman named Teresa who had emigrated from Poland earlier in life. Her training in Poland and then the US, as a Radiologic Technologist, seemed to fit well into what I needed even though she was employed elsewhere and would be available only part time. Her hourly rate was also modest and she helped us a great deal.

Since our equipment was inexpensive by the standards of those days, it was a battle to deliver films of high enough quality to be useful in the screening and diagnosis of breast cancer. Fortunately, Teresa was able to help by directing the most knowledgeable California radiology inspectors to us for further advice.

Overall, we suffered from too rapid growth and too little capital. To propel us into the big time would have required an investment of a few million dollars. In those days, such investment capital was hard to come by. There was also the added pressure of seeking a malpractice insurer for the breast centers. I opted for putting up the American Breast Centers for sale. They were sold for six-hundred-thousand dollars to a larger radiology group. There were various equipment contracts that I had to settle and I achieved a profit. Without the breast centers, my medical practice looked good from a malpractice point of view. I was able to transfer to an excellent insurance company at a reasonable price.

My medical practice in Garden Gove saw continued growth and I took another daring step. I learned that a small practice next to the Fountain Valley Regional Hospital was offered for sale at an asking price of fifty-thousand dollars. Fountain Valley is an upscale community about 10 miles from Garden Grove The practice was not expensive, based on location and proximity to the excellent hospital. From the proceeds of my sale of the mammography centers, I purchased the practice from the eccentric physician who had become frustrated by the increasing paperwork associated with billing the insurance companies. He planned to move to another state. His small practice did not accept the MediCal patients as the reimbursement was small, thus far. His patients were more upscale and they enjoyed the extra attention that I could offer them. The main problem was that his practice was small for the expensive rent at the medical building adjacent to the hospital. I hoped to be able to make the practice more popular but that would take a long time.

Assisting At Surgery

My medical license, like all others of that class, bears the heading of 'Physician and Surgeon.' While this may give permission to the bearer to engage in heavy duty surgery, there are major restrictions. The hospitals limit surgeries that can be done in their hospitals to those types and levels where adequate proficiency can be proven by training, licensure, board certification, and insurance coverage. As a general practitioner, I can perform minor surgeries such as removing skin lesions, benign or malignant, as well as others where we have proven proficiency. We are also permitted to assist in surgery with the surgeon present when there is proven proficiency. This has always been an enjoyable part of my medical practice. However, as my practice has gotten so busy it has become much more difficult to take the time to include the surgical assists. There are frequent delays such as when the prior surgery runs into a snag, and the surgeon and I sit there waiting for our turn. I have to factor in that when I run behind schedule there are ill and angry patients in my waiting room. As a result, I have had to limit my surgeries sharply. However, I have had to take any courses ordered by the hospitals or medical board to keep me trained.

Meanwhile, the field is changing. For the sake of efficiency, we generally no longer care for our hospitalized patients while they were in the hospital. A new classification of a 'Hospitalist' has appeared. A hospitalist's training is more specific and their presence in the hospital is usually all day, while physicians and surgeons don't have that luxury.

Many hospitals, as careful as they may be, have had surgical mistakes during an operation. They are a disaster to the family, hospital, and professional staff, such as operating on the wrong side of the body. Elaborate training procedures have been set in place, which have reduced the incidence of these problems. They are rare, but some still occur.

One day, I was ordered to take one of the presentations. The instructor had an excellent video display to back up the program. The theme was on how group awareness of everything present can help guard against accidents. One video began with a group of young men and women fixed in the position of passing or bouncing basketballs from one to the other within the group. The instructor assigned the various tables of seated physicians with the job of counting how many passes were bounced and how many were passed in the air from one to the other. He pressed a button and the action began. I counted six bounced and three overhead when the video stopped. He asked each table for their scores. He asked if anyone saw the gorilla walking among the players. Only two physicians said they had. He fired up the video and, sure enough, there was a gorilla, nonchalantly, walking through the crowd. I was stunned at this powerful example of how concentration on one task can blot out all others.

Physician Assistants (PA-C)

I had fortunately been an innovator in the use of physician assistants which began about one year earlier. Most physicians were reluctant to employ physician assistants for various reasons. For one, patients were not accustomed to professionals other than physicians treating them. This was changing. There were doubts about the quality of their abbreviated medical education. This was changing as well. The PAs admittedly had not been more subject to malpractice claims than the physicians. I had begun to look for a bright PA on a part-time basis to cover both of my practice locations on an alternating schedule.

My third year medical student, from UC, Irvine, told me about an Iranian-born woman, Parvaneh, who was studying to be a physician's assistant. She had just graduated at the top of her class and had started to work part-time for a group of internal medicine physicians. I offered her a position working several days a week and she accepted. My patients liked her. She was popular with the young unattached men, as she was quite attractive. They frequently asked her to go out with them but she was selective and rarely accepted invitations.

Generally, it is not a good policy to mix business with pleasure activities but I did not object. One day, an elderly Scotch patient, during several office visits, tried to persuade my assistant to meet her nephew. Parvaneh finally accepted but something about him did not please her. She turned him down the next time he asked her out. My patient was so offended that her nephew was rejected that she left my practice. If not for that rejection, I was convinced that the Scottish lady would have remained my patient for the rest of her life. This reinforced the policy of not mixing business and pleasure.

Putting that disappointment aside, I was able to offer Parvaneh full-time employment and she accepted. We then were able to cover both practices shifting back and forth on designated days. The Fountain Valley practice slowly began to increase in popularity.

Shared Space

The Fountain Valley office showed promise for the future. Meanwhile the rent and the need to cover the facility myself, or by Parvaneh, made it a financial drain.

A family physician, Dr. L. Davow, who was a friend of mine, approached me with a proposition. His Fountain Valley family medicine practice had been quite stable for many years. The Fountain Valley Regional Hospital that was next to our office building decided to follow the new national trend of hospitals purchasing and operating medical practices. The administration of the hospital made him an offer that was quite attractive since he was getting on in years. They moved his practice, after purchasing it, into a free standing building about one block from the hospital. They equipped the large number of exam rooms with the necessary supplies and apparatus, as well as installing furniture and office equipment. The hospital employed him and a recent medical school graduate to handle the anticipated flood of patients. An advertising campaign was begun which produced little activity. Even Dr. Davow's former patients did not show up en masse. The effort went on for about ten months when suddenly the administration of the hospital told him that they were closing the new offices and that he could have all of his patients back.

Dr. Davow had intended to retire shortly anyway but he was willing to continue on a part-time basis. The main drawback was that he had no office of his own and to start a new office would be a costly operation. He asked me to consider allowing him to rent one exam room for two days a week. I would supply the medical assistant and front office personnel to answer the phones, as well as help his patients fill out the necessary paperwork. My office would do the necessary billing and we would share the amount received on a fifty-fifty basis.

After entering into this arrangement, we continued it for about a year and neither of us had any complaints. During that year, he remained moderately busy for the two days which left him free to pursue his favorite pastime, golf. One day, he came to me apologetically and told me that he had sold what was left of his practice to a physician that would use the patients to expand his practice. We still remained friendly. Later, he confided that his sale of what was left of his practice turned out to be a bad deal for him.

Dr. Davow leaving would have worked out better for me about one or two years later. The vacuum that he left caused me to watch for a similar opportunity.

The next opportunity for someone to share my office space presented itself several months later. A pediatrician entered into a similar arrangement with me. The pediatrician was much busier than Dr. Davow and the arrangement soon became complicated. Trying to grow the practice, the pediatrician kept pressing me to transfer my pediatric patients. As those patients were important to my practice, I refused the request.

The picture became cloudier when I accidentally received a check in payment of a pediatric office visit of which there was no record. When confronted, the pediatrician said it was an experiment. It was obvious that this was a blatant attempt to receive both 50 percent shares. I reasoned that I needed to remain more vigilant and I continued with the arrangement. To my dismay, I learned that I was not vigilant enough.

On further investigation, I discovered that my front office assistant had been offering my newly pregnant patients a choice of obstetricians that were not the usual ones that I normally chose. Upon delivery of the baby, the regular obstetricians we had been referring them to would suggest that I be called to check up on the baby. This would occur while the infant and mother were in hospital. That had been beneficial to my practice as I would often wind up being the family doctor to the whole family. This was done only if the parents did not have a relationship with their own family pediatrician.

It was obvious that the altered choice of obstetricians would favor a different doctor to check up on the baby. It was easy to fathom who that would be.

I served notice on the pediatrician to leave my Fountain Valley office as soon as possible. I also took immediate action to ensure that the front office assistant would have no role in future referrals. The disengagement was troubled and the pediatrician rented space in the same office building. While the suite was being prepared, I was asked to transfer my telephone lines that I had been using for the pediatrician to the new suite. I declined as we were obviously going to compete with each other for the same pediatric patients.

Somehow or other, the lines got transferred anyway. When I questioned Pacific Bell about the transfer, it turned out that it had been done without my signed release. They quickly transferred the lines back to my service.

Once again, I learned that the calls to my lines were being received at the pediatrician's office. I used my engineering training and checked the telephone room of our building. I quickly determined that new wire connections had been added. I removed those connections and threatened strong legal action if the manipulations continued.

Anorexia and Bulimia

Since my internship had been in psychiatry, except for three months of internal medicine, I had been exposed to many alterations in the mental health of my patients. Many of these were related to the self image of patients who pictured themselves as being fat. They would starve themselves, regurgitate food they had eaten, or swallow large doses of laxatives. This disorder was named Anorexia. In the seventies, a wildly popular singer died of that disorder leaving her pianist brother to carry the family name.

The opposite extreme is Bulimia nervosa. The patient binges on enormous quantities of food and tries to make up for it by starving or other methods, as above. There can be a cycle between the two disorders, which is called Anorexia-Bulimia.

I learned that the Placentia-Linda Hospital in Orange County had set aside one floor dedicated to eating disorders. One of my patients had been admitted there. Due to my interest in that field, the hospital directors listed me as one of the attending physicians with training in the eating disorder field. I wound up sharing the patient load with a psychiatrist who had dedicated his practice to eating disorders. I visited the hospital daily for several years until the hospital needed the floor to their regular patients. The eating disorder field had faded in popularity by then.

Even though my offices were quite far from the Placentia, Linda Hospital, several of the patients that I cared for continued to see me at my offices. One female patient has been seeing me for the past twenty years. When I first saw her at the hospital, she had been in the habit of swallowing 95 laxative tablets a day. I felt that I had succeeded when she cut down her use of the pills to about 20 per day.

Royal Army Medical College & 'Sitting' for the RCGP Exam

The troubling scenario with the pediatrician I shared my office space and staff with, reminded me of a troubling thought that was always in the back of my mind. It involved Kaiser Permanente, Fontana, when the company sent me a letter in 1979, asking me why I turned them down in the Match program which would have led to board certification in family practice.

From their point of view, I would have been an experiment due to my advanced age. From my point of view, the extra two years of training past the internship would have taken a chunk out of the time I could actually practice. That is, if I lived to the male average length of life of about seventy-five years. That number assumed that I would remain in good enough health for all of that time to practice. On the other hand, some of the medical insurance companies were threatening to cut out physicians who were not board certified by a set deadline. This was true of the MediCal program as well. They had become better payers to a large extent.

From an article in one of the journals, I learned that the American Board of Family Practice allowed Fellows of the Royal College of General Practitioners (RCGP), to take the American Board of Family Practice exams. If they passed the exam, they became board certified, Fellows of the ABFP. I reasoned that I had a good chance to pass the exam in England. I applied and was accepted after paying a hefty fee.

The exam was given in Westminster Abbey and was lengthy. I had studied from some text books that gave some insight into the way the locals practiced and so I felt prepared. At the mid-day break there was always a mad rush for the 'Loo.' The male loo was more spacious than the female. It was also more adapted for mass urination with two-meter-long urinals so the female candidates simply used the men's' loo.

No one seemed to find it strange. What I didn't realize was that the RCGP exam was graded on a special curve to limit the passing rate to a select few. That restriction eliminated me from the competition by including into a few, carefully tailored questions. For example, "Which of the following numbers would you use to allow a pregnant woman to extend her maternity leave by three months: BC309, AG976 or ......?"

I resolved to retake the exam but be better prepared. I checked out how the UK students were preparing for the same exam. I did some research and found out that many of the candidates for Fellows of the Royal College of General Practitioners were enrolling in a special class given at the Royal Army Medical College. The fee for this enrollment was reasonable so I sent in my money after converting it into British pounds. I was the only Yankee in the class. After two weeks of preparation, we were all pronounced certain to pass the exam.

British physicians don't take the RCGP exam, they sit for the exam. It really didn't matter whether I took the exam or sat for the exam, the hard fact was that I flunked the exam again. All that I had to show for the effort was a big photograph of more than one hundred students of the Royal Army Medical College, all standing in front of the building dressed in gray or black suits except for one Yankee who didn't know better and was dressed in a brown suit.

Like the proverbial bulldog, I was determined never to give up. I was suspicious of the fancy grading system in England. I called the administrators of the RCGP a few months after the exam and they read my grade to me which seemed respectable enough but didn't qualify for the Fellowship.

A few years later, I was still smarting from the licking I took. I did some research and learned that the same ABFP (American

Board of Family Practice) acceptance granted to those who pass the RCGP worked for the RACGP (Royal Australian College of General Practitioners). I applied for permission to sit/take the Australian exam and it was granted.

The exam administered by the RAGCP was different. There were about seven separate rooms with two physicians in each room to question each hopeful applicant. They were essentially free to question the candidate, in any detail they desired, just as long as they stayed within their field. Much of it had to do with physical examination techniques. If any of the seven sections of the exam are failed, the candidate has to repeat it within two years.

I made the long trip to Australia. The exam began early in the morning and continued until late afternoon. Some of the areas for examination were ophthalmology (evaluating vision study exams), pulmonology (use of metered dose inhalers), cardiology, physical examination, and applied clinical knowledge.

As I made my way through the various sections, I got varied responses such as agreeable, guarded, poker-faced, or slightly hostile. At the last section, which was in cardiology, I was questioned at great length with one of the two general practitioners acting as the patient.

He described having mild angina pains on strong exertion. He read off test results including the lipids like cholesterol (HDL and LDL). He explained what his doctors had offered, like surgery (Coronary Artery Bypass Graft or CABG for short) or conservative measures. I opted for conservative measures and what I would like him to do for his general health. I couldn't read either GPs facial expression. I was ushered out of the room by one of them. He asked me to sit outside until they could come up with their decision. I sat there for about fifteen minutes. Suddenly, the door to the exam room opened and out came the "patient". When he spotted me, he rushed over and threw his arms around me. He gave me a powerful bear hug with a big smile. He said, "What are you doing all this for?" He expressed his opinion that I had experienced a great life and didn't need an additional title. I guess they had read up on my background in the papers that accompanied me and were impressed.

I certainly appreciated the warmth with which he greeted me. From that experience, as well as others during my preparations and stay in Australia, I've felt nothing but warm feelings for the Australian people.

Unfortunately, the time I spent in Melbourne for the exams and then Sydney on the way home ended in tragedy. I was awakened during the night by a phone call from my daughter, Leslie, with the news that my wife, Etta, had passed away. For many years, she had had a mild foot deformity in which one toe crossed over the adjacent toe. The raised knuckle of that toe was subject to irritation from any shoe that she was wearing. Since her immune system had been weakened by the (CLL) Chronic Lymphocytic Leukemia that I described earlier, a minor infection by the bacteria, Streptococcus Pneumoniae, raced rapidly up the leg and into the abdomen. It had been noted that her lymphocyte count had been climbing and treatment by IVIG had been recommended but she always declined it. She had died at the Aultman Hospital in Canton, Ohio, where my daughter lived. She had traveled there for the Passover holidays. At the Aultman Hospital, the day before she passed away, she had told Leslie to try to reach me. Leslie was to inform me that on my way back to the US I must stop at our home in Orange County, California, to make sure that our parrot, Arturo, was well cared for. I arrived in the US too late to see her still alive. I attended her funeral services in Canton, Ohio, after stopping to check out Arturo in California who was fine.

In Canton, Ohio, I was called on to deliver the eulogy before the giant crowd of friends and family that had traveled there to pay their last respects. I spoke about the wonderful, proud woman that I had married, loving mother of our three children, our life on two continents, and her powerful religious dedication. There was not a dry eye in the funeral chapel. I was weeping as well. I closed the eulogy with a heartfelt, "See you soon, my love." I did not know I had such a long time ahead of me.

The Subject Was "HMOs AND IPAs"

I dedicated myself to hard work with long hours. My children tried to help me by calling often but caring for the sick was the most helpful of all. I made sure that I took the time to think through the changing face of medicine and how we could adapt to it. By then, all but one of the insurers had accepted my practice's two offices without a whimper. We had an estimated six thousand patients. Their computers were generating records of the patients enjoying better health and longer life.

When I entered medical practice in 1979, fee for service was still popular and there were insurance companies like Blue Cross and Blue Shield, as well as many life insurance companies, that collected premiums from which they paid the physicians' charges. The other big players were Medicare that served our elderly and disabled population, as well as Medicaid (MediCal in California and later, CalOptima, in Orange County), which served the poor and disabled.

During my years in practice, the insurance companies gained more control and competed for employers' health plans. Medicare and Medicaid were getting costly as the population grew and lived longer. Medication became more expensive as drug companies developed new blockbuster drugs for reducing cholesterol, controlling blood pressure and heart disease, as well as many other great health promoters. They also found that they could raise their prices, at will – particularly for their popular medications.

As insurance plans became larger and sophisticated, the patients moved into large medical groups like Kaiser-Permanente, Anthem-Blue Cross, Blue Shield, and Healthnet. The smaller medical groups entered into contracts with the large insurers with payments of fixed amounts per patient, as negotiated by contract.

Solo practitioners and tiny groups of a few physicians would band together into Independent Practice Associations (IPAs) of hundreds, even thousands of physicians. The giant insurers now were being called Health Maintenance Organizations (HMOs). Medicare, the government super-giant, single-payer organization, started a Medicare

Advantage Program in which they contracted with insurers to deliver health care to the senior population. The Medicaid program remained a fee-for-service program. There were some exceptions such as CalOptima in Orange County, California, where they contracted with the HMOs as part of an experimental program.

There was a lot of shifting around and phenomenal changes going on within the medical profession. It all came under the banner of 'Managed Care.' I plunged into that field early and joined several young IPAs. Backed by my local hospital, I helped form a fledgling IPA myself and signed up Primary Care Physicians (PCPs) and specialists. Before we could get our first HMO contract, an IPA where I was a PCP, which had gained its support from a nearby hospital and had HMO contracts, lost its support as its affiliated hospital went into bankruptcy.

Almost at the eleventh hour, our hospital stepped in and financed the merger of the two IPAs. As I had bought a few hundred dollars worth of shares in my startup, I now bought a few hundred dollars worth of shares in the combined entity. I remained as a member of the Board of Directors. The president of the new combined IPA, a colleague I will call Dr. Charles, was a dynamic individual that had been the president of the other IPA that had joined with our IPA. It was like a board game.

Dr. Charles had been a popular general surgeon in the Garden Grove area. After many years in practice, he was found to have become infected with Hepatitis B. This probably was caused by contact with an infected patient's blood during a surgery. During a major surgery, the surgeon's glove sometimes gets pierced by syringe needle sticks or bony projections. Whatever the cause, he stayed in treatment, which kept the virus count to tiny levels, but he was never allowed to perform surgeries. He had excellent disability insurance and devoted himself to managed care business. I considered him one of my best friends and my wife and I would celebrate our birthdays by going out to dinner with them.

My philosophy of participating financially in IPA activities was simple. Whenever I had bought shares in the stock market, they most often turned bad. Here, I was involved with entities at a small investment.

My popular practice might make quite a difference in the outcome. I set aside the shares and assumed they were essentially worthless as there was no market to resell them. Time would tell.

I joined several more IPAs but only one of them allowed me to buy into ownership. After several years of being an important PCP (Primary Care Physician), with two offices and thousands of patients, I was offered one share for $2,500 which I bought albeit pessimistically. I was part of their Board of Directors and attended the board meetings regularly. You don't learn this at medical school, at least not back then. You had to learn as you go and I was learning managed care by the seat of my pants.

The largest of my neighboring IPAs was one affiliated with the Fountain Valley Regional Hospital. Since I had a Fountain Valley office, I had accumulated several hundred patients in that IPA but I had no seat on their board nor was I permitted to purchase any shares.

From time to time, every medical practice gets a complaint from an irate patient. I have learned to pay a lot of attention to them as the HMOs and their supervising government agencies are vigilant about those complaints. One day, I received a complaint letter from the Fountain Valley IPA, which I dismissed as being superficial. The complaint was initiated by a woman that stated that she had called my Garden Grove office where her family had been treated in the past. She alleged that she requested to have her child seen and was given an appointment date and time for the following Saturday. She arrived with her family on Saturday, at the appointed time, but my office was closed. They waited but the office was never opened, so they left.

The IPA's letter demanded an answer and requested my appearance before their Board of Directors. I prepared a letter stating that our office is never open on Saturdays and I denied her complaint thinking it a simple misunderstanding. At the board meeting, the response was not only lukewarm but one of the board members quoted an old saying, "Yes, but, where there's smoke there's fire. We will have to record this on your record as a justified complaint. If it happens again, we will take severe action."

I replied, "If you don't believe what I am telling you, then I will resign from your IPA," believing that they would back down at the prospect of losing a few hundred patients. I stalked out but they never asked me to return. I was brought down a notch or two by assuming that these patients would all insist on having only me as their PCP. Things don't always go the way we assume. They simply switched the few hundred patients that I had to other PCPs probably to the board members themselves. I tried to profit by the knocks like this one and often I did.

Healthnet

While the downers hurt there are also uppers. One such was my experience with Healthnet, the giant HMO. After doing some hospital rounds, I returned to my office and my office manager informed me that I had received a call from the Chief Medical Officer of Healthnet. When told I was not in, she asked that I call her back when I returned. This was scary as it came from way up the ladder at Healthnet. I was afraid that there might have been some major complaint. I called her back and she made my day (and year) with her request, "Dr. Gendler, you have been highly recommended to us. Our CEO's mother lives in Garden Grove. Would you do us the favor of accepting her as your patient?" I was absolutely stunned as I couldn't imagine a finer tribute from a lofty source. I still get goose bumps when I recall this incident. I accepted her into my practice with great pleasure. My assumption was that the Healthnet computer system was sophisticated enough to track their patient base with outcome scores and each PCP was rated according to that outcome score. If that assumption is correct, then my score must have been one of the best for my area.

After several visits to the CEO's mother, I excused myself as she was also under the care of an excellent specialist in her problems whose office was quite close to her residence. My office was at the other end of town and traveling back and forth was stealing time from my busy schedule.

Cigna Healthcare

Few patients realize what goes on behind the scenes in terms of their doctors and the insurance companies that service their claims. It can be dramatic at times. With the intense competition among the various small IPAs, they were all doing quite poorly as they did not individually have the large patient census to negotiate a substantial payment from the HMOs each month for each patient (PMPM – Per Member, Per Month). Since the PCPs usually belonged to most of the various IPAs in their area, the HMO could threaten that they would not increase the PMPM per month. It would be take it or leave it. They had that much power.

On the other hand, PCPs were not receiving payments for each office visit by a patient but were receiving a capitation payment (PMPM) which usually ranged anywhere from $8 to $10. This low payment per month, which added up to about $100 per year, obligated them to provide the medical services for the patient all year long. The IPA paid some of the other obligations like specialist charges, vaccines, injections, hospitalizations (the latter was usually shared with the HMO), and sometimes medications. It was a mess. Most of the IPAs were close to bankruptcy.

The capitation payment scheme led to some abuses by the PCPs. These included restricting patients' office visits to one or two per year, instead of the mandated three to four. The less frequent visits make it easier for the PCP to accept more patients into his practice but increased the tendency to send patients to specialists rather than treat them. This raised the cost of medical care for the IPAs and pushed them towards bankruptcy.

One IPA which grew up in the south of Orange County achieved a huge census of several hundred thousand patients. They wielded lots of clout with the HMOs due to their large size and so could command a substantial increase in the PMPM rates. I was an active PCP in that IPA as well, and my two offices had about a thousand of that giant IPA's patients in our census.

They helped me in one additional respect other than paying me the capitation rate. As I mentioned before, the one HMO that had never accepted me was Cigna healthcare. I had applied for acceptance as a qualified PCP years earlier. My application was submitted to them as part of a contract negotiation with a smaller one of the IPAs of which I was a PCP. The contract was accepted by both CIGNA and the IPA. Somehow my application with CIGNA was lost. By the time they reviewed my replacement application, their administration had instituted a rule that only board-certified PCPs could be enrolled in their HMO. This was done to support their claim that they were champions of high-quality healthcare. This new rule resulted in their rejection of my application.

I wasn't deterred. I appealed and went to a meeting with their California administration staff to present my case. The meeting was chaired by their medical director. I noticed that while the members of the audience were smiling and nodding at my presentation, the young medical director was standing stiff necked and tightlipped to one side of the auditorium. He did not ask any questions and I knew that he was the enemy. As expected, my appeal was rejected. I learned by hearsay that, after I left the meeting, he addressed the group and pointed out that the national CEO and vice presidents had mandated board certification. He implied that it would go badly with the staff here in California if they had approved my application and appeal. He thought that was that. But it wasn't.

I tried again when new medical directors took office but to no avail. Years later, I caught the opportunity to apply more pressure. A new medical director took office at the same time that CIGNA was negotiating a contract with the giant IPA that I previously described. I emailed the new medical director, congratulated him on his appointment, and facetiously pointed out that I admired CIGNA's high ethical standards in never bending their rules against permitting acceptance of a PCP that was not board certified. In my case, I said they had maintained their high standards despite the fact that, with my census of about 6,000 patients in my two offices, 1,000 of them should have been CIGNA patients, instead of zero, which showed that they prized ethics over profits. That tongue-in-cheek email plus the giant IPA's pressure did the trick. I was accepted as a CIGNA PCP.

More recently, after about ten years of treating CIGNA patients, I received a special letter that stated that CIGNA had recently adopted a new classification for outstanding physicians, which normally had been assigned only to the best of only their specialists by naming them 'Physician Designates.' CIGNA was now going to extend that title to their best PCPs. I was one of the first PCPs to receive that new title. For the next open enrollment period, the catalogs of medical groups and physicians, from which the patients could choose their PCP, would indicate the highest quality physicians with an asterisk (*), indicating their 'Physician Designate' status. Sweet victory.

The giant IPA made it obvious that in order for an IPA to exist and pay their PCPs and specialists a decent income, there had to be higher payments from the HMO's to generate higher capitation rates. That could not be done without a much higher census in the IPA. The logical conclusion was for the smaller IPAs to merge together to gain the necessary clout.

At the somewhat larger IPA that we had formed under Dr. Charles, from the merger of two smaller IPAs, we ran an efficient organization. It generated a small bonus each year for the PCPs and an even smaller one for specialists. My practice, with its certified physician assistant, was particularly efficient. It helped all of the IPAs to which we belonged earn a profit. Each IPA received a payment per member per month (PMPM) for each of our patients enrolled with them that substantially exceeded the capitation rate (PMPM) that we were paid.

Since my use of a physician assistant proved practical, and even profitable, Parvaneh had been working full time as a permanent member of my staff. That is until she met a young electronics engineer and got married. A few years later, Parvaneh resigned since she was expecting their first child. Over the next few years, I employed other physician assistants and/or nurse practitioners (NPs). The practical difference between the two classifications is that I was required to review and sign the charts of my physician assistants but not my nurse practitioners. In fact, a nurse practitioner could open her own office and advertise for patients without a physician's signature on the charts.

With the employment of auxiliary healthcare providers, I was able to staff my two offices fully for five days a week. The physician assistants were not popular at first, but the patients got used to them. As the physician assistants appeared in more offices around the area, they were considered part of the team. Those patients of mine who were impatient often preferred them to selecting me. Typically, I ran late due to the extra time I spent with my patients.

Forming a Master IPA (AIPA)

Dr. Charles was a rigid taskmaster and his basic principle was that the IPA was essentially an organization of PCPs. The specialists were something extra. If there might be some money left over at the end of the year, it was given to the PCPs mainly. Specialists got a smaller bonus. It was slim pickings for years.

If any physician retired or lost his license, he was entitled to receive only what he paid for his shares without any interest. Over the years, they were more opportunities for the IPAs to earn extra money, especially from the Medicare population. The giant IPA, with its several hundred thousand patients, was earning many times the amount that all of the smaller IPAs earned together.

Dr. Charles proposed the idea of a Grand Master Plan to combine our IPA with several IPAs that competed with us. We would merge to form a much larger IPA with a census of about 50,000 patients. Each of the IPAs that were part of the merger would have representation on the board of directors. Dr. Charles would be the medical director and the board would elect a president and secretary from the board members. There was lots of discussion and bargaining but the plan went through. Each of the IPAs that had merged into the big one, which I will call 'American IPA' (AIPA), would elect two or three board members depending on the number of patients in each of the IPA components. Each of the IPA members would elect an advisory committee that met outside of the board. They would submit their resolutions and recommendations for consideration to the main Board of Directors. Each of the founding members was asked to buy in with a minimum payment of ten-thousand dollars for their shares. Any shares that belonged to shareholders of the merged IPAs had to convert their shares into an equivalent percentage of AIPA shares.

After the merger was completed, AIPA had to negotiate with each contracted insurance company (HMO) and negotiate new rates or continuance of the old rates. This was done mostly at the old rates just to get approval. With an increased census of about 50,000 patients, instead of 5 to 10,000 patients per each IPA, it was expected that the overall PMPM rate would improve greatly.

Despite all the careful planning and negotiating, AIPA almost floundered as the component IPAs were losing money. My practice, with its two offices, was part of the Garden Grove Division that was way out in front in earning money for AIPA. We earned six dollars PMPM above the monthly payment we were receiving for caring for our patients. The Fountain Valley division was next with earnings of twenty five cents PMPM. The rest were all losing money. I was also a member of the Garden Grove division committee.

While it might seem more like some major takeover on Wall Street rather than the medical field, the dust started to settle. When AIPA finally reached a profitable level after some years, and was even generating a bonus each year, I was not happy with the distribution. That's because my Garden Grove Division was earning the most money for AIPA. Yet the money was distributed equally as bonuses rather than proportionately, according to the biggest earners. I pushed hard and campaigned to become a member of the Board of Directors. I also watched for my opportunity to try to move to the chairmanship of my Garden Grove committee.

The Garden Grove division committee had joined with the Anaheim division committee to form the Garden Grove/Anaheim division. The

Anaheim division chairman had been the head of the joint committee for many years. When he retired, I put in the effort to become the Chairman of the joint Garden Grove/Anaheim committee. After each two-year period, the individual committees nominated their candidates for the AIPA board of directors. I prepared a stack of letters to be mailed out to all shareholders and committee members, urging them to elect me to the board and to the Garden Grove/Anaheim committee. The timing of the mailing had to be exact. Not too early and not too late. This would not allow time for an organized negative response of any kind. I was successful, being elected to the AIPA board and to the Anaheim/Garden Grove Division Committee.

After many years on both boards, I pressed to become the chairman of the Anaheim/Garden Grove Division Committee who was retiring. The members of the committee were comfortable accepting me as their chairman. I never pressed to become an officer rather than a member of the big AIPA board of directors.

As a member of the AIPA board of directors, I had to vote on their distributions of bonuses and many important matters that came before the board. Every two years my term expired. I electioneered to retain my position as a member of the board, which had to be approved by a meeting of the shareholders of AIPA. As a major shareholder of AIPA and probably the highest earner, I was approved every two years for my seat on the board. With overall increased earnings, the annual AIPA bonuses to the PCPs grew and semi-annual dividends were voted in for the shareholders.

At one of our committee meetings, I recommended that we request a larger share of the annual bonus due to our much larger earnings for AIPA. My Anaheim/Garden Grove Division Committee voted to request an increase of our annual bonus by $1.50 PMPM due to our $6 PMPM earnings which far exceeded the rest of the PCPs in AIPA.

At the next meeting of the board of directors, I presented the recommendation. The opposition was as fierce as expected.

Dr. Charles was one of the loudest opponents. As I had seen happen before with him, he turned furious. I finally achieved a small increase of about a third of what was requested for my division. As I left the board meeting, I passed him on the way out and he stopped me. I thought he was going to congratulate me, but he shouted, "Do you know why you were able to earn an extra six dollars PMPM for AIPA? Your division was getting paid less." I was shocked.

This man, who had been my good friend for years, had been hiding the numbers that each division was getting paid. In his fury, he gave away the secret. This should have been open information for the board to approve. I felt betrayed and never trusted him again. I vowed that I would make every effort to be on top of every matter that AIPA was considering. It helped that my practice was the top earner of all the PCPs.

Here again was the proof that everyone should be watchful, in every situation. Do not assume that you can trust someone just because he or she is a good friend, another physician, or practices the same religion.

New Partner, New Life

I didn't dwell on it. I moved on. My two offices kept me busy in seeing patients and directing the operations. My hospital work was diminishing and the new arrangement was that hospitalists would take over in seeing the patients in the hospital. I only limited my hospital practice to seeing newborns late in my career. The toughest part of the hospital work was the emergency admissions which could occur anytime of the day and night.

My hospital visits involved all of the hospitals that I had signed up with. They were numerous. Of special interest was the University of California Medical Center, my Alma Mater. After all, I was an 'Associate Clinical Professor' in family medicine and I lectured at the university occasionally, with most of my teaching activity in my office.

On one of my trips to that hospital, I encountered a twist of fate. As my patient was having a bedside radiology study done, I quickly recognized the radiologic technologist as the same young lady who had helped me in my mammography venture, Teresa Leyko. We chatted and I noticed that her strong Polish accents had smoothed over to add a charming touch of an accent to her English.

I invited her to have lunch with me during the next weekend at the nearby Doubletree Hotel. She agreed and it was enjoyable. I found her intelligent and unattached. Little by little, our friendship became much deeper and I introduced her to my friends, including Doris DeHardt, a well-known clinical psychologist that I knew well since my VA Hospital internship. Doris commented to me after our get together that Teresa would make an excellent wife and life partner. She magnified that by stating her opinion that Teresa would always do as I say without any quibbling. That prediction turned out to be as wildly incorrect as when Custer ordered his men to "Go and surround the Indians."

For us to get married, we had to face various considerations. She was Catholic and I am Jewish. She is about thirty years younger than me. I had children about her age, while her son was in his first year of medical school in Poland.

When I expressed my plans to marry Teresa, my children were much against the idea. My oldest son, Jeff, and his wife, Pam, were first to accept the idea. They offered to be the best man and bridesmaid at the ceremony.

That wedding ceremony was at Temple Beth David in Westminster, California. The marriage was excellent. She took early retirement from UC, Irvine, and worked with me in my medical practice. Sometimes she encountered problems in the practice which I was able to remedy. One example was that my office manager, who had been doing the billing, was overwhelmed but never reported the problem. Teresa tackled the problem and found that the billing was seriously delayed. She even found several insurance checks amounting to thousands of dollars each that had never been deposited. The solution was to outsource to a billing service. That shift was a problem at first but was gradually straightened out. The end result was increased income. Teresa helped us achieve a great prosperity with a net income of about $500,000 per year. We established a trust to handle our estate when one of us passes on.

She was a great help in other ways in my medical practice. She was always available to recommend the best type of x-ray, CT scans, or MR's, from her many years of radiology experience. When she retired from UC, Irvine, as 'Senior Radiologic Technologist,' the University had to hire two technologists to replace her.

The MediCal organization in Orange County was named CalOptima. They mandated that every practice accepting their patients has to prepare Policy and Procedure Manuals for every procedure done in the office. Teresa had experience with them. She devoted herself to working on those manuals for our practice. She did this at home. After I ate my supper, we would work over the project until late at night. Mostly, I corrected spelling mistakes. When the manuals were completed, I delivered them to the office. At the next CalOptima inspection, their team was so impressed with the results of our work that they sent us a letter of commendation. From time to time, they sent us staff to impress them with what the manuals should contain and how they were to be used as reference.

Things were the best that could be expected. Even Teresa's family accepted me quite well. Shortly after we were married, we visited her parents living in a small city in the northeast of Poland, Augustow. Her father, Mietek Prawdzik, now retired, held an important post in that part of Poland. He had been the chief forest manager for a very large resort area of forests and lakes with several hundred men working under him.

From his photos, I was impressed with his noble appearance and bearing. I could see where Teresa's good looks stemmed that had so attracted me. Teresa's mother, Romualda, was good looking but in a different way. Communication was a problem among us as I just knew a few words of Polish. They knew very little English. Once again, Teresa had her work cut out for her and had to do lots of translating.

A few years later, Teresa's parents came to visit us so I planned some events. One patient of mine who was a full-blooded Native American had described to me an annual event in Indio, California, called a 'Pow Wow' that was to be held during Teresa's parents' stay. The pow wows were intricate dances by the various tribes in their native costumes which were both elaborate and expensive, particularly those with much feather decoration. At the end of the pow wow, the elders rolled out a blanket to receive donations for the poorest Native Americans. It gave my father-in-law a distinct pleasure to walk over to the blanket and place our contributions.

Back in Orange County, I rather capriciously took advantage of a special event. It was by a drug company. They invited me and my wife to a dinner meeting on a boat that was sailing around the Newport Harbor. I asked the sales representative that invited us if I could bring my in-laws from Poland to the event. I described my father-in-law as a Polish physician who did not speak any English. It went off beautifully and Teresa's parents enjoyed the dinner and tour. One thing that I did not anticipate was that the sales representative, at the beginning of his presentation, would introduce_my new in-laws as 'Doctor and Mrs. Prawdzik' (pronounced PRAHVchik), visitors from Poland.

My father-in law passed away a few years ago. Teresa went to his funeral in Augustow. She discouraged me from making the trip since it is arduous and included a lengthy railway trip. She described that most of the population of the city turned out for his funeral, as well as more distant groups that had contact with him. They paid tribute to the noble leader that had done so much to keep the Polish forests and lakes clean and healthy, so that they could enjoy the beauty of their countryside.

After his passing, Teresa's mother came to visit us on a tourist visa. We had invited her to come to the US and live with us. She held a green card, or permanent visa, that she obtained when she visited and worked here in the eighties. That type of visa was considered permanent in the past but the rules had changed. Now it was considered abandoned.

She agreed to stay in the US but required a new application as a permanent resident. I prepared the paperwork and paid the fee but there was no response from our immigration people until her tourist visa was about to expire. I prepared another application, this time for an extension of her tourist visa. One month later that new application was answered from the Mission Viejo division of the immigration service saying that they had rejected her application. The reason given was that it was unnecessary to have her tourist visa renewed since the records show that she was a legal resident of the US. That was an unusual letter and apparently it changed the immigration services own protocol for processing her permanent visa which was approved shortly thereafter.

She lived with us for a while. She later opted to travel to her son's home in Issaquah, Washington, where she presently resides.

Moving Again

I was planning a move myself. This time my Garden Grove office had proved itself with its efficiency of scale and location. Thousands of motorists passing that intersection saw my name emblazoned on both avenues. Under managed care, the patients had to make choices of their PCPs from the HMOs' catalogs when they signed up.

For the people of Garden Grove and the surrounding neighborhoods, my name was recognizable. My Garden Grove office was getting crowded with the Fountain Valley office not far behind. As my lease was coming up for renewal in Garden Grove, I asked the onsite property manager of the mall about a renewal of the lease. He told me that he would discuss it with the new owners of the mall, a Japanese company. A few weeks later, he visited my office and told me that they wanted to know the terms by which I would renew. I laid out some simple requirements such as maintaining the present rent structure and painting the awnings. He said that sounded reasonable and he would let me know promptly.

Weeks passed by with no further word. I was getting concerned. I received a telephone call from the business development manager of Garden Grove Hospital. She alerted me to the fact that a new physician to the area was looking for office space and his real estate agent offered him mine. I investigated further. I found out that there was a lot of turmoil. A large mall, which was somewhat decrepit, was located diagonally opposite to my office suite. A financial group was proposing to renovate the entire mall to an upscale shoppers' paradise. They had run into trouble with the financing but were fighting hard to resurrect the project. Starbucks, which had its eye on the potential of the new enterprise if it ever took off, was dangling an interest in taking over the whole structure on the diagonal corner which contained my office. My office would be the first prize since it was up for lease renewal.

I confronted the property manager with what I had learned. His only reassurance was that if the mall project revived itself I would receive ample notice to give me time to find a new location. Since so much had been hidden from me for so long, I had little confidence in his reassurance. I began to make plans for a new move.

I had confidence that I could forgo the marketing power offered by the corner location, especially since I had achieved an excellent reputation and popularity. The Garden Grove Hospital was only a few blocks east of my present location. Its adjacent medical office building had space to offer. The suite that was available was appropriate for a somewhat smaller practice as it had the disadvantage of a long corridor into the waiting room being carved out of a larger suite.

But, as they say, beggars cannot be choosers. I accepted and negotiated a five-year lease with the hospital management. It worked out well but I kept watch for a better space.

At the end of the five-year lease, I transferred to a larger suite on the top floor of the medical office building. Before I settled that matter, I looked for office space in the medical office building on the opposite side of the hospital. While that building was more elegant and had better elevator service, the rents were higher and the suite was not as well laid out.

Independent Contractor

There were few surprises in the coming years. I began to give thought to retiring. I was in my early eighties. The workload, which now included lots of paperwork, was growing. My shares of ownership and the Board of Director positions in AIPA were providing me with an auxiliary income. Each board and committee meeting, as well as the semi-annual dividend payment, was rewarded with a check. The annual PCP bonus was substantial as AIPA was generating large profits. This would vanish if I sold my practice and retired.

The overwhelming factor in this internal debate was the fact that I must wind down. I was in my early eighties. I worked hard for over half the week with lots of extra activity in my spare time. Due to the increasing patient load, I had set up an additional half day of practice on Saturdays for my staff. This was to avoid having my patients go off to Urgent Care Centers. The care in those places was quite variable and even capricious.

With frequent surgeries on my health record, the odds favored that my continuing to work would be interrupted from time to time. I kept receiving requests from some of the local medical group practices to discuss a possible sale of my practice. Their offers were miniscule. This was due to the philosophy that a medical practice was essentially worthless as a business. I didn't buy into that type of thinking. Non-medical businesses, whether with one owner or several, were valued at three or more times their net earnings before taxation. If the owner or owners were working in the business, replacing them had to be factored into the equation as well.

Only one suitor was coming up with a willingness to negotiate. The business name was the Pathway Medical Group and they had integrated about ten private practices into their own. In general, the owners of those practices continued to see their own or the group patients while working at a reduced or full schedule according to their choice. The reputation of the owner was outstanding in that it was known that his word was his bond.

That might have been so but we negotiated for more than two years. Several times the negotiations floundered but the interest was there. We finally agreed on the terms of the sale with a total price of $1,000,000 payable at $500,000 on signing the agreement. The remaining $500,000 would be paid out at a sliding scale over the next two years. The work schedule was programmed at four days per week for the first eight months, three days a week for the second eight months, and two days a week for the last eight months. The owner confided that the $500,000 was the largest check he had ever seen, as well as the largest amount of money he had ever paid out for something. We signed up with a contract date of May 1, 2005, for the beginning of our merger.

Maybe it was from all the stress, but a few weeks later I developed a UTI (urinary tract infection). At my age, a UTI is usually a frequent complication of an enlarged prostate gland restricting the flow of urine. An antibiotic I had taken for the infection had also caused a rupture of my Achilles tendon. I had surgery for rejoining the Achilles tendon, and reaming out the constricting prostate tissue (TURP) in tandem. I was fitted with a plaster cast until the reunion of the Achilles tendon gained strength. As it did that, I got on track with my prostate.

Upon discharge from the Garden Grove Hospital, the CEO, Maxine Cooper, saw to it that I would be sent home by ambulance. Two strong attendants were to carry me in a Gurney up the steps to my home. She procured two wheelchairs for me, a full-sized one and a portable one, as well as a portable potty. The only problem was that one of the two attendants was a small woman. They came close to dropping me. It's not easy for a doctor to be a patient, but I persevered.

I was paid by Pathway steadily through the several months of incapacity but I began to work after three months when the full length cast was replaced by a short one. I got around that month by renting two electric scooters, one for each office, GG and FV. Teresa kept me mobile by wheeling me in a wheelchair around my home as well as to my doctor visits.

I filled the two years of my contract. Aside from being the oldest person on staff, I was treated by them as an advisor and counselor. There were PAs working under me and I made myself available to them for patient and HMO problems. The owner expressed willingness to continue our arrangement as the contract ended. I asked for the same pay for the last contractual four months at two days per week for my new employment as an independent contractor. He gulped once or twice but acquiesced.

First Prize

The giant IPA that had dominated our area held semi-annual staff meetings. To encourage attendance, they started each session with a medical knowledge quiz for which they awarded three prizes. In 2007, I won the first prize for which I was awarded $500.

One of life's mysteries cropped up when I won the prize, which was awarded late at night. I proudly told a patient about the competition the next morning. I told him I had beaten one hundred and fifty doctors the night before in a medical quiz. He surprised me with, "And you won $500. I read about it in the morning paper." I questioned him as to which paper but he didn't remember as he reads several each morning. Each time he comes to see me we talk about it. It remains a mystery. It is unusual for something so routine to make it into the morning papers so early the next day.

An interesting incident related to that prize took place a few months later. A regular patient of mine used to travel from Seal Beach, California. It was a 20 mile trip to my office. He had some cardiac problems that I was handling but I felt that he should be referred to a cardiologist as the heart problems were getting serious. I spoke to him about this referral and he was agreeable. I sent him to a young but knowledgeable cardiologist, Joseph Westley. At his next office visit to me, I asked the patient how he liked Dr. Westly. He said that he liked him a lot. He felt that the examination had been thorough. He added that there was something that might be uncomfortable telling me but that he would do so anyway. Dr Westley had asked him if he had ever considered switching to a younger primary care doctor. He had replied that he was quite satisfied with me.

A few weeks later I ran across Dr. Westley at the Fountain Valley Regional Hospital. I took advantage of the timing. I spouted, "Hey, Joe, I have some interesting news. I beat one hundred and fifty doctors at the Monster IPA staff meeting recently and won $500." He looked glum. I was elated to have that opportunity. I still kept referring patients to him but I did note an increased respect in addressing me.

About one year later, I came close to winning it again but I was marked wrong on a question that involved arthritis in older patients. I checked out my answer to that question. A few experts concurred with the answer I gave. The tie-breaker question at the end was about epilepsy. The correct answer, according to the IPA, was sixty and my estimate for that question was fifty-nine, which would have won first prize had I been considered right on the arthritis question.

IPA Business

Throughout the negotiations resulting in the sale of my practice I remained as an independent contractor for the Pathway Medical Group. I also continued my duties as a board member of the AIPA and as chairman of the Garden Grove/Anaheim committee. All of my patients that had been transferred to the Pathway medical group remained listed to me as their PCP. They were still helping keep the IPA quite profitable. That conserved my position as a member, shareholder, and officer of the IPA.

At this point, I was in my mid eighties. I had already moved partially towards retirement. I gave a lot of thought to the value of my shares. The board of directors consisted of shareholders and non-shareholders. As we shareholders were all getting older, we began to consider whether there was some way of revaluing our shares toward a much higher market value due to AIPA's tremendous earning power.

This was opposed by the non-shareholders, but even more vigorously by Dr. Charles. He opposed it on the premise that there would be no increase of share value above what was paid for the shares on retirement or disqualification of the shareholder. Any payout for shares returned to AIPA was not to exceed what the shareholder paid for them, and without interest added.

By a quirk of fate, one of the first shareholders to suffer from that restriction turned out to be Dr. Charles. After he passed away, his widow received a puny payout for his shares. Had he not opposed the restriction and it had been lifted, his family would have had a larger inheritance from the proceeds.

The board of directors ordered a listing of shares of stock held by each shareholder. Of the approximately 600 shares outstanding, I owned 33.9 shares after all of my shares in the component IPAs were converted into AIPA shares. This was almost 50 percent more than the other highest shareholders in AIPA.

We shareholders called a vote by the Board of Directors. We prevailed in a motion to revalue the shares to their true present market value. The administrators of the IPA reported back to the Board of Directors that, according to the IPA counsel, it would be necessary to order an appraisal of the IPA's value based on standard accounting principles. The Board of Directors approved an order for that appraisal.

A few months later, the IPA administration reported that there were complications in the appraisal process. They asked for more patience as it would be somewhat delayed. The months stretched into years. In response to the board's inquiries the IPA's CPA addressed the Board of Directors at their next meeting. He stated that IPA's have no real value, especially since we had no year-end earnings, having always distributed a bonus consisting of those yearly earnings. I challenged those statements. I pointed to major non-profit medical groups with zero year end accrued earnings having been purchased for billions of dollars.

I consulted an attorney skilled in healthcare matters for a consultation. He agreed that the IPA had a substantial market value but he was not an accountant so he could not venture a guess as to what that value was. He did suggest that there were prior law suits where draconian limits were placed on payouts so that only a tiny fraction of the true value was allowed to be paid according to the contract. He believed that some of those law suits were successful. It was an interesting consultation but the prospects of an expensive law suit were not acceptable.

I thought the matter over carefully. I came up with a daring plan. I called the Board of Director's secretary and asked for her to block out half an hour of time at the next board meeting for my two motions. She agreed. I spent time preparing my documents for the meeting.

I contacted two board members that were good friends of mine and begged them to make sure that they attend the next board meeting to second any of my motions. I did not furnish any further details to them but I assured them that it would be exciting. It was.

The board of directors meeting opened with the usual noise and cross talk. After the reports were read and voted on, the president of AIPA was getting ready to close the meeting. I signaled him and pointed to the meeting schedule. He acknowledged the schedule and gave me the time I had arranged.

I asked for silence and asked the board to pay strict attention to the serious matter that I was about to propose. I stated that I have prepared legal letters of intent for all of the shareholders offering the purchase price of $3,000,000 for the complete purchase of all the shares of AIPA. This brought a stunned silence to the room for a few seconds. There was a hubbub of objections.

I demanded silence and asked, "Do I hear a second to my motion?" The response was still more shouting of objections. I added, "I don't hear any second to my motion so I withdraw my motion."

With that, the board members began to leave their seats. I shouted loudly, "Hold it. I am not finished yet. I have a second motion. Please listen carefully." I told them that since they turned down a legal and serious offer of $3,000,000 for the six hundred shares of AIPA, we therefore have to realize that my offer, which amounted to $5,000 a share, was insufficient. I stated, "Therefore, I make a motion that we declare that our shares' value to be at least $5,000 until such time as the administration comes up with a legally determined accurate price."

That started a veritable storm of arguments. Shareholders agreed and the non-shareholders objected. The shareholders won the battle. Finally, the shares had a low but serious price. There was a brief setback. The AIPA counsel reviewed the motion and decided that the method used was not quite suitable for determining the value of the shares. A variation was set in place which confirmed the minimum value of shares was indeed $5,000 each.

That was hardly the end of the struggle. The shareholders realized that their shares, whether they held one or twenty, had a substantial value. This enthusiasm set in and grew. It led to the administration engaging a skilled negotiator to probe the market. Within the next few months, there was a bidding war for the shares of AIPA. Increasingly higher prices were brought before the board at each board meeting.

I watched this feeding frenzy with trepidation, not knowing where it would end. Several months elapsed. Even after the board of directors meeting had established the $5000 minimum price, there was always the possibility that someone might throw a monkey wrench into the works. It was decided by the Board that we would accept an offer from a much larger IPA that promised to commit to an annual substantial bonus for the PCPs. The agreed-upon price was about $26,000 per share.

That was really a bonanza for me since I owned by far the largest number of shares. At the final closing, the purchasing IPA medical group distributed checks to the stockholders of AIPA. I took home a check for a little over $1,000,000, which is the largest check I had ever seen. This was the giant upper in my life that made up for the downers. I felt grateful for the support and confidence of my wife and the rest of my family, as well as my mentors that had confidence in the bushy-haired youngster.

Arizona

My unpaid volunteer faculty appointment at the University of California, Irvine, had been a satisfying one. I worked with third-year students and, in the three months of internship with me, saw them grow in confidence and skill. After many years of teaching, there was a decision by the university to keep their third-year students on campus for their training. This was replaced by sending occasional second year students to me and others with similar faculty appointments for a few weeks of part-time training. I found them far from ready to do any more than follow me around and discuss the case afterwards.

My wonderful relationship with the University of California, Irvine, began to fall apart. It had been gratifying to work with the third-year students and I felt that my many years of training them had saved the university thousands of dollars. That helped me repay the help they had given me by accepting me into the Fifth Pathway Program. I had certificates from the university thanking me for my great service.

The climate had changed when the new 'Chief of the Family Practice Department' appeared on the scene. When the new chief took over, the trickle of second-year students shut off. I did hear some rumors of a new attitude, which was that the university had trained me. Now, without even bothering to become board certified, I was taking away their patients. I assume that came from the reports of third-year students that had been sent to me. Perhaps when they returned they had described to the department how busy my practice was.

This change of attitude was reinforced by a warning that since I was planning to move to Arizona, I would not be able to meet the minimum seventy-five hours per year of service required to maintain my faculty appointment. That information was in response to my routine request for backup information on my teaching duties and time spent to support my application for Arizona licensure. I had been spending more time in Arizona visiting my wife's family, which was limited to a few weeks a year. I wanted to be licensed in Arizona to be able to teach there or share a part-time practice with another family medicine doctor.

Another letter sent to me by the Associate Dean of the University of California, Irvine, informed me that it had been brought to their attention that I listed my title of 'Associate Clinical Professor' on my website, www.doctorsam.com. He pointed out that this was against the university rules. I checked other websites and that did not support his statement at all. I had my volunteer faculty title taken out. Most informative of all was that, below his signature on the letter, it was copied to "Acting Chair of the Family Medicine Department." Oops.

I resigned from the university after well over twenty years of service. I still refer patients to their wonderful hospital. They have prospered and grown and I wish them the best.

Paradise Found

When I received that $1,000,000, I was eighty-nine years old. I still worked two days a week for the Pathway Medical Group. My energy level remained high and my attendance at work went smoothly with rare absences. At the time of my sale with him, the owner of Pathway was concerned about employing a physician in his mid-eighties but I had proved to be a strong member of his team. I was also an unusually popular PCP with the patients and the rest of his staff. I pointed out to the owner, who was reluctant to hire a physician in his eighties, that he would not have that problem much longer since I would soon be in my nineties. It was a dilemma for him perhaps, but not for me.

Remembering my several months of recuperating at home, a year earlier, Teresa and I had been searching the real estate market for a property with at least one bedroom and bathroom on street level. With no steps to negotiate. Since she was an avid gardener, we looked for a small farm. Our search took us far and wide from our home and was disappointing. We searched through listings in surrounding states.

One night, I was exploring the Internet for real estate properties. I came across a foreclosure sale for a small farm property. Not being aware of where the property was located, I looked it up. It was a quaint area and, most importantly, rural. Just right for Teresa's gardening.

The next day we contacted the real estate agent that had listed the property. We learned that it had been sold by its owners in 2005 for $1,200,000, but, perhaps because of the financial crisis of 2008, the buyers could not maintain the payments and the lenders foreclosed on it in 2009. It was then bought by some banks for $795,000.

When we looked at the abandoned property, it had been neglected. The trees and plants appeared to have been languishing for months. A retaining wall that held back the mountain behind the house had failed and the girders were twisted. The red barn and the bridge across Oak Creek, which ran through the property, needed much repair.

Inside, the house was great with lots of beautiful woodwork. That also needed work. Its potential was obvious to us. You could say it was just what the doctor ordered. I offered the banks that owned the property $600,000. They quickly accepted.

We were able to bring in a smart contractor who helped us whip it into shape for much less than the prevailing rates. Teresa shifted gears and knew just what to do. Wasting no time, she fixed the irrigation system and put in a conservation type of watering system. She planted rows of fruit trees. The previous fruit trees blossomed when the new watering system was in place.

By the summertime, the property was covered by a riot of colorful plantings. It was as if we had found paradise, an 'Eldorado.' Not the airport in Bogotá (the El Dorado International Airport) that I departed from years ago but the Eldorado, the legendary utopia and city of riches that early Spanish explorers believed existed somewhere in South America.

Taking up residence in Eldorado seemed like a grand Hollywood-style ending with cameras panning out over the mountains at sunset. I felt at supreme peace. That shortly ended as the property blossomed and became even more of a visual feast, we ran into a situation which threatened the peaceful enjoyment of our newly found paradise.

It all began with a phone call to my mobile phone. A woman called me stating that she worked for EPC (Electric Power Company) and, as I may have heard, a utility pole had snapped. It had torn down the electric power wiring for a long distance. Since the broken utility pole across the road from our home was the source of main power for our home and its red barn, they might have to place a utility pole on our property to make the connection. She asked me to call back, *at my leisure.*

I called EPC as soon as I could and reached the field engineer on the project, Dan Hall. He told me the shocking news that the utility pole had already been installed on the property and there was nothing I could do about it. He agreed to meet us to prove that statement.

We arrived for the meeting and were shocked to see that there was a huge utility pole installed in the garden area, smack in line with our prized picture window. We confronted Hall and he said that EPC had an easement that extended from the road well into our property. The utility pole was on the line of that easement which extended 6ft on each side of that line. Teresa challenged him, stating that he had no right to intrude on our property and he had to get the monster pole removed immediately. He responded that the best we could hope for was to pay $17,000 to move the pole. Then we would have to pay the same amount to install a new one in a different location. It would have been better for him not to rush to snap judgments like that because we were prepared to do battle.

I went to the Real Estate Office in the county where the easement records are kept. There I found that EPC's easement covers the road passing our farm and no easement existed for private property. Hall had got that half right - or half wrong depending on your point of view.

I complained to his superiors and then to the regional supervisor for EPC for the area and got a more sympathetic response. We agreed to meet with Hall again to establish a new location on the curb (between the road and the creek) which did not interfere with the view from our picture window. We also engaged an electrical contractor to make the necessary changes to our electrical service from the new utility pole to the barn and house that EPC required.

With the proposed new installation, EPC insisted on obtaining an easement that was agreeable to both us and them. They gave the job of obtaining the easement to a company that they engaged for that purpose. The drawing needed to identify the easement area for the county records which was drawn by Hall himself. The easement company sent me the documents to sign with the drawing. I rejected them as Hall had drawn the easement area on the wrong side of our little bridge, right back in front of our picture window.

A meeting at the property was arranged for me with Hall and the easement people. Hall pointed to the agreed-upon easement location where there was a small post with a red flag and then to his drawing. It was incorrect by about 60 ft. The easement expert told Hall he was wrong and that I was right. Victory at last.

While Hall might have walked away angry and befuddled over the whole affair that day, the matter was settled at long last. We were left to the peace and enjoyment of our surroundings. Not bad for that bushy-haired boy who, decades ago in another century, ran around with his elbows sticking out of the sleeve of his torn sweater. Like Don Quixote, we tilted against windmills but the picture had changed and we had won the battle.

I continue to make trips to the office on a consulting basis and on an intermittent schedule that would not interfere with my retirement.

We have found our Eldorado and it is enough.

Epilogue

Now at age 93, I have found the time to try to analyze a major puzzle in my life, which becomes more evident as time passes. I am aware of the puzzle, which is why have I been able to reach old age with minimal infirmities and strong brain function.

My family, friends and patients have pointed this out to me but I am very much aware and grateful for the near-miracle. In fact, I have faced old age, with confidence, for many years, without pointing it out to anyone, and just letting it happen. In this discussion, I will advance some of my thoughts and facts. But, I will leave it to my readers to extract whatever they feel applies to their particular situation. If you are content with your prognosis for a long life, please feel free to bypass this epilogue and I thank you for reading the story of my life.

1. I was fortunate to be born to Becky and Clement as they passed on excellent genes. My father, Clement lived into his mid-eighties despite high blood pressure and high cholesterol, which caused him to have a series of strokes. My mother lived into her low nineties despite a severely damaged heart from childhood Rheumatic Fever. My grandparents lived to ripe old ages.

2. My inherited high blood pressure and cholesterol were treated by me, with medication, resulting in very tight control over the many years. Before cholesterol was identified as the cause of heart problems, I had a few warning angina pains, which were due to blocked heart arteries. An excellent surgical repair bypassed the blocked blood vessels.

3. I never really smoked except for occasional cigars and experimenting with a pipe at times. I never experimented with drugs. My consumption of alcoholic beverages is no more than a few glasses a year mostly at parties or religious events.

4. My Colombian Professor of Internal Medicine recommended a large dose of Vitamin C so I have been taking 1000 mg a.m. and bedtime for over 40 years. Studies done with Vitamin C never proved to be advantageous but I believe that my professor knew better.

5. My parents taught me to be a happy person, which suited me fine and I have avoided depression even when I had setbacks in my life. I became unhappy when things became gloomy but I always felt that I could work my way out of the bad situations.

6. My brain function has remained excellent probably due to my intense interest in keeping my brain busy. At the medical practice, I have had to handle multiple medical and emotional problems for each patient adding up to hundreds of such problems each day when I was in full practice. At present, I am reading heavily into the structure of our universe.

7. My wife controls my diet emphasizing healthy eating with little meat but frequent fish, green vegetables, fruits and fruit juices, as well as wheat bran for fiber.

8. I drive carefully although around the speed limit when traffic is light. My car is kept in good condition with excellent brakes and tires. I haven't had an accident or a traffic ticket for at least 20 years.

9. At home, we have fire, smoke and burglar alarms. I am leery of heights so I don't go for hikes along mountain tops or climb roofs. My engineering training and education helps me analyze when a dangerous situation could present itself like on a roller coaster.

10. I know who the great physicians and surgeons are in my region and I use them, if needed, for me and my family.

11. I take a few medications and vitamins each day including the high dose Vitamin C.
12. I try to get about 8 hours of sleep each night, but unfortunately that is difficult although I will not take sleeping pills other than Melatonin OTC.

Sam Gendler, M.D.

Printed in the United States
By Bookmasters